Dear Lindsey

Live life big.....
Remember to always
practice mindfulness!

Always With You

Much love.
Steph

12/7/18

Always With You

A true story of love, loss… and hope

By Shalini Bhalla-Lucas

Published by Just Jhoom! Ltd
PO Box 142
Cranleigh, Surrey
GU6 8ZX
www.justjhoom.co.uk

Cover Design: Angela Basker
Author Photo: Sian Tyrrell

ISBN-13: 978-1721800629

For Jeremy.

My best friend, my lover, my soulmate.

You are my reason, my heart, my home.
In every way you complete me,
in mind, body and soul.

Until we meet again…
Kyunki, hum phir zaroor milenge.

Table of Contents

Life is messy. And so it goes without saying that our stories will be messy too.

The story I tell here is of me and Jeremy. And yes, it is messy.

People don't always come out looking their best, situations aren't always seen in the rosiest of lights. Where I have recounted what Jeremy said to me, the conversations and experiences we had, I do so from memory. They are as I remember, from his perspective and from mine. And so, if there are any discrepancies to how someone else may remember the occasion or situation, this is completely unintentional.

I also write about depression, suicide, religion, the afterlife, Indian culture – all complex, emotive and sometimes painful topics. I don't write to influence anyone in my way of believing or to suggest any actions are taken. Rather, I hope to give you my perspective, my understanding, of these topics.

I am a better person for knowing Jeremy, for being with him and for being loved by him. In every way he completed me. By telling our story I hope to show this. At no time whilst writing this book did I want to hurt anyone or cause any distress. But I believe a story should be told from a place of truth.

This story is my truth. It is Jeremy's truth. It is *our* truth.

Shalini Bhalla-Lucas
Cranleigh, Surrey, 2018

Prologue

He is here to meet me. I know he is here because I can see him: strong now, he stands tall, straight-backed, smiling. Our eyes meet and there is the same fluttering in my chest that I always get when he is near. And his smile… he smiles in a way that makes me feel safe. And complete.

A wave of love pulses through me, enveloping me, encircling me, lifting me up and flooding through my whole being. I am transformed by this love. I am pure energy, pure light and the same light is within him, pouring through and around him. I see his face and it is clear and open, free from pain and suffering. He is just as he was when we first met. His skin, translucent, seems to shimmer and glow with health and his eyes, always laughing, are bright and sparkling blue. I hear him talk to me but there are no words. His voice is within my heart: 'I am here to bring you home. There is nothing to separate us now.'

An intense feeling of peace settles over me. This is how it has always been with us. After every journey I took, he was there to greet me. I never had to search him out; he would be there, ready to take me home. Except now I'm not getting off a train, nor dragging a heavy suitcase up a ramp towards a station barrier. There is no need for me to reapply my lipstick, comb my hair or smooth down my journey-worn clothes for our reunion. I have no need of any luggage. No need of a physical presence at all. I am unencumbered by those concerns. No longer restricted by the heavy weight of being, I am free at last.

Now I stand in front of him and his arms envelope me. Our bodies entwine, our beings merge. I am safe and secure, held here in this perfect moment. All the pain and suffering of our separation melts away. There is no need to worry, no fears for the future or regrets about the past. All that is over and I am becoming whole again. In this moment, there is only peace. The light of love flows through us both now as we are once again connected. We are this love and, in this moment, my heart feels only joy.

There are no boundaries between us.

We are one.

Chapter 1 – A Rabbit in the Garden

"Destiny will place you in those particular circumstances; it will dictate that you will encounter a certain person, at a certain time, and perhaps in a certain place."
—Dr. Brian Weiss[1]

There is a rabbit in my garden eating my freshly planted flowers! I watched, outraged, from the upstairs window of my new home as a very fat white rabbit hopped around my lawn, helping himself to all the new flowers I'd planted just the day before – a riot of brightly-coloured wallflowers, pansies and camellias. *The cheek of the thing!*

I raced downstairs and out onto the lawn to get a better look at my unwelcome visitor. I knew practically nothing about gardening but I'd done my best in the last few days to make the place look a little better than when I'd moved in a few weeks before in early February. The garden had looked pretty bleak back then but as the weeks passed, the winter frost loosened its grip and hopeful buds of spring began to poke through the ends of bare branches. I had arrived in the UK the previous year, in September 1996, and the long, cold English winter had come as a real shock to me. The dark nights drawing in so early, the cold damp that seemed to penetrate my bones, bitter winds that made breathing difficult and the greyness that seemed to pervade everything. It was a far cry from the warmth, sunshine and colour of Kenya – my home - and a strong feeling of homesickness had gripped me throughout the winter. But my mood had begun to lift as the pretty cherry blossoms emerged on the trees along our street and the sun enticed small flowers from bulbs in the ground. It was enough to tempt me into a garden centre with the aim of cheering up my own garden. I knew little about plants, other than what I thought looked nice. So, I filled a trolley with the most colourful and healthy-looking flowers I could find, learning their names from the plastic labels at the front of the pots; invested in a trowel and some compost and got to work on the beds, digging up weeds, removing stones and planting an eclectic mix of flowers. Hours later, I sat back on my heels to admire my work. *Not bad for a girl who had never attempted gardening before!*

Now, I was dismayed to see that most of the flower heads had been chewed off and a good many leaves sported tell-tale nibbled edges. I sighed. My mother would have been so proud to know I was giving our house a makeover. An astute businesswoman, it was her idea to buy this place, 15 Miller Road, on the outskirts of Guildford in Surrey. While I studied for my masters in Tourism Education at the University of Surrey, my mother decided to invest in the UK property market – and provide a place for me to live at the same time. We agreed that she would put down the deposit to buy the house and I would be responsible for the mortgage and bills while I lived in it. Then, when I was due to return to Kenya to join the family business, we would sell up and both profit from the joint investment.

My mother was herself a wonderful gardener, filling the beds in our garden at home with dozens of sweet-smelling roses. There was no competition to be had here, I thought miserably. *Where had this rabbit come from?* It was still there, barely giving me a second glance as it sat on his well-fed haunches, munching through my garden with impunity. I peered over the fence to my neighbour's garden on one side – no clues there. Then I walked to the other side, where I looked over and saw a couple of young girls, aged about 10 or 11, playing with two rabbits. *Aha!* In the corner was a large homemade hutch, which was clearly where my hungry friend belonged. The girls were engrossed with the other two rabbits and didn't seem to have noticed that the third had escaped.

Who were they? I racked my brains for the answer. I had met several of my neighbours already and some had introduced themselves to me when I first arrived. But I hadn't met this one yet... what was his name again? A divorcee, he lived on his own and his name was... Jerry? Or Jeremy? I remembered that he had three daughters who came to stay on the weekends when I often heard them playing in the garden.

The sun was shining and a warm breeze rustled the trees outside so I didn't bother putting on a coat. I just slipped on my Kenyan *bata* slippers and left the latch on while I walked up the path to Jerry/Jeremy's front door. His front garden, I noticed, was beautifully tended. He must be a pretty good gardener, I thought, admiring the attractive tulips and colourful rock garden. The rabbit clearly hadn't found its way to the front of the house yet. I rang the doorbell.

In a matter of seconds, the door swung open to reveal a striking-looking man with piercing blue eyes that perfectly matched his crisply-ironed shirt.

'Hello?' his voice was both deep and soft at the same time. It had a smooth, pillowy quality. For a second I completely forgot why I was there. *Wow! Those eyes!*

Instinctively I smiled and he smiled back - a broad, handsome grin which lit up his whole face. My stomach did a little somersault and I had to fight the urge to giggle. *My goodness! What's going on?* The whole reason for my visit suddenly seemed utterly absurd.

'Hello,' I finally managed to blurt out. 'Hello. I'm your new neighbor, Shalini. I moved in a few weeks ago.'

'Oh yes,' he grinned again and nodded. 'Hello Shalini – lovely to meet you. I'm Jeremy.'

He put out his hand to shake and when I offered him mine, he grasped it firmly and pumped my arm up and down a couple of times. His grip was strong and firm and his hands, warm. *How very English*, I thought.

'Welcome to the area. I hope you're settling in all right. You know, if there's anything I can do…'

'Yes, well, there is actually. I think your rabbit has broken into my garden and he appears to be eating his way through my flowerbeds.'

Jeremy had looked so confident and cool at first – now his face collapsed in confusion.

'Really? Oh no, I'm so sorry.'

'Yes, it's a big white fluffy rabbit. Is it yours?'

'Erm… yes. At least, I think so. Just give me a minute.'

Jeremy disappeared and I heard him shout through the hallway, 'Jenny! Katie! Have you got Fluffy?'

A pause, then footsteps again and Jeremy reappeared at the doorway, looking awkward and embarrassed.

'I am so sorry about this, Shalini. The girls got the rabbits out and he must have slipped under the fence somehow. They hadn't even noticed he was gone. What a little rascal! I'll come round now and get him back.'

Jeremy stepped out of the doorway and joined me as we walked towards my house.

'I wouldn't mind, really, it's just that I planted all these flowers yesterday and now, well, there isn't much left,' I said, as I opened the front door and we crossed the living room through to the patio doors.

'You didn't, did you? Oh no!' Jeremy appeared genuinely upset about the situation. 'I can't apologise enough. Really, Shalini, I'm so sorry. Here's you moving into a new home and it's not exactly the best start, is it?'

Opening the back door we both saw the rabbit sitting, rather proudly, in the centre of the lawn.

'Yes, that's Fluffy Right, come here, you little rotter…!' Jeremy lunged towards the bunny, who darted away in a split second. He might have been a hefty fellow but he certainly moved fast.

'You cheeky bugger!' Jeremy exclaimed.

Now that Fluffy was alert to what was going on, he bounded off into a corner of the garden, right up against the fence, and sat there watching us warily.

'Come on Fluffy…' Jeremy called out in a singsong voice as he crept forward, crouching low, arms outstretched.

'Come here…come on then…'

Fluffy sat, immobile, his little nose twitching suspiciously. Jeremy edged closer and closer. He was going to do it this time, I felt sure. I held my breath as he crept nearer and nearer to his target… then… pounced! But once again, the agile creature bounced off in the opposite direction. Jeremy ran after it now, not even attempting the singsong voice. He literally jumped on it this time but somehow Fluffy managed to wriggle out of his arms. I burst out laughing.

'Hey!' Jeremy said ruefully, straightening his back. 'Whose side are you on?'

'I'm sorry,' I laughed. 'Don't get me wrong; I want him out of here. I'm on your side, but he's cleverer than he looks.'

'We'll see about that,' Jeremy whispered, his face set in solemn determination. 'We'll see...'

It must have gone on for about ten minutes, this crazy game of cat and mouse, or, more accurately, man and rabbit, as Jeremy chased his pet from one side of the garden to the other. As he ran, he couldn't stop apologizing for all the disruption and for messing up my garden. It was sweet, funny and completely ridiculous. I had completely forgotten about my flowers, but I didn't mind. Not one bit. The entertainment was well worth it and I *loved* the way Jeremy said my name. *Shalini. Shalini.* It sounded so right in his voice. I could have listened to him all day but finally he caught up with his dastardly pet and managed to scoop him up in his arms.

Beads of sweat peppered Jeremy's forehead and his blue eyes sparkled triumphantly as he held the rabbit aloft, as if brandishing a first-prize cup.

'Got him!' he panted.

I clapped appreciatively.

'You're going back into your cage, you blighter!' Jeremy addressed the rabbit before turning to me: 'Lovely to meet you, Shalini, and again I'm really very sorry. I'll get this one back home now and later today I'll work out where it he got out and fix it. I promise he won't be bothering you anymore.'

'Okay,' I said. 'Thank you. It's been nice to meet you too.'

He had such charming manners, this man. I felt sure that if it weren't for the large rabbit in his arms, he'd be trying to shake my hand right now.

Later, as I sat down to start a course assignment, the memory of that day made me smile again. *I like him!* I knew that straightaway. He was handsome, of course, and I noticed his strong, athletic physique as he raced around my garden. But there was more to it than that. There was something special about this man and I felt that I wanted to get to know him better.

Although I had experienced crushes before, I'd never really had a proper relationship with a man. And that didn't bother me because I hadn't been interested. I had been brought up in a fairly strict Indian family, where it was expected that I would eventually marry a good Hindu boy with a successful career and from a well-off, respected family – very much the suitable boy. Even with my western education and outlook I would still in the end be required to go back to Kenya and be the good Indian girl. But it was something I was not wholly comfortable with. I was fiercely ambitious and independent and knew I would never need a man to make me feel complete. I was a strong woman, a proud feminist and I laughed at the folly of those women who obsessed about men and the state of their love lives. What for? I had bigger aspirations than making a man happy. I was set on achieving a high-flying career and I certainly wasn't going to let a man get in the way of my ambition. Still, when I put my mind to something, I usually saw it through. And since it wasn't likely I would get another bunny invasion any time soon, I had to think of another way to see Jeremy again.

So, the following week, I walked over to his house and knocked on his door.

'Shalini!'

'Hi Jeremy,' I said, quite casually. 'Since I'm new to the area, I'm doing a little bit of entertaining… you know, trying to get to know my neighbours. I wondered if you'd like to come over for drinks one evening next week?'

'Yes, that sounds lovely.'

'Great – which night are you free?'

Yes, it was brazen but I didn't care. I had chosen my words carefully, making the invitation sound like a friendly and neighbourly get together, nothing more.

'Tuesday's good for me,' he replied.

'Tuesday it is. Shall we say 8pm?'

I felt a thrill and a sense of rebellion that I had never felt before. I had always towed the line with my parents and always met their expectations. I had always been the dutiful Indian daughter. Until now.

Chapter 2 – The Good Indian Girl

"And in the sweetness of friendship let there be laughter, and sharing of pleasures. For in the dew of little things the heart finds its morning and is refreshed."

—Kahlil Gibran²

Calm down! I told myself sternly as I wiped down the surfaces in the kitchen for a third time that evening. It was 7.55pm and he was due any minute. I straightened my dress and checked my hair in the mirror again. This wasn't like me at all. I wasn't normally the nervous type. Usually I was pretty confident in most situations but there was something about Jeremy. I wanted to make a good impression. I glanced at the clock again... 7.58pm. He wouldn't be late, I knew that. No, he was too much of a gentleman, too considerate to keep people waiting. Sure enough, at 8pm on the dot, the doorbell rang.

Jeremy was wearing an azure blue polo shirt tucked into a pair of chinos and an infectious grin, which seemed to light up his whole face. We shook hands – I was getting used to this now – then I showed him through to the kitchen where I had a plate of chocolate chip muffins and a bottle of red wine waiting on the kitchen table.

'Am I early?' he asked, looking around.

'No, no,' I replied. 'You're right on time.'

'Oh, oh right. That's good,' he said.

'Please sit down,' I gestured to one of the hard backed chairs around the table. 'I'm sorry about this but the only decorating I've done is in the kitchen and the bedroom...'

He looked at me for a second. Then he blinked.

Realising what I'd just said, I felt a warmth creeping over my cheeks, but I blustered on: 'But, erm, we'll stay here!'

I poured Jeremy a drink and we talked for a little about how I was settling in. I told him that everyone had been very kind and welcoming so far and he said it was a good area and for the most part, we had very friendly neighbours

'How long have you been here?' I asked.

'Oh, now you're asking!' he smiled. 'Let's see if I can work this out... my ex-wife and I moved here a few years after getting married so that must have been in the mid-80s... So, well over 10 years? Something like that anyway.'

'But you're not married now?'

'Well no...' a shadow crossed his face.

'I'm so sorry. I don't mean to pry.'

'Not at all. No, I'm afraid things didn't work out quite how I imagined they would. We're divorced now but we were together a good number of years and we had our girls. Jenny, she's the eldest at 12, then Katie, 11, and Amanda, she's 8 years old. All good kids. They're at mine most weekends - I'm sure you've heard them over the garden fence and you've already met their naughty pet! But during the week I'm here on my own. And it's been like that for nearly three years now.'

He smiled again, but there was a sad, resigned look in his eyes. I wondered how much more he wasn't saying but I knew it would be impolite to question him further about something so personal.

'Is this where you're from? Originally, I mean?' I asked, pouring him another glass of wine.

'Oh yes, I grew up in Eastwood Road, in Bramley. It's not that far from here – about 7 miles. I spend most weekends there playing golf or fishing. During the week I work as a manager for Barclays Bank.' He drained his glass.

'What about you Shalini? I'm guessing you're not from Guildford?'

'No!' I laughed, as I poured us both another large glass. Normally, I didn't drink but as the evening's hostess I felt it was only polite to join in. Also, the wine was definitely helping me to loosen up and feel more relaxed.

'No, my family are from Kenya. We're Kenyan Indians. I miss them very much and I know they miss me. I also don't have any family around here, my closest extended family is in north London, so I'm having to adjust to living alone.

We couldn't have been more different, Jeremy and I. For a start, there was clearly quite a difference in our ages. Though I couldn't exactly place him I guessed that he must have been almost double my 21 years. And while he had spent most of his life in Surrey, only venturing abroad for the occasional family holiday to Tenerife or golfing trip to Spain, I was already a well-seasoned traveller.

As Jeremy and I relaxed into in each other's company, I began to tell him about my background. I came from an affluent Indian family in Nairobi. We were either third generation Kenyans or fourth, depending on whether you started from my father or mother's side of the family. My mother's grandfather, Himatlal Jani, had emigrated to Kenya in 1890 from Gujarat in Western India. He settled in a small outpost called Voi in southern Kenya and worked as a stationmaster for what was at the time called the

Uganda Railways. His son, my maternal grandfather, worked for Barclays Bank in Tanzania and was later transferred to Nairobi, where my mother was born, in 1945.

My paternal grandfather emigrated to Kenya in 1908. Originally from Punjab in northern India, he came to join his elder brother who had emigrated a few years before. He found work as an assistant in an Indian corner shop in what was once the tiny town of Eldoret. He did well and eventually moved his family to Nairobi, where he started a business selling firewood. Each of his five sons would follow him into the business. It was here in Nairobi that my Punjabi father, born in 1948, the youngest of the five sons, met my Gujarati mother in the early 1970s.

At first, both families were opposed to the relationship; it was unusual for a man and a woman from different Indian sects to get married. There was also a class difference, my father's family was very rich and my mother's much less well-off. Also, my father was seen as a real catch in Indian society. He was young, fair and handsome and a sought-after bachelor. My mother was short, with a dark complexion and from a simpler background. But finally, after a five-year courtship, their families relented and my mother and father were married in 1974. It was a lavish affair with 2000 guests - a true Punjabi and Gujarati celebration with all the colour, noise, laughter and exuberance that Indian weddings seem to evoke.

My parents became successful business people in their own right. While my father, Ashok, ran a chain of successful Indian restaurants, my mother, Sharmi, established a secretarial business and organised conferences in the city for major international groups like USAID and the UN. They were bright and driven people and I was proud of them both.

My father's business, in particular, gave us a certain standing within the community. He had spotted a gap in the catering market in 1980 and set up a Mughlai restaurant in Nairobi called Minar, which quickly became very popular. More restaurants followed and by the time I was growing up in our affluent Nairobi suburb, they were well-known and very popular. Even today, people talk about Minar as being the pioneering restaurant of its kind – and my father was the man behind its success for many years. My younger sister, Shivani, and I would often stop off at one of the restaurants after school to be given some new dish the chef was experimenting with, like succulent *shish kebabs* with herbs and spices, drenched in mint raita or spicy *dum aloo* in a creamy coconut sauce. We attended good private schools, ate out frequently and spent our weekends visiting wildlife parks all over Kenya to see lions, cheetahs and elephants. In the holidays we made frequent trips abroad and often visited the UK, as most of my mother's family had emigrated to north London.

But there was one thing that most defined my childhood: dance. From the age of three, my mother had taken me to Indian classical and folk dance classes, which I absolutely loved. Dancing came naturally to me. It became central to my childhood and I took it very seriously. Of course our studies came first - my parents made sure of that – but after academic success, dance was the only thing that really interested me. My mother sent us to lots of other classes too, cramming horse-riding, swimming, Spanish and piano lessons into our busy timetables. But it was dance that was my real passion, one I had inherited from my mother. When she was younger she wanted to learn to dance but her family were too poor to send her to classes. Later, with Shivani and me, her success allowed her to give us the opportunities she had been denied. But while I took to it naturally, my sister hated it and endured the classes until the age of 10 when she put her foot down and refused to dance anymore.

Dancing gave me a wonderful sense of peace and contentment. I was very studious from a young age and always felt pressured by my parents to do well in school. Dance gave me time out from my studies. It gave me a sense of freedom and a chance to escape from the books for a while. The music always moved me from within and I loved telling the stories of Hindu gods through movement. I'd practice for hours and hours in our living room until at the age of 16, all that hard work culminated in my *Bharata Natyam* dance graduation, called an *Arangetram*.

Native to South India, *Bharata Natyam* is one of India's eight classical dance forms. It was originally performed in the temples by *devadasis*, young girls and women who were dedicated to serve the temples for the rest of their lives. Like the *devadasis* I had to learn numerous steps and dances normally performed in a very low demi-plié – with the feet and knees turned out and stylised hand gestures. The hand gestures have two main usages. The first is for aesthetic purposes to accentuate the line and tension of the body, and the second is as a medium of expressive and descriptive dance – or storytelling. I also learnt various eye, neck and head movements. After years of rigorous training, we are allowed to showcase what we've learnt at an *Arangetram*, a Tamil word which means the 'etram' or ascending of the 'arangu' or performance stage.

My parents spent a fortune on the event, hiring a beautiful theatre and flying in garlands of bright orange marigolds from India as well as a group of renowned musicians for the big day. The invitations to each of our 450 guests were hand-delivered, the same way an Indian family would hand-deliver a wedding invitation. And it *was* like a wedding in so many ways - it was as if I was marrying my art form, becoming a bride to Shiva - the God of Dance. There were news reports in the local papers and TV and on the day I was inundated with flowers from my family in the UK who couldn't be there. I felt like a star! It was held on the evening of 14 September 1991, my 16th birthday, and for three hours straight, alone on stage, I danced in that enormous auditorium, in front of all our invited guests...

'Wow!' Jeremy exclaimed. 'That must have felt amazing.'

I remembered how I felt that night, as I stepped out onto the stage, the *ghungroos* on my ankles jangling, the tips of my fingers and toes stained red with *alta* dye, the jasmine *gajra* in my hair and my body draped in a beautiful Kanjivaram silk sari. But it also felt distant, like watching a film, as if it had all happened to another person. *Who was that girl? Was that really me in front of all those people?* I shook my head.

'What is it?' Jeremy enquired gently.

'Well, it's funny...' I smiled wryly. 'But looking at my life as it is today, you would never guess I had devoted so much time and energy to dancing.'

'What happened?' asked Jeremy.

'I gave up dancing after leaving Kenya at 18. I had wanted to make a career from it but my parents said that wouldn't work. It would be too hard to make a decent living as a dancer and they were right. Anyway, it was important to them that I got a degree. So I decided I would work with my father in his restaurant business. I did a diploma course in London then I went to Switzerland to study for a degree in hotel management. We had the occasional cultural show there - where all the international students dressed up in traditional costumes and performed dance routines - but I haven't really danced since I came to the UK.'

'Do you miss it?'

'Yes and no,' I mused. 'I mean, there's so much going on in my life now I can't even think about it. I'm studying for my Masters and I waitress part-time in the hotel down the road. Plus, I've got this place to sort out... and when it's all decorated, the plan is to take in a lodger to help me with the rent. With all of that going on, there really isn't much time for dancing.'

'That's a shame. I'd love to see you dance.'

'Maybe I'll show you one day.'

Our eyes met briefly and my tummy did a back flip. *Was I flirting?* I wasn't sure because I'd never really been very good at flirting. This wasn't like me. I had always been brought up to be fairly conservative. My father had been particularly strict with my sister and I, never letting us go out in the evenings, not letting us have boyfriends and making sure that any free time we had was spent with the family.

The wine continued to wear away at my inhibitions and I described to Jeremy how I had always been the good girl that my parents expected me to be – diligent at school, focused entirely on work, rather than friends and socialising

At Les Roches, the Swiss hotel management school I went to, it was made very clear to me by my parents that I was there to learn, to work hard and to make them proud. That was the most important thing to me and it informed everything I did. Even when my friends were out drinking and socialising, I'd stay in and study. I was the model daughter, 'a good Indian girl' in every sense and I was pleased that in the end, all my hard work paid off.

'I came third in my whole year,' I boasted to Jeremy. 'They gave us gold medals. Even now, while I am here at university, I am expected to study hard. My father wants me to come back and join him in the business. And, I suppose in the end I will be expected to do what all good Indian girls do – get married to a suitable boy and have babies.'

I said this with less conviction because deep inside me I knew that marriage and having children would not be something that would come to me naturally. I did not believe that one needed to be married to be happy or to be in a relationship. For me marriage was an institution that I was not convinced by. But I didn't say this to Jeremy at the time. I did however tell him that I didn't want children. I had made that decision when I was only 16. My mother and I had been talking about careers one day and my mother, in passing, and without much thought, said, 'I would have gone much further in my career if I hadn't had children.'

Even though she was talking about me and my sister, I wasn't hurt. I realised that I, too, wanted a career and in order to do so, I probably shouldn't have children. I wouldn't want to make a child feel like an obstacle in life. As the years passed and I saw the state of the world, the environment, war, terrorism and the perils of social media I felt that the world was a dangerous place to bring a child into. If anything, I would sometimes think about adoption – there were so many children already in this world who could do with a loving home, an education and the safety and security that were their birthrights. But, I also never really had a maternal instinct, or at least I never allowed it to rear its head. And so, from a very young age I decided that my life would be childfree, rather than childless. I was just too scared to tell my parents – especially my father.

As I explained this to Jeremy I realised that I had painted a rather harsh picture of my parents.

'Don't get me wrong,' I explained. 'Growing up, I never felt unloved. My parents were kind and loving to both of us, but they also expected a lot in return. It felt like a lot of pressure to be under all the time.'

I suddenly became aware that I had told Jeremy so much about my life but had asked him very little about his. His eyes clouded over as he explained that he had been through a tough divorce but was now coming out the other side and looking to the future.

'Why see the glass as half empty? You know what they say… life begins at 40!' And with that Jeremy burst out laughing.

Aha – so he was 40 years old! He really didn't look it. He had such a boyish charm about him. I grinned and reached for the bottle of wine.

'Oh!' I giggled, as I realized the bottle was empty. 'We seem to have drunk it all!'

'Really?' said Jeremy. 'Well it's probably just as well because it's nearly midnight.'

'How did that happen?' I asked, incredulous. *Had we really been talking for four hours?* It felt like no time at all. We had been so open and honest with one another, I marvelled.

'Sorry about the chairs,' I winced, as we both stood up. I felt woozy and clung to the table for support.

'No need to apologise. It's been a lovely evening but I'd better be getting back. Got to get up early tomorrow.'

'Of course. It's late!'

We walked to the front door and I opened it to let him out.

'By the way,' he turned back to face me, 'Did you invite anyone else tonight? I was sort of expecting to see the other neighbours here.'

'Oh no,' I replied. 'I didn't invite anyone else. Just you.'

He smiled as he turned away and I closed the door.

Chapter 3 – Sweet Surrender

"The real lover is the man who can thrill you by kissing your forehead or smiling into your eyes or just staring into space."
—**Marilyn Monroe**[3]

*B*eep *Beep Beeeeeeep… The time is 7 o'clock on Monday 9*th *June. These are the news headlines…*

The radio clock next to my head startled me awake. For a second, I wondered where I was. This wasn't my bedroom… But then it all came flooding back. I pulled the turquoise duvet cover around my shoulders and snuggled a little further down the bed. Next to me, I felt Jeremy move and opened my eyes to find him watching me.

'What?' I asked self-consciously. 'What's wrong?'

'Nothing at all' he whispered as he curled himself around me, giving me a tender kiss on my neck 'Just looking!'

And, for a little while we just lay there, holding each other. It had been a perfect night and I didn't want to break the spell that bound us together in this moment. It felt like torture to spend a moment apart from Jeremy. I wanted to be with him all the time and in the past month we had spent many evenings in each other's houses, getting to know one another better. That night, like many before, we had spent a wonderful evening together, talking and drinking the Rioja that he had brought back from Spain on his last golfing holiday.

'You know, I really thought this case of 12 bottles was going to last me about a year,' Jeremy reflected as he uncorked the last of the Faustino VII bottles.

'We've got through them very quickly,' I agreed.

During the past few weeks Jeremy and I had been seeing one another, I'd consumed more alcohol than I had my entire life. I was normally so restrained. I had never even been drunk before meeting him. All that falling over and throwing up, it seemed so sordid and undignified! I had felt quite smug next to my student friends in Switzerland as, one by one, they all succumbed to the temptations of alcohol while I remained stone-cold sober. But with Jeremy, it felt okay to let go a little. He made me feel safe.

We had become incredibly close in such a short space of time. I felt like I could tell him anything and it would be okay. He seemed to accept me completely. Before long our handshakes at the door turned to hugs and then, one night, he took me in his arms and kissed me tenderly on the lips. It was a perfect moment and I suddenly knew that he felt the same way I did. That was 18 May, the date our feelings for one another became real and known. From that point on, it felt as if we were a couple, although Jeremy had a little wobble when he found out that I was only 21 years old.

'21…? Really? You're younger than I thought,' he said.

'What do you mean? How old did you think I was?'

'I don't know – 25, 26 maybe? I mean, here you are, alone, living in your own house. You've lived abroad… you just seem so… I don't know… mature!'

'Well I am mature!' I retorted. 'Age is just a number, wouldn't you agree? I've lived apart from my family since I was 17. Does it bother you, that I'm only 21?'

'No!' Jeremy was quick to reassure me. 'It doesn't bother me in the slightest. It's just the way it will look to other people.'

'Oh, I don't care!' I exclaimed. And I really didn't. It was far too late to worry about other people. 'I don't care what other people think. Let them think what they like.'

We had been watching *Dirty Dancing* together on the sofa, our fingers entwined, when I realized the time was right to take the next step.

'Take me upstairs,' I whispered to him.

'Oh,' his face fell. 'Okay then.'

Well, that was weird. And definitely not the reaction I was expecting! Maybe he hadn't heard me.

'Take me upstairs, Jem,' I repeated.

'Oh!' Now his eyebrows shot up and his expression transformed into one of joy.

That was a bit more like it.

'What did you think I said?' I asked.

'I thought you asked me to take you home…'

'No…' I giggled. 'I want to stay here tonight. With you.'

And without another word spoken between us, he got up and led me upstairs to the bedroom.

Now a warmth spread over me as I recalled our exquisite night together. It had been my first time with a man but I wasn't scared or nervous at all. He told me I was only the second woman he had taken to bed, so it felt very meaningful for both of us. Just as I imagined, he was tender, passionate and generous. We'd hardly slept a wink, delighted by the discovery of each other's bodies. Occasionally we would both doze off but then we'd wake again, surprised and excited all over again to be together in this way. I wanted the night to last forever. But we'd fallen asleep eventually and now the harsh daylight bullied its way through the curtains. Jeremy pushed himself onto his elbow and glanced at the alarm clock.

'Oh no!' he groaned. 'I'd really rather stay here with you, sweetie, but I'm afraid I have to go to work.'

Then he kissed me on my head, cheek and neck before finally planting a soft kiss on my lips, before rolling over to his side of the bed, flinging off the duvet and walking stark naked to the bathroom.

*Whoah! There's no self-consciousness with this man...*I admired his body confidence. I certainly wouldn't have left the bed so boldly. In fact, I was very relieved Jeremy had to leave before me so that I could hide my nakedness, under the covers, instead of hopping about, looking for my clothes.

I watched from the bed as Jeremy returned, dripping wet from his shower, clutching a small towel around his middle, and dressed himself in his smart work clothes. From the radio next to me the newsreader kept up her patter, though I hardly paid her any attention until Jeremy looked over and addressed the radio:

'It's *post*humously, not post*hum*ously.'

'What was that?' I asked him.

'She pronounced the word wrong,' he said absentmindedly, pulling up his socks. 'She put the emphasis on the second syllable but the word is *post*humously.'

It was such a throwaway comment but inwardly I smiled to myself. *Cute and clever!* Once he was fully dressed he sat down on the bed next to me and kissed me again on the forehead.

'I've got to go to work. You can sleep longer if you like. Just let yourself out when you're ready and I'll see you later.'

A few minutes after that I heard the front door slam and then I lay there, wondering how the hell I was going to get home without all the neighbours noticing. I had only lived on the street for a few months. Leaving my divorced neighbour's house at 7.30am - how was that going to look? I imagined curtains twitching down the length of the street. I got out of bed and started to gather up my clothes. Opening his front door just a little way, I quickly checked up and down the street for any familiar faces before bolting down his front path and back up towards my front door.

All that morning as I showered and got ready for university, little memories from the night before kept popping into my head. It had been such a special evening and everything felt so natural between us. Even as I walked to class, it felt as if I was floating on air. After class, my Portuguese friend Silvia made a beeline for me and nudged me in the ribs.

'Okay, spill the beans!' she demanded.

'What?' I laughed.

'You've just grinned your way through a bloody statistics exam, Shalini! I don't consider that normal behaviour so you better tell me what's so amusing or I'm going to have to start guessing.'

'Really?' I couldn't believe it. Had my happiness been on show for everyone to see?

'Really!' Silvia nodded. 'You're looking radiant! I'm guessing it's probably got something to do with that neighbour of yours you've been seeing... hmm?'

I didn't say a word.

'Aha! It *is* him!'

'Oh Silvia, we just spent the most amazing night together!'

'What… the whole night?'

'Yes!' I squealed. 'All of it!'

Silvia and I were good friends and she knew this was a big deal for me.

'I suppose that explains all the grinning. What can I say - congratulations! I guess you must really like this guy?'

I nodded. 'You know what, I think he's perfect for me.'

It wasn't long after our first night together that Jeremy told me he loved me. We had been in my kitchen making dinner and while we were waiting for the food to cook, he had pulled me onto his lap for a kiss. He was always doing things like that - it was as if he couldn't get enough of me. He told me all the time how beautiful I was and how much he adored me. He left beautifully-written cards and notes for me to find. He made me feel like a princess. He had even taken to making me tea every morning and bringing it up to me in bed. After we kissed, I got up to check on the food and, as I walked away he said, 'You know, Shal, I think I love you.'

My heart stopped a moment. *Oh my goodness. He loves me!* It was such a big deal and yet he had said it so easily, like it was the most normal thing in the world.

'Oh. Okay. Thank you,' I squeaked, feeling shocked and embarrassed.

We had only been going out a few weeks and I didn't know if it was normal to feel this way so quickly. I would tell him I loved him too, in time, when I felt ready. I glanced back at him and saw that he knew I felt the same way.

A few days later Jeremy introduced me to his daughters - Jenny, Katie and Amanda – and his mother, Gladys, a petite woman with perfectly-groomed hair and immaculate nails. Although she came across as very English in her mannerisms, Gladys was actually half French and occasionally threw French sentences into her conversations. She was fiercely loyal and protective of Jeremy and at first seemed a little wary of me. Who could blame her? Her son had been hurt not long ago and now he was opening himself up again. Would I do the same to him? Would I break his heart? But it didn't take long for her to see that I was sincere.

Jeremy's daughters were polite, if somewhat shy at first. But once they relaxed they began to talk quite openly, giving me some wonderful anecdotes about Jeremy and telling me how he took them fishing, golfing and boating. I showed them around my house as they were curious to see how similar it was to their Dad's house. I was relieved that our first meeting went so well.

On the weekend of the Summer Solstice Jeremy surprised me with a weekend away to Swanage, on the Dorset coast. Until then, the weekends had always been strictly off-limits as they were the only times when Jeremy got to spend time with his daughters and I respected that. But on this weekend Jeremy had rearranged things so we could spend some free time together, unencumbered by work or university.

'Let's go away!' he suggested. 'Let's go to the seaside!'

I should have been nervous – after all, we were going to be spending two whole days together without a break – but I wasn't. I called it our 'first dirty weekend away' and I couldn't wait. We found a lovely country house hotel situated along Studland Bay with uninterrupted views of the sea and long stretches of sandy coastline.

Our days were punctuated by mealtimes, long morning and evening walks on the beach and time just being with each other talking and making love. As we spent time in the beautiful country house landscaped gardens there was a deep sense of ease that we felt with each other, a feeling that being together felt right, an innate knowledge that this is how it was meant to be.

On our return, Jeremy surprised me with a stunning sapphire ring, my birthstone. As he opened the box, I was taken aback. It seemed such a very big gesture, but there was more to come.

'Shal, these past few weeks have been the best in my life,' he started, hesitantly. 'I could never have imagined meeting you and how much happiness you've brought to my life. I want to marry you, if you'll have me?'

I was amazed. We had only known each other for two months and had only been seeing each other properly for a few weeks. I was astonished that he was ready to marry again, having been through such a dreadful divorce. I gazed at Jeremy's beautiful ring.

'My goodness, Jem.' I didn't know what to say. 'This is beautiful but, the truth is, I don't see myself getting married, to anyone. Ever! I have so many other things I want to achieve in my life.'

Seeing his face fall, I hastily continued, 'Look, I really want to be with you too but I don't think we need a piece of paper or a ceremony to prove our feelings for one another. Do you? How can you even think of getting married again after what you've been through?'

'Actually, I thought we had a good marriage,' he said quietly now. 'But that was nothing compared to the way I feel now. Look, I know it's quick. I know it's a big commitment. Please just take the ring as a token of my love for you. And if you ever decide to change your mind about marriage, I'll be right here.'

There was another reason I couldn't contemplate marrying Jeremy - a reason I had been ignoring up until this moment: my parents. In their eyes, a man like Jeremy was the opposite of marriage material for a 'good Indian girl'. For starters, he was white and not a Hindu; secondly, he was nearly double my age, thirdly he was divorced and fourthly he had three children in tow. My parents would have seen him as completely unsuitable for me. He was not the well-educated, financially well-off Indian boy from a respectable family that my family would have chosen for me. And yet, riding this wave of our love, I felt certain that I could convince them to accept Jeremy and my love for him. My sister, Shivani, who was studying Zoology at Lancaster University, had already met him and she agreed with me that he was a real gentleman. But she also knew that no matter how good a man Jeremy was, they would never accept him – the cultural differences were just too huge. Good Indian girls did not behave in this way; they did not let themselves fall for divorcee neighbours.

It will be okay, I told myself as I packed my suitcase in preparation for a planned holiday in Kenya at the beginning of July. *We love each other and that's all that matters.* I was looking forward to going home and seeing my parents again, spending time with Shivani and going on safari together. I would tell my mother and father about Jeremy then. I would let them know how much we cared for one another. Suddenly Celine Dion came on the radio singing *Because You Loved Me...*

I felt my heart swell in my chest. Until now I had never known what true love felt like. My friend Cheeku, who I had met at Les Roches, and I had laughed ourselves silly when we'd first heard the lyrics to this song – what a weak and stupid woman, we'd agreed. It was anathema to me, the idea of giving myself so fully to a man. A strong feminist, I believed in standing on my own two feet and not relying on someone else for my happiness. The idea of surrendering myself mind, body and soul was so alien to me, I couldn't imagine it. But now, listening to the song again, I heard the gentle strength in her words and yes, it rang true.

It would be okay, I assured myself again. It would have to be.

Chapter 4 – Feet Away, Worlds Apart

"Being deeply loved by someone gives you strength,
while loving someone deeply gives you courage."
—Lao Tzu[4]

'Shal!' Jeremy's eyes widened in shock. *Oh, it was so good to see his face again.* He grabbed me and enveloped me in a massive bear hug. After four long weeks apart, I had yearned for this moment, to feel his arms around me again. Now I let myself melt into his body.

'Wow! Look at you – you look stunning!'

He pulled me back to admire me and I let him twirl me by the shoulders, pleased he appreciated the effort I had gone to. Despite a gruelling nine-hour flight from Nairobi to London, arriving in the early hours of the morning, I'd managed to get home by taxi and shower before putting on this pretty red floral dress with big white buttons down the front. I knew he loved to see me in colourful clothes and I probably looked healthy and refreshed after my month-long stay in Kenya.

'I thought you weren't due back until this evening,' he went on, ushering me into his house.

'I managed to catch an earlier flight. Surprise!!'

'What a wonderful surprise! Oh Shal, I've missed you so much. Oh, my love!'

And with that, he pulled me to him again and covered me in kisses. Reunited with the man I loved, I should have been ecstatic, but something didn't feel right. His love for me was so big, so strong, it was everywhere. It was… overwhelming. My mouth felt dry all of a sudden.

'Can I get a cup of tea please?' I asked. I was probably dehydrated from the flight.

'Yes, of course! Sit right there, sit down, let me make you a cuppa.'

For the next hour Jeremy fussed over me, asking me questions about my trip to Kenya and all the while taking every opportunity to touch me, grab my hand and cuddle me. As he did so, I began to withdraw into myself.

'What's wrong?' he asked, breaking a long silence that had filled the room.

'Nothing,' I snapped. 'Nothing's wrong. Why do you ask?'

'Well, it's just that you seem very quiet, Shal,' he said, looking hurt and confused.

'I'm just tired, that's all,' I made an excuse. 'Sorry, Jem. It's been a long journey and I probably need some sleep. Do you mind?' I asked, as I stood up.

'No, of course not, not at all…'

But I could see the bewilderment in his eyes. We had been apart for a whole month and now I could barely spend an hour in his company. I couldn't make sense of it and yet I knew I wouldn't be able to think clearly while we were together. I had to find some space.

As soon as I shut the door to my house, I collapsed in tears. *This can never work!* I knew that now. I had been living in a dream world, a fantasy where I could do exactly what I wanted and there were no consequences. But my life wasn't really like that. I had seen that on my return to Kenya. It was so obvious and yet I'd been fooling myself until now, fooling myself into believing Jeremy would ever fit into my parents' world – *my* world in Kenya. Returning to my parents' home in Nairobi, I had been reminded of the reality of my life, my childhood flooding back to me and eclipsing the new life I had built for myself in England.

I was five when we had moved into the red-roofed stone bungalow in a northern suburb of Nairobi. I remember very clearly the day we had moved in and the excitement I'd felt on coming to live in such a beautiful house. My parents had bought the place for 1 million Kenyan shillings, which is only about £7,000 in today's money, but considered a fortune back then. Ours was one of several houses surrounding a man-made lake, each sitting in a half acre of lush vegetation.

My parents, too, were proud of their new home. My mother grew beautiful roses among the tall cypress trees in our garden and built a pond with lilies and a pretty *banda* - a painted wooden Kenyan summerhouse with a thatched roof. Both my mother and father worked all hours to make a success of their businesses and that meant that my sister and I were looked after by our *ayah* (nanny), Esther. We also spent a lot of time with my mother's older sister, Usha, She was our Ushamasi (Masi meaning aunt) and she was like a second mother to us. Since she herself had only sons, she lavished love and praise on me and my sister, calling us her only daughters. In turn, we grew up calling her Mom.

Now, as I wandered from room to room, I was reminded of the years I had spent here practicing my dance routines in the sunken lounge next to the fireplace, doing my homework in my bedroom or playing hopscotch on the tiled slabs of the courtyard with my sister. We were never bored in this house, I reflected, never allowed to 'do nothing', as my mother called it. That was considered 'lazy' so every hour of our days was filled with non-stop activity. There was a constant striving to achieve, to reach one's goals and beyond. It wasn't enough to come second in my class, I had to be first. It wasn't enough to get a B in a test, I had to get an A. I was taught to be the best I could be – and that was what I wanted too. Our mother had instilled in us both a drive to succeed and, back in this house, I felt again the heavy weight of expectation settle on my shoulders.

My education had been built around the idea that I would return to Kenya and take over my father's restaurant chain. And yet, living away from home for so long and establishing my independence as a woman, the goal of eventually returning to Kenyan life and taking on the responsibilities of the family business had been lost. Blinded by my love for Jeremy, I was convinced that the relationship was compatible with this plan. I thought that I could persuade my parents to accept this man as my chosen partner in life and all would be well. But with every day that passed in Nairobi and in my parents' company, my dream seemed more and more impossible.

In Kenya I returned to being Shalini, the good daughter, a child in my parents' eyes, who needed to be chauffeured around, told what to do and whose future was clearly mapped out in front of her. How could Jeremy fit into this? He would never move to Kenya, not while his daughters were still growing up. And my parents would never allow him – a white, middle-aged divorcee with children – to become part of our family. No, the world that Jeremy and I inhabited in England simply didn't work with that of my parents' in Kenya.

It took returning to Kenya to see the reality and I knew that telling my mother and father about how I had fallen madly in love with a completely unsuitable man would only bring them pain and heartache. These were the people who had loved and cared for me all my life. They mattered more to me than anyone and I couldn't hurt them. For a while, I had pushed these uncomfortable feelings to one side but the moment I had been reunited with Jeremy, all my fears for the future resurfaced. Now, back in my house in Guildford, I fretted, trying to work out what to do. In the late afternoon, a hand-delivered letter dropped onto the mat.

19th July 1997

My Dearest Shal,

We are now only yards away from each other and are not seeing one another. Why are we doing this? Weren't we blissfully happy together? Is it so wrong to be happy in another person's company? I feel dreadful — how about you? I won't ultimately get in the way of your goals or upset your folks. I realise that your ambitions in life are, and will be, your main drivers for your happiness. I also think I understand your worries for the future.

There must be a great deal more behind your concerns which I may never understand or know about.

Please speak to me sometime soon. I pray for you and for peace in our hearts. I love you, with all my heart and much, much more…

Jeremy xxx

Jeremy knew something was wrong. I sensed his anguish and confusion through his beautiful swirly handwriting, which seemed to belong to another century. This wasn't fair! I couldn't leave him in limbo. I needed to explain to him just why this wouldn't work. Fighting back the tears, I started to write.

My Dearest Jeremy,

Two months ago, I started something that I never should have — something that has got us in the position that we are in now. A difficult and painful time for both of us. When I first met you, I was inexplicably drawn to you. I wanted to get to know you. The more I learnt, the more I wanted to know. Eventually I couldn't stop thinking about you and I guess the inevitable happened – I fell in love with you. The most amazing man who has ever entered my life. You made me feel beautiful, special. Everything I dreamed the right man would do or say, you said and did. You were perfect for me.

What I really didn't count on was the impact I would have on your life. I never thought I could have such an effect on anyone. How can I be the best thing that has ever happened to you? All I will do in the end is hurt you like I've already done, like you've been hurt before. I trust you totally, but it is myself I do not trust. It is me who will mess up this relationship. The reason is that my parents will never accept you or my love for you. I know I've always said we should live in the present and not in the past or the future but the future worries me. Four weeks without you was hell. How will I live the rest of my life without you? You make me so, so happy but this whole relationship is tearing me up inside. I had so many conflicting feelings whilst in Kenya because being with my parents brought me down to earth. I had been living in a dream world with you. I thought that when I came back I would be able to put all my doubts and guilt behind me and we would be able to go back to how it was before I left. I was wrong.

Now not only do I carry the guilt of hiding this huge secret from my parents but I also carry the guilt of hurting you. You opened yourself up to me, you trusted me and I've betrayed that… and for that I am so sorry. I really wanted to believe that everything would be fine. I love you enough to fight the world for you… but not enough to betray my family's trust in me. I already have done. But they will never know. I will not hurt them. I will not choose you over them. If this continues, one day I will have to make a choice, and they will come first. Yes, it is my life, but it was given to me by my parents and they will always take priority whenever I have to make a decision that will affect any of us. I can't give you just a part of me – it is all or nothing - and I can't give you my all. I can't introduce you to and share you with the most important people in my life. I can't ever show you where I'm from, what my life before you was like. There will always be a part of me – a big part – that you will never understand, you will not be able to share with me. How can we continue a relationship based on this?

I love you. I love you so very much. I've shared things with you that I've never shared with anyone. I've given you me. Please don't hate me, but I can't go on like this. You are a wonderful person – so much to give, so much love. I cannot describe how you have changed my life and how special you have made me feel. I feel so sad, so empty today. Exactly the opposite of what I thought today would be like. I've hurt you and I'm sorry. Forgive me if you can. Today, I'm asking you to release me from this relationship. Of one thing I am sure, that to love you and to be loved by you was all that I asked for at one time. And all that time that we spent together will always be really precious to me and I will cherish all the memories forever.

I love you Jeremy. This has been one of the hardest things that I've done in my life and I am sorry for all the pain I have caused. If you ever feel that you can stand to face me, I'll be here. Just to see you once in a while will be enough.

Take care my sweets.

I love you.
Shal

It was the only way forward, I knew that now. The only way out of the mess I had created. Yes, it would hurt us both in the short term but not as much if I allowed the relationship to continue down the same path. It was, on balance, the least destructive thing I could do, but knowing that didn't make it any easier. My heart broke as I posted the letter through his front door and I retreated back to my house. I couldn't contemplate a future without my parents - after all, they had supported me all these years, loved me, encouraged me and given me the opportunities to pursue my goals. After everything they'd done for me, I owed it to them to do the right thing. It didn't feel right for Jeremy and me but this was the sacrifice I had to make in the deliverance of my duty to them. That night I cried myself to sleep, imagining Jeremy in his room, just a few feet away, so close and yet a world apart.

The next day I set about my daily tasks, opening letters, paying bills, dealing with my university admin and trying to distract myself. I tried not to think about Jeremy because it was simply too painful. *What was he doing now? What was he thinking?*

Did he hate me for what I'd done? I felt wretched at the thought of hurting him and confused at how something which felt so right and good was causing us both so much pain. *It wasn't fair.* I'd never done anything against my parents' wishes before, never rebelled in the slightest. Was falling in love really such a crime?

Jeremy didn't put up a fight, come round to my house and throw himself at my feet. He didn't make any sort of objection at all. He was too respectful of the difficulties that I faced, too sensitive to my feelings to make this any harder than it already was. He left me alone. But his absence was monstrous. I kept recalling the love he had poured into the letters he had written while I was in Kenya. We had come to mean so much to each other in such a short space of time. Physically and emotionally I already depended on him so much. Alone in my house, I felt desolate and adrift. I couldn't turn back the clock, pretend we'd never met and fallen in love. And why should I? Pain quickly shifted to anger... Why was I putting myself through this when the man I loved was just on the other side of this wall? Why was I sacrificing my future happiness? Who would benefit?

After all, I reasoned, my parents had fallen in love themselves, defying the wishes of both families. My Gujarati mother had fallen for my Punjabi father, which, according to both sides of the family, was a terrible decision. After all, they argued, weren't Punjabis and Gujaratis fundamentally different? Each had their own language, culture and ideas. I mean, how could they ever understand one another when those deep ancestral stereotypes were so fundamentally opposed? The Punjabis looked at the Gujaratis as puny, tee-total, vegetarian money-minded mercenaries while, on the other side, the Gujaratis considered all

Punjabis to be flashy, loud, whisky-drinking, meat-eating chauvinists.

Just like the Scottish and the English, they had an entrenched mistrust of one another. My paternal grandfather was so against the marriage that he had even threatened suicide if it went ahead. The fact that my mother came from a family with a lot less money than my father's only compounded the situation. My parents did not want to hurt their parents but neither did they want to break up their relationship. Finally, after years of waiting for the dust to settle in their homes, the families agreed to their marriage and they settled down in their own home, something very unusual in Indian families, where it is customary for the wife to move into her husband's family home. My mother, who had been picked on by the wives of my father's older brothers, felt unwelcome in his parents' house and insisted he buy them a flat of their own. She was a strong, independent woman and she wasn't afraid to rock the boat. Was my situation really so very different?

If my father struggled to accept a non-Indian man as a son-in-law, surely my mother would be on my side? She had always been my biggest champion, supporting me in all of my decisions. I looked around – hadn't I proved myself by taking on this house and being responsible for the mortgage? She trusted me and I felt sure that if she knew my true feelings she would find a way to placate my father.

She was due to visit me in six weeks' time - perhaps then I could tell her. Surely, if she met Jeremy she would realise what a special person he was. If she just gave him a chance we could persuade her to smooth the path with my father. It would never have worked if I'd told them in Kenya, in their home. But here in

England, I wasn't a child. I was an independent adult in my own right. *I'll explain it to her… I'll tell her… she'll support me. Yes, mum will be on my side.*

That night, only 24 hours after ending things with him, I walked over to Jeremy's house.

'I can't live without you. It's too hard. We'll find a way through this. I promise. We'll work it out.'

Chapter 5 – Love, Eclipsed

"Love is from the infinite, and will remain until eternity."
—**Rumi**[5]

*Y*our father will never accept this,' my mother said quietly. 'Never.'

Then she straightened her back, folded her hands in her lap and fixed me with a stern look. I knew what that look meant: *conversation over, there's nothing more to say on the matter.* This was worse than I had anticipated. I knew it would be hard but I hadn't expected my mother to be so closed off. I turned to my Ushamasi for support. She too was in shock at the news, but I could tell she wasn't as rigid as my mother. It was clear that my mother's mind was fixed on one thing: my father. How would she ever be able to tell him? He was really short-tempered, we all knew that, and when his anger was up, he could be quite frightening. But, surely, she could persuade him?

It was early September, six weeks after my return from Kenya, and I had travelled to my grandmother's house in Bounds Green to meet my mother and aunt who had flown in for a visit. My mother had a big family – there were eight siblings in total, six sisters and two brothers. The story went that my grandmother kept having girls and was determined to have sons. So, she just kept going until my two uncles came along. Over the years most of the family had relocated to London to study and work – it was only my mother and Ushamasi who had stayed in Kenya.

I had found my courage in Guildford and of course, the past few weeks reunited with Jeremy had been wonderful. A DIY enthusiast, he'd helped to redecorate the hallway and lounge in my house in preparation for my mother's visit. I discovered that he was one of those men who could literally turn his hand to anything – hanging curtain rails, putting up wallpaper and grouting the tiles in the bathroom. There was nothing he couldn't do and of course I had no end of jobs for him to tackle in my new home. He also helped me landscape the garden – and re-plant what his rabbit had eaten. I had found a tenant already - a friend from Les Roches – and I was also waitressing to help pay the bills. I wanted to show my mother that I was worthy of her trust. Now, determined to brave her condemnation and find a way to win her approval, I had come to London to reveal my big secret.

'Mum, I've got something to tell you,' I had started. 'I've met somebody. I love him, he loves me and we make each other very happy. The thing is – he's English. He's also divorced, he has three children from his previous marriage and he's 19 years older than me. He lives next door to me in Guildford.'

There was no point sugar-coating it – they had to know the truth right from the start.

My mother turned pale, put her hand to her mouth and broke down completely.

'Look, I know he's not what you would consider suitable...' I desperately continued, as Ushamasi tried to comfort her. 'And I did try to break up with him, but it didn't work. Mum, I really, really love him. I want you to meet him because he is the person I want to spend the rest of my life with.'

She gasped at that and continued to cry. Her face a mixture of pain, fear and confusion. I felt awful. I couldn't bear hurting her like this, but I knew that I couldn't keep this from my parents any longer.

'When you come to Guildford, I'd like you to meet him...' I ploughed on. 'Then you can talk to him and get to know him for yourself. He's wonderful - he's very caring and he loves me very much and I really think you'll like him.'

'Shalini, don't be so foolish!' my mother whispered, more in despair than anger. 'This will not be acceptable to your father. You know that. It can't happen.'

'Mum, just meet him. Please.'

'Okay, okay Shalini.' My aunt was keen to diffuse the situation. She put a hand on my shoulder. 'We'll come to Guildford. We'll come and meet him and talk to him and work all this out. Okay?'

I nodded.

'I think it's better if you go home now. Give your mother some time. This is a lot to take in, hmm?'

It didn't take long for the news to spread like wildfire. There were no secrets on my mother's side of the family and, one by one, my aunts called to urge me to end the relationship.

'Think of your family,' they implored. 'You are bringing shame and disrespect to your parents. How can you do this to them? It is so selfish and ungrateful. You know nothing about this man – he is too old for you and is taking advantage of you.'

'Don't do it, Shalini!' my Mum's younger sister begged, when she called me. 'This is the worst mistake of your life. Don't put everything at risk for this man. It's not worth it.'

Back at home with Jeremy, I was tormented by their words.

'Am I being selfish?' I asked him. 'My family have put all their faith in me. It feels like I'm betraying them.'

'You are the least selfish person I've ever known,' Jeremy reassured me. 'You do so much to make others happy and you're always concerned with how other people feel. I'm sure that when you see your mum and explain things to her, she'll understand.'

'Will she?'

'Of course! I mean, look at what you've done with the house!' he gestured to my living room which together we'd spent many hours decorating.

Everything had been carefully picked out and arranged and I'd cleaned and scrubbed every surface till they gleamed.

'She'll be really proud of what you've achieved with this place. It looks great and it shows how much you care.'

I nestled into his arms.

'They made me feel like the worst person in the world,' I murmured. 'They said Mum and Pop will really suffer because of my selfishness.'

'Shhh,' Jeremy stroked my hair. 'Don't think about it. Don't take it to heart. Whatever happens, just remember I'm here for you and I'll do everything I can to support you - always. You can depend on me.'

Two days later, my mother and Ushamasi arrived in Guildford. Nervously, I showed them around the house. Ushamasi made admiring noises at all the improvements I'd made, while my mother carefully inspected every inch of the place, running her hands along banisters, feeling the curtain for quality and checking the finish on the worktops. Nothing escaped her laser-like attention.

'And I've already brought in a tenant,' I babbled as I sat them down in the kitchen. 'My friend from Switzerland is studying here in Surrey and she will take the second room and I hope to have another tenant soon. Tea?'

Mum made a non-committal sound.

A second later the doorbell rang - it felt like the cavalry had arrived. I jumped up from the kitchen table and practically ran to the front door to find Jeremy on the other side, wearing a smart mustard-coloured shirt and his most reassuring smile.

'Don't worry,' he whispered and squeezed my hand. 'It'll be fine.'

I showed him through to the kitchen and, trying to control the waver in my voice, I announced, 'Mum, this is Jeremy!'

I had imagined this moment so many times in my head, playing out the scene in so many different ways but nothing could have prepared me for my mother's dismissive response.

'Oh hello,' she said flatly, barely giving him a second glance. My heart sank. She wasn't even going to give him a chance. As if to make up for my mother's rudeness, Ushamasi rose from her seat and put out her hand to shake his.

'Hello Jeremy – it's nice to meet you.'

The next hour was torture. I made everybody a cup of tea and Jeremy sat down at the kitchen table between my mum and Ushamasi, while I hovered next to him, one hand protectively on his shoulder.

'So… Shalini has told us a little bit about you, Jeremy,' my aunt said. 'But I think we'd like to know a little more. She says you're divorced. Is that right?'

'It is.'

'What was the reason for this?'

Patiently, Jeremy explained the painful breakup of his marriage. He talked about his three girls and the good relationship they shared. My mother started firing questions at him. What was his job? What were his financial commitments to his children? What were his intentions towards me? On and on it went, Jeremy answering every question with good-humour and honesty. But after an hour of this grilling, even he became weary. He placed his cup down on the table in front of him and turned to my mother.

'Look, Mrs Bhalla, please understand I'm not here to hurt your daughter,' he said. 'I know the age difference is going to be a problem. I know that if my daughter went out with someone so much older I would be uncomfortable. I know I've got all the baggage and on paper I'm the wrong person for her. But I really love her. I will not hurt her.'

He was so sincere, so compassionate. Sadly, my mother wasn't listening and Jeremy's heartfelt appeal fell on deaf ears.

'It's not a good idea,' she said simply. 'My husband will not accept you.'

For a long while no one said anything. Then my aunt spoke,

'Jeremy, thank you for your reassurances. It's very nice to meet you and I can see you and Shalini are very much in love. But the problem, you see, is that my sister is very worried about her husband. Ashok will not agree to this.'

'But you can both talk to him can't you?' I asked, hopefully. 'Tell him that Jeremy is a good man, that we love each other and we want to be together.'

My mother shook her head. No, that was her answer. No, she wouldn't support me on this. No. She wouldn't stand up to my father. No. No. No.

'Perhaps now is not the right time,' my aunt suggested gently. 'Yes, we will tell him. It will be fine, I'm sure. But I think that maybe we should keep this from him. For now, at least.'

I looked at my mother. *Please support me.* I willed her to be on my side but she refused to return my gaze.

'No, we can't tell him now,' my mother agreed. 'Ashok doesn't need to know this.'

Jeremy nodded. 'Of course, I'll go with whatever you feel is best.'

He got up to leave and he shook hands with both my mother and my aunt. Then, just as he had started to walk out my mother said to him,

'Well, Jeremy, you better know that Shalini is a very stubborn, strong-headed girl. But she's your problem now.'

It cut me to the quick, those words. As if she was washing her hands of me. *She's your problem now.* I never realised I was a problem to her! I'd never felt like a problem before now. All these years I had done everything in my power to please her, to make her proud and now, in one day, I had disappointed her so much that she wanted nothing more to do with me. And yet... and yet... I still hoped that my mother would come around. That she would see how much happiness he brought me and relent. I still wanted her to find a way to make it work with my father. She just needed more time. I was sure that it wouldn't be long before she told him.

In the end, it would be two years before my mother told my father about Jeremy and me. During that time, our love for one another only deepened. Jeremy built a little gate between our garden fences so we no longer had to brave the neighbours every time we wanted to see each other and our houses became almost interlocking. Our lives became completely intertwined as we spent every night together, cooked for each other and introduced each other to our respective friends. We also had some fun-filled days out with his girls and his mother and I felt relaxed and happy in their company.

In July 1998, for our first proper holiday together, we stayed in an idyllic hotel overlooking Coverack beach in Cornwall. The journey was a long one but it didn't feel that way. Seated next to Jeremy in my short white sundress, as we sped down the small winding B-roads towards the Lizard Peninsula, I felt so free and happy. We had been a couple for almost 14 months now and life together felt right and comfortable. We had an amazing week – our hotel was right on the bay and every afternoon the husband and wife team who ran the place served traditional afternoon tea on the lawn. Most mornings we walked along the beach and for lunch we enjoyed cold beer and hot chips at the pub on the peninsula.

It was just the start of the many holidays we took together. Later that year we went to Bournemouth and stayed in a little B&B in Christchurch. Seeing our names written down as Mr. and Mrs. Lucas in the checking-in book at reception gave me a little thrill. We giggled a lot that holiday because our bed creaked and we were conscious of making a terrible racket at night. Every evening we'd share a bottle of red wine with our chateaubriand at The Crooked Beam- a cosy, candle-lit restaurant with low wood-beamed ceilings and a romantic ambiance.

Nairobi and my familial responsibilities became more and more distant for me. I knew my mother was tormented by my relationship – my sister reported back to me whenever she visited - but she didn't tell my father about Jeremy. During that time, she also went through some sort of an 'epiphany', whereby she abandoned her Hindu religion and turned to a very extreme Christian belief system. She started going to church, to preach to whoever would listen and attempted to convert us all. I found it all rather strange and annoying. I begged her to tell my father about the relationship but she insisted that the time wasn't right and swore us both to secrecy.

It meant that when I graduated from the University of Surrey in December 1998 and my parents came to stay, I had to hide Jeremy away. We even had to replace the gate between our gardens with a fence panel so as not to arouse my father's suspicions. For a whole week I couldn't see Jeremy and it was painful for us both. Thankfully, I managed to get him a ticket to my graduation and he crept into the back of Guildford Cathedral without my family knowing he was there. But it felt wrong to sneak around like this and unfair that he couldn't be part of the celebrations.; that he had to watch it from afar.

These were the moments of frustration, though they weren't very frequent. Generally, Jeremy and I got on with our lives and didn't think too hard about my parents back home in Nairobi. They were out of sight and out of mind and, as long as my father didn't know about the relationship, I didn't have to face the truth: that if he decided he wouldn't support our relationship, my life would be changed forever. My mother had her reasons for keeping it from him. She probably hoped the relationship would fizzle out.

But as it became clear this would never happen, the pressure got too much for her and she realised that she had to tell him the truth.

On 11 August 1999, Jeremy and I had invited all our friends and colleagues round for a solar eclipse party. We opened up the gate between our gardens and started with drinks at my house at 10am. Then we moved into the garden for the eclipse, before crowding into Jeremy's house for the food he had prepared. Jeremy was a good cook and he enjoyed catering for people, while I enjoyed being the hostess with the mostest, flitting around, filling glasses, chatting and entertaining our guests. We had about 30 people – some friends of mine from the hotel in Haslemere where I worked, university friends, Jeremy's golfing pals and their wives. It was the first time we had entertained jointly and we both had a good time. By 6pm, everyone had left and we were clearing up the glasses at my house when my landline rang.

'Shalini, I've got your father here,' my mother's voice was strained. 'He wants to talk to you.'

'Don't do it! Don't do this, Shalini,' my father pleaded down the line. 'You can't be with him. Please, don't do this to us.'

'But Pop I love him,' I whispered, when I finally found my voice, which sounded thin and weak, like that of a small child. I could hear my sister crying in the background – it broke my heart to know how much she was suffering.

'No, *Bete*, said my father, using the Hindi word for child. You can't be with him. You know that. You really know that you can't be with this man…'

Hearing my father speak like this made me feel like I had been punched in the stomach and I fell to the ground. Until I met Jeremy, he had been the only man in my life and until now, I had done everything he said. He was my father. How could I betray him?

'You have to make the right decision, Shalini,' my father went on. 'You can't be with this man. Don't make a bad choice.'

In the moment, I suddenly realized that I wasn't just beholden to my family. I was beholden to the Indian society that my parents were a part of, that I had once been a part of. It was my family's *izzat* that I was destroying. Family respect. Family honour. In Indian culture it is considered that the whole family's honour rests in the behavior of the daughters, particularly the eldest. By falling in love with the wrong man I was destroying my family's reputation and honour. All those years my parents had spent building up a good name for themselves and I was throwing it all away in the self-interested pursuit of happiness. In Jeremy I had found the most unsuitable of men – and he would never be accepted.

As soon as my father hung up, I burst into tears.

'He won't accept you,' I wept, as Jeremy took my in his arms. 'What can I do? What can I do?'

'Shal…'

'No, Jeremy. You don't understand. He is my father! I cannot go against him. If he doesn't approve of us then there's nothing else I can do. I can't lose my family. I just can't. Please go. I need some time. Please leave me alone.'

Staring into the darkness that night I went over the events of the day. The eclipse had been weird, otherworldly even. Jeremy and I had watched, side by side, as the sky slowly turned to black in the middle of the day and one by one, all the birds in the garden fell silent. Suddenly it was dark as night. Everywhere there was a heavy silence, a stillness that was beautiful yet unnerving in some ways. Standing next to Jeremy, I had felt anchored, complete. The world could tip on its axis and fall into oblivion but as long as he was there with me, I knew I could cope. Choosing a love affair that had lasted for two years over a 21-year family bond was the hardest thing I could imagine, but I knew that Jeremy and I were meant to be together. Until this moment I had believed that the mere fact of our love would bridge barriers and cultural differences. I knew now that it wouldn't. My mother had refused to support me, my father refused to accept us. It was time to face reality.

'I choose you,' I told Jeremy later that night, having slipped back through the gate into his garden. 'But this is it now. My family will disown me – they have made that very clear. There's no going back. I need you now more than ever. I can no longer be financially tied to my parents so I'll have to make some changes in my life.'

'I'll support you, whatever it takes,' he said, tears in his eyes.

We both knew this was a huge turning point in our lives.

'I'll never let you down. What you have done for me is astonishing, overwhelming and I won't take it for granted, not for one second. You do know that, don't you?' he said as he stared intently into my eyes.

'Yes, I do. I trust you, Jeremy, with all my heart. I know we are meant to be together. This is going to be really tough but I know with your support I'll make it.'

'We'll make it,' he corrected me. 'Together.'

Chapter 6 – A New Start

"Every moment is a fresh beginning."
—T.S. Eliot[6]

'*C*heers!' Jeremy lifted his glass to mine and we clinked them together.

'Cheers!' I smiled. 'Here's to us, to our new home and a new start.'

Having dinner in the conservatory of our new home, I felt genuinely happy for the first time in ages. It didn't matter one bit that we were surrounded by the boxes that the removal men had lugged in earlier today, we were in our own home and it felt good. I gazed out onto our beautiful garden, still dappled with summer evening sunlight. *At last, we were heading in the right direction!*

It had been such a struggle the past few months. From the moment I had told my parents that I intended to stay with Jeremy, I knew that my life had to change drastically. To begin with, it was clear that I would have to leave the house I had lived in for the last three years. The house was sold and I began to reconcile myself to the fact that I had made a decision which had changed the course of my life. Now there was no way I could return to Kenya to work with my father in his restaurant business. I moved into Jeremy's house in the New Year of the new millennium. My mother and I never spoke of the house again but I knew that selling it had been just as distressing for her as it had been for me. I quickly discovered that there wasn't much room at Jeremy's house.

'Where am I supposed to keep my clothes?' I asked him, on finding every wardrobe in the house packed full with either his clothes or the girls' toys.

'I'm sorry,' he said. 'I'll clear out some of the clutter and put it in the loft.'

It was the same story in every single room – the whole house was full to the brim with Jeremy's and his children's possessions. I suppose, given that this had been their family home for many years, it was hardly surprising. But the history of the home made it hard for me in other ways too. When the girls came over for the weekend they had the run of the place. We got on well enough but now they were young teenagers, I felt overwhelmed. Previously, I'd been able to escape to mine at the weekends, giving Jeremy and the girls their time together. Now I no longer had anywhere to go. It felt like I was a guest, which was unsettling after three years of owning my own home and having my own space.

'Jeremy,' I can't live like this,' I told him a few weeks into our new arrangement. 'It's too hard. I've got no space here. I feel crowded out.'

'Really? Well, we can make some changes. I've thought about this. Perhaps we could build an extension onto the house, make a new room for you, extend the kitchen…'

'No,' I interrupted him. 'No, I don't want you to make changes to the house. I just don't want to live here. It's hard enough to lose my home and my independence but now I'm living next door to my old home and I have to watch the new people undo all my work in the garden.'

I got up and wandered round the room, pointing at all the old photographs of Jeremy and the girls on the walls.

'These pictures, this place... it's... I just feel like there's too much history here, too many memories of your old life. It is like living in the past, *your* past. We need to start again. We need a new home for our future together.'

'Move out?' Jeremy was incredulous. 'But this is the girls' home, the family home they've known all their lives.'

'Exactly!' I said. 'It's *their* home. It's *your* home. It's not mine. It's not *ours*.'

This was a subject we returned to many times over the next few weeks but somehow I couldn't get through to Jeremy. I couldn't get him to understand how claustrophobic I felt living under his roof. Eventually, I ran out of options.

'I've found a flat,' I announced one night.

'A flat? What do you mean?' Jeremy was flustered, caught off-guard.

'I mean, I've found a flat to move into and I'd like you to come with me to check it out.'

'Okay,' Jeremy said reluctantly.

The next day we arranged to meet the estate agent outside the small, one-bedroom studio flat I had picked out in Guildford town centre.

'Yes, this will work,' I murmured approvingly as we took in the mouldy bathtub and the poky bedroom-come-lounge, complete with peeling wallpaper. *God, what a pit!*

'I like it,' I told the agent. 'I'll probably take it but I'll give you a call in the next couple of days to confirm.'

Jeremy was silent all the way back to his place. We got in, I put the kettle on and he sat down, a dark look on his face.

'What is it Jeremy? Don't you like the flat?'

'You can't move into that place,' he said. 'I just...no! There's no way. You can't move in there.'

'But I told you, I'm not staying in this house. I need my own space.'

'Okay, okay I hear you,' he said, shaking his head resignedly. 'We'll put this place on the market and start looking for a house of our own.'

It had been a bluff of course; there was no way I was going to move into that dingy and over-priced studio flat but I had to show him that I was serious. He was so attached to his home he couldn't understand why I found it so hard to live there. We started looking at properties in earnest. In terms of location, I had to concede to Jeremy's wishes – he didn't want to move too far away from either the girls or Bramley, where his mother lived. Gladys had another son and step-daughter, but her husband Fred had passed away some years before and Jeremy now visited her regularly, helping out with small jobs around the flat. She was highly dependent on him. We saw quite a number of properties before we went to view a house in a quiet cul-de-sac in the pretty village of Cranleigh.

'Oh, hello Jeremy!' said the man who opened the door.

'Nick!' Jeremy exclaimed in surprise. The owner, it turned out, was an old school friend of Jeremy's brother and the pair recognized each other straight away. We were greeted like long lost friends and it may have been this surprisingly warm welcome or the house itself, but I got a good feeling about the place immediately. It felt calm and tranquil and best of all there was a wonderful conservatory at the back overlooking a sunny, south-facing garden.

'I like it,' I whispered to Jeremy as we were shown round and he nodded. That evening we put in our offer. Later, I reflected that it must have been fate because, although another couple had also made an offer, the old school connection convinced Nick to sell to us.

On a warm July morning, we packed away the last of our possessions and drove away from Miller Road and the two houses which had brought us together. It was, in Jeremy's words, the end of an era and yet from the moment we left, neither of us looked back.

Now the dynamics in our domestic arrangement shifted. The girls would have a room of their own to sleep in when they came to stay, but the rest of the house belonged to us and that meant a few new ground rules. I'd noticed in the months I'd lived with Jeremy he tended to bend over backwards for the children, a consequence no doubt of the guilt attached to being a 'weekend father'. They ate whatever they liked, behaved how they liked and there was little effort made to help out around the house. I felt that they should now try to fit in with us, instead of the other way round. From now on everyone would take their plate to the sink after dinner and everyone would leave their shoes at the door. I had understood that the previous house was theirs and they could behave in it however they liked, as long as their father agreed. But now things were different and I felt I deserved a little space and respect in my own home.

The new rules were quickly and easily adopted. Nobody seemed to mind and in fact the girls appreciated that the house was a lot bigger than the one in Miller Road. Now, if I felt the need for a bit of time on my own during a weekend visit, I could go upstairs to our cosy master bedroom or into the den and close the door, something I hadn't been able to do before. We could all enjoy a little bit more space. Yes, things were definitely looking brighter on the domestic front, though I was still struggling to adjust to the estrangement from my family. Previously I'd been very close to my parents, speaking to them on the phone at least once a week, and regularly visiting my extended family in London. But, apart from regular calls from my sister, who supported me and Jeremy throughout, I lost contact with everyone else. It was heartbreaking and very, very lonely. In one last-ditch effort to win my parents' approval, I flew out to Kenya at the end of July.

'Let's talk this through,' my father had urged, persuading me that there might be a way to reconnect with one another.

The plan was to spend some time in Nairobi before travelling to Mauritius together for a family holiday, just like we used to do, like old times. We would talk, try to understand each other and perhaps, at last, my parents would accept Jeremy as my chosen partner. But from the moment I landed, I knew that there was no going back to the way things were before. My relationship with my mother had changed irrevocably. Once, I could tell her anything; now a gulf yawned between us. Yes, I had disappointed them but they had disappointed me too. Why couldn't they accept my life choices? Why did they need to put their own strict beliefs before me, their daughter? And, given all that they had gone through with their own families all those years ago when they had met, why didn't they understand?

As the days in Mauritius passed, it became clear their minds were made up. They had no intention of listening to me or accepting Jeremy. Instead, they asked me to rethink, pointing out all the things that made Jeremy an unsuitable partner. He was too old, he had children, he was taking advantage of me! He wasn't Indian, so he could never understand me or my culture, which meant we could never enjoy a fulfilling relationship. It was all horribly depressing. One night I overheard my mother commenting to my father that I had put on weight.

'*He's* done that to her,' she whispered.

Back in Nairobi, I came to accept that the whole trip had been a waste of time. I missed Jeremy terribly and all I could think about was getting home to him. It was pointless to hope that my parents would relent. Realising that this was probably the last time I would be in their house, my childhood home, I went to the cupboard in my old bedroom to retrieve some precious dance mementoes from my past. To my surprise, I found the cupboards empty.

'Where is everything?' I asked my mother.

'I got rid of it.'

'What do you mean got rid of it?'

'I didn't want it in my house.'

I felt shattered by her coldness. I knew this was in part related to my mother's conversion to Christianity. She had turned her back on Hinduism completely, removing all the old statues of Hindu Gods that they used to own, and was trying to convert everyone around her. But why take away *my* things? It felt like she was trying to remove me from her life.

I discovered that she had thrown out all my beautiful, hand-made *Kanjivaram* dancing outfits that had been specially hand-stitched in India. A box full of South Indian temple jewellery had disappeared, as well as my precious *ghungroos* – the foot bells that I considered sacred. My *Bharata Natyam* pictures, hand-written notes, books, photos, the video of my dance graduation… everything, gone! Every trace of my childhood dream, my dancing life, had been disposed of, as if it meant nothing.

'Why didn't you ask me before you threw it out?' I cried.

My mother just shrugged. She saw nothing wrong in her actions. *What sort of mother could do this?* I started to cry. I couldn't bear to be around her for a minute longer, so I called Sheela, my cousin's wife, to come and pick me up. I needed to get out of the house.

I waited and waited on the side of the road. Finally, after an hour, I walked back to the house. But I found my mother had gone out and locked up. With no phone and no taxis to be found for miles around, I was stuck. Finally, after four hours, my mother returned and let me back into the house again. I spoke to Sheela on the phone and she told me my mother had called her straight after I'd spoken to her and told her not to pick me up. Then my mother had gone out, leaving me stranded. *What a spiteful thing to do to your own daughter! How had she become like this*? I wondered.

The following day I spoke to my parents for the last time.

'I'm leaving. I'm going back to Jeremy,' I said quietly.

I felt no anger for them, just sadness at the knowledge that this might be our last meeting.

'As you know, we have bought a house together and we're a couple. That's not going to change. You can either accept Jeremy as my partner or there is nothing left to say here.'

'No, Shalini,' my father said. 'He can't be the right person for you. Can't you see?'

'It's over, Pop. I'm leaving now.'

'Don't leave. Please, let's work this out.'

'There's nothing to work out, Pop,' I said, tears in my eyes. 'I'm sorry. I have to go.'

There really was nothing left to say. Their minds and hearts were closed; they had chosen to cling to dogma and convention and tradition, rather than try to understand their own daughter. I felt utterly heartbroken.

Back in England, Jeremy and I picked up from where we left off and I tried to put the rift with my family out of my mind and concentrate on my career.

Previously I'd been working at the Lythe Hill Hotel in Haslemere but that had been based on the idea that I would one day return to Kenya to help in my father's restaurants. Now I thought about a change of direction and, over the next two years, went back to waitressing, taught hospitality and tourism at Farnborough College and worked as a recruitment consultant at a hospitality recruitment company. I seemed to flit from one job to another, feeling no passion or commitment to anything. I was bored and unenthused by the work I was doing.

Something felt wrong, but I didn't quite know what to do about it so I pushed down the uneasy feelings and carried on. It had been drummed into me that if I worked hard, I would achieve my dreams and that would bring me happiness. So, I kept going. Except some days I woke up feeling more tired than when I went to bed. And I carried a sort of grey fuzziness around in my head which engulfed my mind and stopped me thinking clearly.

But still, I carried on.

It'll be fine, I told myself over and over. *You have no right to complain. You have Jeremy, this house and a wonderful life. Everything is fine. There's really nothing wrong.*

Chapter 7 – The Crash

"It is very hard to explain to people who have never known serious depression or anxiety the sheer continuous intensity of it. There is no off switch."
—**Matt Haig**[7]

*M*y eyelids popped open and for a moment I lay still in the darkness, staring up at the ceiling. Without looking at the clock beside me, I knew the time. It was 3am. I sighed. It was always 3am. Now I wouldn't be able to get back to sleep for another couple of hours, which meant I would be shattered for work. I rolled over and pulled my knees to my chest, curling up into a tight ball. My mind whirred and with every minute that passed, I felt myself getting more and more tense. I couldn't stop thinking about work at the recruitment agency I was at, about the deadlines I was missing, the targets I hadn't reached. *Be quiet*, I told my brain, *just stop thinking about it and go to sleep*. I screwed my eyes tight shut. *Please go to sleep… please.*

Four hours later I dragged my heavy limbs to the bathroom and propped myself up in the shower as I tried to wash away the weariness of yet another broken night's sleep. My head felt thick and heavy; my whole body aching to return to bed. It was a bleak November morning and as I sipped a cup of *masala chai*, I gazed absently at the trees in our garden, already bare of leaves. Then I gathered up my things, put on my winter coat and scarf and headed for the door.

But as my hand reached for the handle, something stopped me. All the strength left my body. *I can't push down, I can't physically open the door.* My hand started to shake, and then my whole body. *What's happening to me?* My chest contracted. *I can't breathe.* I opened my mouth and gulped in air, like a fish out of water, but it didn't seem to make any difference. It felt like I was suffocating. *Help. Help!* I screamed but no sound escaped my lips. I collapsed on the floor in the hallway, my body shaking with sobs. In desperation I reached for the phone on the shelf above my head and dialed Jeremy's number.

'Something's wrong,' I gasped. 'I can't move. Please, you have to come home.'

It took him two hours to get back from London, where he worked, and in that time I didn't move from the hallway floor. By the time he found me, the terror had subsided but I was wrung out, exhausted, barely able to move an inch.

'We're going to see the GP,' he told me in a soothing tone as he lifted me tenderly to his car. 'Don't worry, Shal, I'm here. It's going to be okay.'

I let him drive me to the surgery and there, our GP, Dr. Robin Fawkner-Corbett, gently questioned me about my health and state of mind.

'Have you been under a lot of pressure recently?' he asked and I nodded.

'Have you had any suicidal thoughts?'

'Yes, I have,' I admitted in a flat emotionless voice, and beside me Jeremy shifted in his seat. 'I've thought about it quite a lot actually.'

I remember talking – strangely calmly – about a hill nearby that I could drive my car off. I thought it would be quick that way. Dr. Fawkner-Corbett scribbled something down on a pad.

'Shalini, it sounds like you had a panic attack this morning. You need specialist help so I want you to go see a colleague of mine, Dr. Tim Cantopher. He's a consultant psychiatrist who holds consultations in Wonersh, down the road. Are you on private health insurance?'

'Yes,' Jeremy answered for me.

'Good. You'll go see Tim tomorrow then.'

The next day Dr. Cantopher welcomed me into his office and we had an hour-long chat about my life. He asked me about my background and I told him the whole story about falling out with my family over my relationship with Jeremy.

'My parents disowned me and I feel like I've disappointed them,' I concluded.

Tears rolled down my cheeks and I swiped at them with tissues from a box on the table in front of me. Dr. Cantopher told me that he suspected I was suffering from clinical depression.

'Now this may come as a surprise to you, because undoubtedly you are a strong person, but I find that depression is often the curse of the strong mind. We tend to think of depression as an illness of a weak mind, but actually it's just the opposite. It's a physical illness and if you are a weak person, you are like a reed. When the wind blows the reed will just bend in the wind.

'A strong person is like an oak tree: the wind hits it over and over, but it remains standing. But one day the wind will be too strong and oak will fall. You've been battling for a long time. That's what the panic attack was - your body and mind saying "enough is enough."'

He let me absorb this for a minute and then he went on.

'Shalini, it's not your responsibility to make your mother and father happy. It's their responsibility to make themselves happy. If they are disappointed, it is their choice to be disappointed. By your actions, you have done nothing wrong. You've just fallen in love. There's nothing wrong with that.'

I found myself weeping with relief. His words were so reassuring, so comforting. For the first time, I realised that the heaviness and sadness I had been carrying around all this time was real. It was called depression. It was like taking a broken arm to a doctor and being told they could mend it. He had diagnosed a broken mind and he had said, *it's okay, we can help with that.* Just knowing that he could help me was such a relief. And though it took me a long time to fully accept that I was not responsible for my parents' feelings, just hearing him say that was revelatory. My choices as an adult were okay. I was validated. It was okay to choose Jeremy.

Dr. Cantopher said he would refer me to The Priory as he felt I was danger to myself. He wanted to admit me immediately. But I was not at all keen and refused. I'd heard about The Priory, of course. It was, notoriously, the place where drug and alcohol addicted celebrities checked in for treatment. I couldn't go there. The shame would be too much. But Dr. Cantopher was insistent.

'Shalini – I want you to go home and speak to Jeremy and tell him these exact words I've said to you today. Tell him I said: *I want you to go to hospital because you are a threat to yourself.* Can you do that?'

Jeremy was as resolute as Dr. Cantopher. I was to be admitted to The Priory at the earliest. But the thought of being admitted to an institution was shameful. Nobody I knew had ever been mentally unwell before - it was a taboo subject in Indian families - and I couldn't bear the thought of people knowing that I was suffering from depression. To me, the danger of that stigma felt far worse than any potential harm I could inflict on myself.

Shame engulfed me. This was all my fault! I had brought this all on myself. I crumpled into a heap and wept inconsolably. Jeremy held me and whispered soothing words in my ear but I felt utterly defeated. How had I got to this point? I couldn't fight Jeremy on this, I knew he wouldn't let me.

Two days later, Jeremy drove me 45 minutes to The Priory, where I was admitted as an inpatient. Once the woman at reception desk had taken my details we were shown to a very small, poky room. I felt the panic rising in my chest.

'I don't think I can stay here,' I whispered to Jeremy, as we waited to be seen by a doctor. The room felt so claustrophobic, I couldn't breathe.

'Don't worry - I'll sort it out.'

Jeremy spoke to the supervisor and ten minutes later, we were shown to a bigger and brighter room. Later, I was interviewed by a rather cold and matter-of-fact Asian woman, who was the locum and on duty that night. She questioned me about my innermost thoughts as I wept rivers of tears. That night, as I lay alone in my small single bed, waiting for the sleeping pills to blanket my tired mind, I hoped that this was the answer to my pain. I hoped I would get better.

I was an inpatient at The Priory for four weeks and I have no doubt it saved my life. I had never allowed the possibility of depression to enter my head until Dr. Cantopher diagnosed me. I had covered it up beautifully, so effectively in fact, that Jeremy never knew that something was wrong. Nobody realised how serious it was, especially not me, until I was at a crisis point and then, thankfully I got the help I needed. At The Priory I went for one-on-one counselling with Dr. Cantopher, as well as a lovely therapist called Tessa, whom I continued to see long after I left. I attended group therapy sessions as well as art therapy and slowly, very slowly, I began to understand what had happened to me.

For the last two and a half years since my family had cut me out of their life, rejected and isolated from everything I had ever known, I had lost my direction. My sense of belonging had been shattered. Until then, everything – every single decision in my life – had been aimed towards pleasing my parents. Now I had made one single choice - to love Jeremy - which had changed all of that and altered the course of my life forever. I had lost my family, my community and been cut off from my own past. At first, I had gone on as if nothing had happened, coping as well as I knew how. But it felt like a part of me was missing and I just didn't know how to fix it.

According to my family, I had brought shame on them and I had taken this very much to heart. My family's *izzat* rested with me, as it did with so many Indian girls. Status means everything in Indian society and I had been told in no uncertain terms that by choosing Jeremy, I had brought dishonor and shame on the whole family. I couldn't fight centuries of traditional culture, but where was *my* respect? Was I not worthy of it? No. Because in Indian families, a son is allowed to go out partying, have as many girlfriends as he wants and sleep around, as long as he settles down with a suitable Indian girl in the end. But an Indian girl has none of those freedoms. Her reputation is often all she has in the world. Even the whisper of a boyfriend can destroy a girl's reputation. So, while families like mine send their daughters to western schools and colleges, at home they are expected to revert to being the 'good Indian girl'. This way, many Indian girls grow up with split identities, trying to find their place in two very different worlds. It is traumatic, especially when the two worlds clash.

Now that I was beginning to understand how the split with my family had affected my mental health, my anger began to surface. These attitudes were so backward, so very sexist and I felt outraged that even I, a Westernised, well-educated and liberal woman, was being judged entirely on my choice of partner. It didn't matter what I thought, said or achieved in life, my status was wrapped up entirely with this decision. I had seen it time and time again. I had heard about similar situations with my aunts and friends and although it was less overt it still happened. I began to see that this was the way Indian societies around the world controlled women. For my whole life I had never questioned these rules and conventions., which I had inherited from my family and from the social hierarchies that permeate Indian culture. It was only now that I found myself fundamentally opposed to these principles.

In The Priory, I learned how to accept my own feelings, to handle my emotions without letting them control me. I was sad. I had to accept that, to feel the sadness, to welcome it almost and in that way, to process it. And while I was learning how to experience emotion in a positive way, I also learnt coping skills that helped me to break out of negative patterns of thinking. The therapists at The Priory were brilliant and in the non-judgmental atmosphere I felt free to talk about my family quite openly. Though I was often challenged, I was never once made to feel bad about myself, or my choices.

Jeremy came to visit every night after work and asked me about everything I had been doing that day. He read books on depression and was eager to help in any way he could, admitting that he had been shaken to learn about my suicidal thoughts. I shared everything with him, told him about the therapy sessions and the insights I was gaining. It was heartbreaking at times, but there were lighter moments too and I found great solace and comfort in the camaraderie I shared with other patients. We laughed and cried together and shared our most intimate thoughts. Each Saturday afternoon Jeremy would take me home to spend a little time together and the next evening, he would take me back in for my week's therapy. I was shocked at how quickly I became used to the routine; how easily I became institutionalized. The Priory was a quiet, calming environment; it felt safe and cocooned from the world. But by the end of just one week, I found it difficult to go into a supermarket – too many people, too much noise. The bright lights hurt my eyes and the loud voices jarred my brain.

One evening, after a long day at work, Jeremy brought in an old cassette player that I had asked him for as we had been told that listening to music could be a good way to relax. After he had gone, I chose a tape at random from the selection he had brought for me. It was an invocation to the Hindu God Krishna and as I heard the melodious sounds of the flute and the *tabla*, something inside me moved. I felt compelled to stand up and to dance. It had been a very long time since I had last danced and I wasn't exactly steady on my feet. My legs and arms shook from exhaustion and the medication I was on. Still, I persevered.

I closed my eyes as I listened to the beautiful voice of the Kathak expert, Pandit Birju Maharaj.

Ananda ranga sagaram

Namami Krishna nagaram

Of many colours – just like the ocean

I bow to him – Krishna – the noble one

As I listened to the evocative Sanskrit lyrics describing Krishna – his distinctive blue skin, his smiling face, the peacock feather in his hair - something just took over. I let the rhythm guide me, my body recalling the choreography as if summoning it up from my depths of my being. I found that my hands and feet seemed to remember where to go, undirected by my mind and entirely of their own accord. It was as if, in some long-forgotten part of my body, the gestures and movements were still perfectly imprinted, just waiting to be summoned again. I had forgotten how much I loved to dance! As I moved, my body gently lifted and lilted to the music and something deep within me stirred.

It was not my finest performance, not by a long shot, and yet for the first time in ages I felt alive. There was a glimmer of hope.

Chapter 8 – The Dancer Returns

"To dance is to give oneself up to the rhythms of all life."
—**Dr. Maya V. Patel**[8]

Jeremy pushed open the front door and I was greeted by a huge *Welcome Home* sign strung across the corridor. I smiled broadly.

'Wow!' I exclaimed. 'Thank you, sweetie. That's really lovely.'

I walked into the kitchen to be met by yet another sign.

Welcome Home – from the kitchen!

I laughed.

'Wait for it…' Jeremy said, a twinkle in his eye. There were signs plastered everywhere!

Welcome home from the cooker!

Welcome home from the computer!

Welcome home from the bedroom!

Welcome home from the sofa!

And on it went.

'Oh Jeremy!' I giggled, pulling him to me. 'This is ridiculous!'

'Don't blame me,' he said in a mock-innocent tone. 'What could I do? They missed you!'

It was obvious that Jeremy was happy to have me back and it felt good to be in my own home again. Although I was worried about re-entering 'the real world', I had missed being 'us'. But work was a different matter. Although my bosses at the hospitality recruitment agency had been very supportive after my diagnosis, paying me throughout my time in hospital and allowing me to return to work part-time, just a week into this new arrangement, I realised that the high-pressured environment wasn't going to work for me.

'I can't cope with the targets,' I said to Jeremy one night. 'It's making me anxious all over again.'

'Your health is the most important thing in the world,' he replied. 'No job is worth compromising your health for. Just hand in your notice.'

So that's what I did. Instead of worrying about money and climbing the career ladder, I handed in my notice and relied on Jeremy for financial support. Although I wanted to work – I certainly wasn't anticipating sitting at home all day long – I knew I couldn't handle a demanding job. Dr. Cantopher suggested I look for a part-time job instead. I scanned the local paper for part-time work close to home. That's when I spotted a marketing assistant job at Cranleigh Arts Centre.

'You'll be doing a lot of photocopying, putting up flyers, posters, that sort of thing,' said Helen, the manager who interviewed me.

'It sounds good,' I nodded, enthusiastically

It was perfect – photocopying flyers and posters and putting them up on noticeboards or around the centre was just about all I could manage. I'd return home at midday, utterly exhausted and make myself a cup of *masala chai*, the old-fashioned Indian way, the way my mum used to make it. First, I'd boil some water in a saucepan then slowly I'd add the spices, then the black tea leaves and finally the milk and sugar, until it all bubbled up into a fragrant mix. I'd perform each step deliberately and carefully, paying close attention to the simmering water, to my stirring and to the wonderfully warm, pungent aromas of cinnamon, cardamom and fennel seeds that wafted up from the saucepan. I found it calming, meditative even, so different from the way I did things in the past. Before falling ill, I was a bundle of energy, always rushing around, performing a hundred different tasks at once: putting on the lunch, taking out the washing, opening the post, all the while talking on the phone or to Jeremy. But I was incapable of functioning like that anymore. My brain was so befuddled that all I could do was focus on one task at a time. And making *masala chai*, I found, relaxed me, it slowed me down.

Once it was made, I'd sit in the conservatory, taking long, slow sips from the hot mug clasped in my hands. Within 20 minutes my eyes would start to close and my whole body felt heavy. I'd drag myself upstairs and sleep for the rest of the afternoon. There were times I didn't even make it up the stairs and I'd wake up with a start, still on the sofa, at 5pm, the house dark and still. At first, I felt horribly guilty for wasting my afternoons in this unproductive way. I could almost hear my mother's voice in my head, chastising me for being 'lazy'.

But, as always, Jeremy reassured me, calming all my concerns, and encouraging me to do what I needed to heal. I decided to give myself permission to sleep in the afternoons, knowing that the only way I was going to recover was by allowing myself time to do so. The Arts Centre also gave me a purpose – a reason to get out of bed in the morning. It was a safe and welcoming environment, where self-expression and creativity were encouraged. I was so inspired by the paintings and artwork in the exhibition gallery, and the many shows held regularly including dance, theatre and music, that I decided to explore my own creativity. Several times a week, I would use one of the Centre's studios to practice Indian dance. In those happy hours, I'd recall all the many steps and routines I'd learned as a child. To my delight, I found that most of the choreography came flooding back. The routines I'd memorized so many years before told colourful stories about the Hindu gods and I revelled in immersing myself in the intricate steps and movements. It was as if I'd learned them only yesterday. In time my mind and body began to feel stronger.

As summer arrived, Jeremy and I expanded our little family with the addition of a pet kitten. My therapist had said it would be good for me to have an animal to take care of, so we went to take a look at a litter at a local stable and, inevitably, fell for an adorable bundle of black fluff. But the kitten was also a feisty little thing. At his first check-up the vet exclaimed,

'Gosh he is a bit wild! You'll never be able to tame him.'

And so we named him Tabasco, after the fiery sauce that I loved so much. We quickly became inseparable and my friends often teased me that he was my surrogate child.

Meanwhile, my job made me feel like a valued part of the local community. Since we were such a small team - just four members of staff, plus a few volunteers - everything we did made a difference. There were days where I had to clean the toilets or man the front desk or take tickets on the door of a show. But I didn't mind. I was being helpful and productive, a worthwhile member of a creative company, rather than just a cog in the corporate machine. My confidence grew and soon I was promoted to marketing manager. Gradually, day-by-day, I felt myself getting better and stronger. I came off my anti-depressants and the afternoon naps shortened and then stopped altogether.

One day a lady approached the front desk and asked whether anyone at the centre knew of an Indian dance teacher.

'Shalini does Indian dance,' Helen replied, having seen me practice in the studio. 'Why do you ask?'

It turned out that the lady was a teacher from a local primary school. For their learning journey that term they were studying India - the food, the culture and the geography. The teacher thought it would be fun for them to learn a little Indian dance too. Helen relayed all this to me in the office upstairs, which overlooked the light and airy gallery below.

'I don't think they want too much – just an hour or so to go in and show the kids some dancing. What do you think?'

My brow furrowed.

'I don't know,' I replied, hesitantly. 'I'll think about it.'

For the next couple of days, I procrastinated. Did I want to teach or did I want to just dance for myself? I wasn't sure. Would I be able to control a classroom full of primary school children? Would they be able to follow the moves? I was tempted by the idea, but also racked by self-doubt. *Just do it*, a little voice inside my head kept urging. *Just do it!* Eventually, I decided to listen to that voice. It wasn't a big commitment, after all, just an hour, so if it all went horribly wrong I'd never have to do it again. I called the teacher and agreed to run a one-hour workshop for their Year 4 children.

In preparation, I choreographed a simple and fun routine using wrist scarves to add colour and interest for the children. Then, on the day itself, despite the butterflies in my stomach, I confidently took control of the class and taught them the whole routine, explaining the story behind the music as I went along. I was thrilled to find that they picked up the moves very quickly and seemed to really enjoy the lesson. The biggest surprise was discovering that the person who enjoyed it most was me. I *loved* teaching dance – from that first class, I knew I had found something that made me feel alive, something I was really passionate about. I walked out of the school that day buzzing with excitement.

The teacher called me after the workshop to say the children had loved the class, asking whether I'd like to teach some of the other year groups. I jumped at the chance! There was something so fulfilling about teaching the children, sharing my love of dance and seeing their faces light up with enthusiasm. I knew that perhaps the kids might forget my name and forget what they'd learnt, in time, but perhaps there would be an image of those classes lodged in a part of their memories. It transpired that the very reason I found dance so helpful to my own recovery was also the reason it was so rewarding to share with others. It was uplifting, fun and made you smile!

Over the next few months, with Jeremy's encouragement, I started a company called SB Dance – Shalini Bhalla Dance – which aimed to work with local schools to teach Indian dance workshops. With every workshop we signed up and with every class I taught, my confidence and skills improved. To a large extent, I had Jeremy to thank for that. I always had high expectations of myself and everyone around me. He realised that in the classroom I was probably no different. So, when I came back from an early workshop raging that the children had failed to 'get' the routine, he made subtle suggestions to help fix the problem.

'Do you think you're tailoring it to the right level?' he'd ask. 'Why not try something a little easier next time and see how it works.'

Wise counsel, as always. Yes, perhaps I was being a little hard on them, I thought. Perhaps I needed to lower my expectations, make the routines a little easier and less complicated. At the next class, this method worked a treat and showed me that as long as I delineated the framework then it was all about having a positive learning experience. Thanks to Jeremy's advice, my classes flowed more smoothly after that. The children had a better time and I got more work as a result. The fact that I could connect with these children through dance gave me a new sense of worth.

Soon I began to think about my lessons more creatively, finding different ways to engage the children. I introduced *dandiya* sticks, traditionally used during dances at the Hindu festival of *Navaratri* - a festival dedicated to the worship of the Hindu deity, Durga. As a child this was my absolute favourite festival. I remember that over the course of nine (nava) nights (ratri), we would go to large community halls in Nairobi to take part in the social, celebratory dance form of *Dandiya Raas* (played by both men and women) as well as the folk dance *Garba* (danced predominantly by women in a circle). I always likened *Dandiya Raas* to a form of speed dating for young people. The typical format is that of two circles of people – one going clockwise, and the other going anti-clockwise. People then 'play dandiya' with the person in front of them for a few seconds, a chance to get to know a boy you might have a crush on before then moving onto the next person. It was great fun. And it was this sense of fun I wanted to instill in the children I taught. The boys, especially, loved them. It was so gratifying to start the lesson with a class full of cynical, grumpy boys, convinced that dancing was 'girly' and definitely not for them and turn them into such enthusiastic dancers!

I was firm but fair and I didn't take any nonsense. My method was simple – I'd teach them a few steps and then put them in pairs or groups and send them away to create their own dance motifs together. They learned to work as a team and that freedom to choreograph independently gave them a sense of creativity and ownership of the dance. They weren't just passive recipients of my knowledge – they were using that knowledge to create something uniquely their own. At the end of each lesson, the different groups would perform for each other. The visible pride on the children's faces was inspiring and gave me such joy. To have this connection to the children, to feel their energy and enthusiasm and to be able to share a part of my world that I had devoted so much time to myself as a child was overwhelming and hugely rewarding.

For so long, I had been cut off from my family, my background and my culture but now I began to reconnect with my past and heritage. It was a way of rediscovering who I was and asserting my identity. Dancing and teaching dance was my healing. It gave me a connection and a sense of purpose I discovered I had been missing for a long time.

Over the next 18 months, I developed and honed my teaching skills further as I continued to work part-time at the Arts Centre. During this time, Jeremy took voluntary redundancy from Barclays Bank and started work as the practice manager for a local physiotherapy centre. Now that we were both working within our community, we felt more rooted in our environment and, for me especially, this was life-changing. It felt good to have a sense of belonging again and putting on shows for the good of the community felt like I was doing something worthwhile. As a teenager, I had been told that teaching was a dead-end profession and had been steered instead towards the corporate world of hotels and restaurants. I was never encouraged to work for any reason other than to earn money for myself. This is exactly what my parents had done, working crazy hours for money and status, but it felt so shallow to me now. I needed purpose in my life, I needed to feel a connection.

By 2005 SB Dance was doing so well, I decided to devote myself to teaching full time. It was sad to leave the Arts Centre – so much a part of my recovery – but it was the right time to go. I began working with a charity in London called Create and they helped me hold large workshops at the Scoop Amphitheatre in Southwark. Teaching dance to people of all ages, from all over the world, at the foot of Tower Bridge was an amazing feeling. I loved being up there, on the stage, in charge and at the centre of attention. I found that I loved using my body creatively and sharing my passion for dance with as wide an audience as possible.

Encouraged by the enthusiasm I felt during these workshops, I decided to start a Bollywood dance class for adults at a studio in Cranleigh. To my dismay, however, the class didn't prove quite as popular as I'd hoped.

'Just two people today!' I moaned back to Jeremy, after yet another disappointing turn-out. 'I just don't know what to do. I put all the posters up, I handed out the flyers. We even managed to get a piece into the local Surrey paper. I really felt sure this would take off.'

'Maybe Cranleigh isn't ready for Bollywood dancing,' Jeremy suggested.

'Cranleigh *is* ready for Bollywood dancing, they just don't know it yet!'

I was nothing if not determined.

Yes, I was back to my normal, confident self and I was pleased to find my chosen career actually paid me a good wage. My mother once said to me that I would never be able to make a decent living from dance but since I was working alone with no overheads, I was doing pretty well. I also decided to study for a Master of Arts in South Asian Dance. I felt that if I was going to teach full-time I needed an official qualification, so I embarked on a degree at the Roehampton University in Richmond. There were just two of us – myself and another woman Payal – on this new course, which consisted of lectures on all manner of subjects, from anthropology to history and culture. Learning felt important to me, it gave me focus and helped to make me feel more professional about SB Dance.

On the whole, I loved being my own boss, deciding my own hours and where to focus my energies. The only problem, I soon discovered, was that there was no one else to take up the slack. I wasn't just a dance teacher, I was now also an administrator, designer, accountant, technical support and marketeer. Instead of relaxing at the weekends, I'd find myself designing posters, putting up flyers and choreographing new routines for my classes. It was Jeremy who noticed me falling back into old patterns again, working till late at night then waking at 3am.

'You need time to relax,' he insisted. 'I want you to start taking weekends off so that we do things together.'

Mindful of my inclination towards overwork, he kept me on an even keel. We took long walks in the countryside, made roast Sunday lunches together and took short holidays to Bath, Dorset, Devon and Wales.

I didn't give up, though. I persevered with my Bollywood dance classes in Cranleigh and slowly, by word of mouth, attendance grew. Two became four and then six and then ten until, after a year, I had more than a dozen regulars. In fact, the class became so popular I had to start a second class.

In 2006, when Jeremy started a new job as Finance Manager at Bramley Golf Club, and we once again had two decent incomes, we began travelling further afield: to Barbados, India, Paris and New York.

I was settled again and happy. But I continued to question my past and my identity. *Who was I? Was I Indian? British? Kenyan? Did it matter? Did I need to label myself?* At times, especially when I was dancing, I felt Indian, but I also felt deeply, so much of my life having now been in the UK.

I decided to explore this question of identity through my dance and, with the help of my fellow degree student, Payal, we took a two-woman show up to the Edinburgh Fringe Festival in August 2008 called *asmâkam* – the quest. The show contained four sections of dance that was set to music specially created by Cranleigh-based singer-songwriter Eleanore Duggan, with storytelling and poetry by the iconic Bengali poet, Rabindranath Tagore. In it, we raised these questions about identity, belonging and the expectations faced by Asian women in a Western world.

Conversely, women who had been given Western educations and a certain amount of independence - women like me - found themselves at odds with the traditional stereotypes of women within our own cultures. Forced to choose between these two worlds, our personalities and inner selves became conflicted and divided.

Where did I belong?

Chapter 9 – Just Jhoom!

"Don't just sit there…Just Jhoom!"
—Jeremy Lucas

'*M*eeeooow!'
'Morning, Tabasco! Is it time to get up?'

'Meow.'

'OK, come on then. Let's get you some breakfast, poppet.'

'Meeeoow.'

'Yes, I'm hurrying, I'm hurrying I know you're hungry'

I lay in bed, listening to this serious conversation between Jeremy and Tabasco, or JumJums, as I liked to call him. The sound of their morning exchange was my very favourite sound in the whole world and now I strained to hear the rest of the conversation as Jeremy carried JumJums into the kitchen for his breakfast. It was November 2008 and Jeremy was up early for his usual round of golf with friends. I was due a little lie-in this morning as the only work I had booked in that day was my Saturday morning Bollywood dance class, followed by a Bollywood-themed birthday party for an eight-year old girl later in the afternoon.

I had been running these parties for a couple of years and had designed a programme which seemed to work pretty well. Over the course of a two-hour birthday party, I would spend the first hour doing dance games and icebreakers and then teach the children a Bollywood dance routine using scarves and ribbons. After a half-hour break for the birthday tea, the girls would all wear *bindis* and bangles and practice the dance routine in time for a performance at the end for the parents. It didn't take long for the idea to catch on and after a few months, I was regularly being booked to run children's parties.

I lay in bed half-dozing and listening to the familiar sounds of Jeremy making himself tea, unloading the dishwasher and getting ready to go to golf. Just before he left he placed a mug of hot tea on the bedside table, gave me a kiss and said the words he said every morning: 'Don't let your tea get cold. Have a lovely day. See you later. Love you lots.'

Half an hour later, I threw off the duvet cover, swung my legs over the side of the bed and stood up. But no sooner had my feet touched the floor when I collapsed. I sat on the carpet, feeling very odd and off-centre. My head was thick and woozy, as if I had a massive hangover, though I hadn't drunk anything the night before. I broke into a cold sweat and a wave of nausea washed over me. Grabbing the side of the bed, I tried to pull myself up but it felt like I was being buffeted around on the deck of a wave-tossed ship and my stomach couldn't take it. I managed to crawl to the toilet just in time to throw up. *What's happening to me?*

I stumbled back to my bed and lay down. Lying flat seemed to be about the only way to stop the terrible nausea. I closed my eyes shut against the morning light and clenched my fists, as my head pounded and I swung between sticky, cold sweats and searing-hot flushes. Terrified, I reached out for the phone on my bedside table and dialed the number of the golf club.

'Hello – it's Shalini Bhalla here, Jeremy's partner,' I said slowly, trying to control the panic in my voice. 'Look, I know he's out on the course somewhere but this is an emergency. Please find him and ask him to come home straight away?'

It didn't take long for Jeremy to get back home and by then I had managed to get in touch with most of my adult students to let them know that the morning class was cancelled. At 11am a GP had arrived and was at my bedside examining me. I braced myself for bad news, but looking at his relaxed face, the young doctor seemed very far from alarmed – in fact, he looked positively laid-back.

'You have vertigo, Shalini,' he explained in a laconic drawl. 'It's a condition of the inner ear – very common, nothing at all to be worried about. I'm afraid it's just one of those things, probably caused by labryrinthitis, an inner ear infection, which is affecting your balance. I can prescribe you something to help with the infection but generally the cure is just rest.'

'Vertigo? I thought that was a fear of heights,' I replied, confused.

'No,' he said, packing away his bag. 'It's a medical condition affecting the balance. Nothing to worry about. Nothing serious.'

God, he was so blasé, I almost felt annoyed that it *wasn't* serious.

As soon as he left, I turned to Jeremy.

'How can I rest this out? There is a mum out there expecting a Bollywood birthday party this afternoon for her daughter and 11 of her friends! I can't let her down.'

'You can't even stand up!' said Jeremy. 'There's no way you can do a birthday party.'

This was a disaster!

'Ok, don't panic,' said Jeremy, calmly. 'I can go down there and help out but I'm not confident I can teach them to dance. Is there anyone else you can call on to do this with me?'

I reached for my phone and somehow managed to cobble together an alternative birthday party for the girls. Georgia, one of my dance students, would lead the girls in some dance-related games and then an artist friend of mine, Louise, would do some tie-dye scarf -making with them.

Jeremy was a rock, as usual, and being the father of three girls he wasn't at all fazed by the prospect of supervising a pre-teen birthday party.

I lay in bed that afternoon and watched the clock tick slowly through those excruciating two hours, feeling increasingly helpless and frustrated. *How was it going? Were the children having a good time?* I had faith in Jeremy and my two friends but it was agony to be lying here, so incapable. At just after 5.30pm I called Jeremy's mobile.

'Well? How did it go?' I asked impatiently.

'It went very well,' he replied. 'Kids had a great time, the mum seems happy. Relax!'

Oh thank goodness for that! We probably got away with it this time, but what if it happened again? What if I was out of action long-term? It dawned on me that I couldn't just rely on myself to do all the work associated with SB Dance. I needed support, I needed to train some assistants.

BAM! It was a lightbulb moment. With SB Dance, I could only go so far. If I wanted to turn this into a real business, I needed to expand my Bollywood dance classes into a professional outfit. After a few days in bed, I was up and about again and then I threw myself into researching the world of organised dance-fitness. After all, if I was serious about a future in teaching Indian dance, I had to find a way to scale up my dance classes, making them accessible to everyone and training instructors so they could teach their own classes and provide cover for me too.

The first thing I did was to sign up to some other dance-fitness classes to see how they worked. Zumba had recently taken off in our local area and this involved aerobic fitness routines choreographed to upbeat Latin music. Dancing and bopping along during a session, I was impressed by the instructors and their approach to the class. *This is what I do*, I thought, *but with a Bollywood theme*. I took a Pilates instructor course too and several other fitness courses, gathering ideas on how to put together my own programme. I even did an Exercise to Music (ETM) course, in order to become an accredited fitness trainer, where I learned all about the anatomy of the body and the physiology of exercise. I was determined to go about this professionally. At the same time, I partnered up with a fellow dance teacher, Beccy. She brought her knowledge of western dance styles and general fitness to the table. Jeremy supported me every step of the way, putting in the start-up capital in order to help me launch the new business. He even got involved by taking promotional pictures and filming videos for the new website.

It took me a year of research and training before I was ready to design my own instructor training programme. I'd learnt a lot from my years teaching with SB Dance - how to make the dances fun and accessible, for example, but now I also had to codify all the different moves I used in these class. These verbal cues would help the class to remember the moves and to follow the instructors more easily. But there was no standard Bollywood dance vocabulary at the time and certainly none that could be taught to a Western audience, which meant I had to start from scratch, dreaming up names like 'bumbling bees', 'sunshine step-touch' 'waterfall lunge', 'washing windows' and 'hopping statue'. It was good fun coming up with these names and I was creative in my approach, borrowing ideas from all sorts of unlikely dance traditions: from jazz to contemporary, flamenco, jive and even Morris dancing. The two Indian folk-dance styles that I drew from were *bhangra* from the Punjab (northern India) and *garba*, from western India – styles I had learnt as a child. The hand gestures that made my dance style unique were from *Bharata Natyam*. I wasn't worried about incorporating moves from all these various genres, in fact the more unusual the better! I knew I had to make my dance classes as original and exciting as possible.

With the help of a local yoga instructor, Sarra, I also designed a slow, cool-down routine as part of the course to help with stretching and core strength. Mine would be a high-impact, high-energy dance-fitness programme, but with strength at its core. Eventually, after months of changing, honing and finessing all the details, I sent off the course materials for evaluation to the Register of Exercise Professionals, or REPs, the UK governing body of fitness. We'd settled on the name Just Jhoom! - *jhoom* being one of the Hindi words for dance. The idea was to take the glitz and glamour of Bollywood and put it into every local fitness centre, a perfect blending of Eastern and Western ideas. It helped that the hit film *Slumdog Millionaire*, had recently ignited a nationwide interest in all things Bollywood...

In February 2010 I trialled the new format of the classes with my students and they loved it. I had designed the teaching programme so that new instructors could choose to teach the class in either one of two ways. The first involved one dance over an hour-long lesson. The second was more in line with Zumba, where you do many routines, one after the other. On 27 May we launched Just Jhoom! at Cranleigh Arts Centre with a party for 80 guests and on 9 July I was thrilled to learn that we had received REPs' accreditation for the course. The evaluator wrote:

'Well done! I wish you every success with the programme. All the materials are professionally presented, informative and well thought out and considered. It would appear, to me, that the integrity of Bollywood and Indian dance has been respected and honoured and at the same time connected to a safe and effective ETM structure – this I congratulate! ... All the very best success and again, well done!'

I was over the moon. Just Jhoom! was now the first ever accredited Bollywood dance-fitness instructor training course in the world!

In October I embarked on my first training session, with 10 instructors. The training took place over two days, during which time Beccy and I taught the instructors all the different moves and a series of routines which they could teach their classes. Once they were familiar with these, they could then go on to choreograph their own routines. At the end of the training, each instructor had to submit a DVD of themselves teaching a Just Jhoom! Class, which would provide the basis of their accreditation. Then they could start their own Just Jhoom! classes locally. They paid an annual license fee which gave them access to new choreography, training opportunities, networking with other instructors as well as the permission to run Just Jhoom! classes. In the space of three months, I ran three such courses, training up 32 instructors. It was thrilling when our first accredited instructors started up their own classes around the country, spreading Just Jhoom! to Kent,

Cambridge, London and Somerset. Over the following months I also designed a course for children called Junior Jhoom!, as well as one for older people and those with limited mobility called Forever Jhoom! I even put together a Bhangra Jhoom! programme, making classes even more high-impact and energetic.

Getting the business off the ground proved a steep learning curve for me and in those early days, I was constantly refining my approach to the marketing and training. Thankfully, I had Jeremy to help with the business side of things. He encouraged me to put in place a team of people to support my fledgling business. We needed online promotion, a media presence and help with the everyday administrative tasks. Jeremy, meanwhile, would take on the role of Finance Manager. At Barclays, he'd spent years supporting small businesses so he knew better than anyone what was needed to make a company work. In this respect he was my guru and his input proved invaluable.

'You know, it could take a long time to get this business up and running profitably,' he warned. 'I'm not being negative, just realistic. You know that I believe in you 100%, Shal, but just with my finance hat on, I'm still not convinced this is a viable business.'

'It *is* a viable business, Jeremy, and I'll prove it to you.'

'I'm very willing to be proved wrong in this instance,' he grinned.

'As long as you're not in a rush to get your money back,' I added, cheekily.

I was determined to make Just Jhoom! a success. This was my baby and my passion. I was prepared to put everything I had into it. So, while the training programme got off the ground, I ploughed every single penny that came in back into the business and employed a PR company to help with the promotion. If we wanted this to become a national business, we needed national coverage and gradually the team at Wigwam PR began to build our profile. We appeared in the local press, the fitness media and even in the Asian media. Before long, we had generated enough interest to get into the national magazines and newspapers.

In February 2011, together with local multimedia company, Freehand, we filmed our Just Jhoom! dance-fitness DVD. Our biggest issue was the music. I was adamant that any DVD we produced would have to have authentic Bollywood music – not the copyright-free tracks that seem to be the staple of most Bollywood DVDs on the market – but proper music from Bollywood films. I knew this was going to be a challenge because, until now, no one in the UK had ever managed to secure music rights from a film company in India to use on a dance-fitness DVD.

We approached dozens of distribution companies without success when, out of the blue, we were contacted by Yash Raj Films. They wanted to talk. Yash Raj are one of the biggest and most respected Bollywood film production companies in India. They also held the license to a song called *Jhoom*, from the film *Jhoom Baraber Jhoom* – a song we used to start all our Just Jhoom! classes. After much negotiating, Yash Raj Films gave us permission to use seven tracks from a variety of their films for the DVD. We were ecstatic! We were using songs from blockbuster hits like *Chak De India* and *Band Baaja Baarat*, both of which were huge in India. The DVD was released on our first birthday, 27 May 2011. It was a fabulous achievement.

Over the course of the next few years we released Just Jhoom! t-shirts, hoodies and water bottles. We also released Cook to Jhoom! a creative and innovative collection of healthy Indian recipes created by my friend, Cheeku. She worked tirelessly to try and test typical Indian dishes, turning them into healthy, contemporary creations suitable for busy people who cared about their wellbeing. We even teamed up with music company, Pure Energy, to present a Bollywood Bhangra double album, filled with a fantastic selection of tracks used in the Just Jhoom! classes. It was exciting, it was fast-moving and it was hugely rewarding. Just Jhoom! was new, something no one had seen before and it began to take on a momentum all of its own.

Just like Just Jhoom!, Jeremy and I shared a relationship that took the best of both our worlds and combined them together to create something entirely new. My mother's fears of us experiencing a culture clash and a lack of common understanding proved to be unfounded. Jeremy and I enhanced each other's understanding and embraced our cultural differences, not just in a superficial sense, like enjoying food or dress, but on a deeper level we embraced even the subtlest nuances of each other's cultural heritage.

I was always deeply impressed by the British response to natural disasters, the charitable impetus to try to alleviate suffering. Fundraising was a part of the national psyche in a way that I hadn't seen in India and I admired it. There was also an understanding of and respect for unspoken social boundaries, which wasn't at all a feature of the average Indian community. For example, Jeremy's mother, Gladys, would never dream of asking personal questions about me in the way that my family felt fully within their rights to question Jeremy.

Conversely, Indians were always very welcoming as a community unlike the British whose reticence and reserved manner could sometimes be interpreted as coldness. If I was going to dinner at someone's house in Britain and Shivani was staying with me, I wouldn't just take her along, I would call up first to see if that was all right. With an Indian person, I would take her without question. In fact, it would be seen as an affront to the host if I didn't take her. Jeremy and I managed to find a way to fuse these cultures and attitudes. As the years passed, I learned that I was very British in some ways and quintessentially Indian in others, and I was okay with that. By creating Just Jhoom! I had managed to carve out a place in society and a career for myself that not only reflected my personality and passions but also managed to integrate the best aspects of British and Indian cultures. Every day I grew more confident and comfortable in myself and my choices, while Jeremy and I became closer and happier.

Despite all the hard work, we were always careful to make time for ourselves, enjoying bi-annual trips abroad. We visited many places over the years – Malta, Portugal, the Gambia, Mauritius and the Maldives, where Jeremy discovered a passion for snorkeling and underwater photography. Our times away were blissfully peaceful, a chance to be together, just the two of us.

'We must come back here!' Jeremy would declare over dinner on our last night of each and every holiday and, although I would agree at the time, in the back of my mind I knew there were other places I was keen to visit.

As time passed, there was one place in particular I was desperate to return to.

Chapter 10 – Cold Rain on Red Earth

"Treat the earth well. It was not given to us by our parents, but loaned to us by our children."
—Kenyan Proverb

From the moment I stepped off the plane and into Nairobi's Jomo Kenyatta International Airport, I felt at home. The familiar sound of Swahili filled the corridors as I led Jeremy through the labyrinthine arrivals hall to collect our luggage. Everything felt the same as the last time I was here, twelve years ago, but so much had changed. I peeked down the stairs that led to the exit and saw my father and sister standing outside, waiting for us. I waved madly at them both; they caught sight of me and waved back. Even my father looked exactly the same, handsome in his red Safari Rally shirt.

Jeremy squeezed my hand.

'Ready to do this?'

I nodded. At last, I was going home.

As we walked outside I breathed in deeply – it had been raining. I could tell. That smell of the cold rain on hot red soil was like nothing else on earth.

It was 2011. Just Jhoom! had really taken off and Jeremy and I had been together for nearly 15 years, but I felt a deep yearning within me for something that I hadn't seen or experienced in a long time. I missed home. Kenya – the land of my birth – was such a vital part of my inner history, but I hadn't realised to what extent until it had disappeared from my life.

After years of travelling all over the world, there was only one place I wanted to return to. I missed the friendliness of the Kenyan people, their melodious language, the changing, dramatic weather and the beauty of the landscape. From its bountiful national parks teeming with exotic wildlife, to its bustling coastline and cool mountain regions, Kenya is a vast and extraordinary mix of geography and culture. Childhood memories of visiting Maasai Mara, Amboseli and Nakuru National Parks where we would see cheetahs, lions and elephants would surface every so often back in England and I felt strongly that I wanted to share these experiences with Jeremy. I wanted him to visit my birthplace and see for himself all the wonders I grew up with. This was a huge part of me, after all, and I felt that it was high time I took him home. As for my parents, well, I knew it would be nice for us all to meet again but I didn't hold out too much hope of a reconciliation.

I had written a friendly and polite email to my parents, telling them that we planned to visit Kenya in the early spring of next year and we would be staying in a hotel in Nairobi for a few days. I concluded with saying that it would be lovely to see them. My father's response was swift and decisive:

You will not stay in a hotel while your father is still alive and has a house in Nairobi – you will stay with us!

He added that he would like to take us down to Mombasa and spend some time there together. When I read his email, I could hardly believe it. I hadn't expected him to respond so positively and the relief I felt was overwhelming. Emails began to ping back and forth between us and, though none were overly emotional, the tone was friendly enough. My father, it seemed, was happy to welcome me home. As for my mother, I still didn't really know where I stood with her. Over the years, she had sent us intermittent emails that more or less acknowledged the longevity - and therefore success - of the relationship, but her messages were also drenched in religious dogma and diktats. Our refusal to marry, she said, meant we were living in sin and God would punish us for that. I had no idea how she would receive us in her home.

'Whatever happens,' I told Jeremy before we left. 'We're a team. I know I can cope with anything they throw at us as long as I have you by my side. We do this together. We'll be strong for each other.'

'Yes,' he smiled. 'We are a team.'

My father was clearly overcome with emotion, as we walked out of the airport. He held me tightly and his eyes brimmed with tears. Then he clasped Jeremy's hand in an enthusiastic two-handed shake and pumped it up and down.

'Jeremy!' he exclaimed, grinning broadly. 'Jeremy, welcome to Kenya! Welcome to Nairobi!'

'Thank you, Ashok,' Jeremy said. 'It's wonderful to be here.'

I had dreamed of this moment for a very long time. Now, to see these two men – the two most important men in my life – smiling at each other with such genuine warmth and emotion filled my heart with joy. From the look in my sister's eyes, I knew that she recognized what this moment meant to me. We embraced and, just for a short while, I had no words to express my happiness.

As Pop drove us home from the airport, I noticed sadly that the green city I remembered from my childhood, and had been excited to show Jeremy, seemed to have all but disappeared. The streets had changed beyond recognition. Ugly grey buildings had sprung up everywhere and huge flyovers and motorways were being built to accommodate the increasingly large number of vehicles on the roads. Where once there had been trees and green spaces, now there was only signs of construction and development. Of course I wanted Nairobi to thrive, to join the developed world, but the old city centre had boasted a certain idiosyncratic charm. Now, choked with traffic and crammed with monstrous skyscrapers, it looked like every other developed African city. Thankfully, as we drove towards the suburbs, the roads became less busy and I began to recognize the streets again, familiar once more with the terrain. This was the Nairobi I remembered!

My mother was there to greet us at the house when we arrived and although she offered us both a friendly hug, her greeting wasn't quite as warm as my father's. Still, I was happy to be there and grateful they were welcoming us into their home. It meant that after all these years we had finally gained their acceptance.

'You must be tired,' said my mother. 'Let me show you to your room.'

She led us through the house and showed us to the room we would be staying in, which happened to be my old bedroom.

'I'll let you freshen up and then you can come through and have something to eat.'

Jeremy opened the door and we walked in. For a second, I just stood there dumbfounded, unable to move or speak. In front of us stood two single beds. Two very single beds separated by at least a metre of space. Lying down, we wouldn't even have been able to hold hands!

I stood there, rigid and unable to speak, but Jeremy put his hand on my arm.

'It will be okay,' he said quietly in my ear. 'It will be fine. We're not staying long.'

Then he brought in our bags and closed the door behind us. He looked at me, and I stared back at him. Then we both laughed. All the tension disappeared as we shook our heads at the absurdity of it all.

'I would never want to have sex under their roof anyway!' I whispered, still giggling. 'But you'd think, after nearly 15 years together…'

'Oh Shal, it's so… so silly! But we're only here for three days,' he sighed, shrugging.

Thank goodness for Jeremy, I thought. *Thank goodness this man has a sense of humour and is grown-up enough to be able to take this in his stride.* I wasn't going to let this bother me.

Once we'd freshened up, we went through to the dining room where my mother had prepared some of her best dishes including *aloo paratha*, a Punjabi wholemeal chapatti filled with spiced mashed potatoes, green chillis, red onions and coriander; *baingan ka bhartha*, a smoky aubergine dish cooked with garlic and spices and a cooling *raita* with cucumber sprinkled with salt, red chilli and cumin powders. She had always been a wonderful cook and now, as she pressed us to eat, I admired her confidence and understanding of such complex spices and textures.

We chatted with Pop and Shivani about our plans for the holiday and dug into the fragrant feast, while my mother buzzed about in the kitchen. Although I was instantly relaxed in my father's company, I felt a tension around my mother that I just couldn't shake. I knew she still disapproved of our relationship and so I felt uncomfortable and on my guard for any slight or insult that might come our way.

'Sharmi, this is truly delicious!' Jeremy enthused, as he helped himself to his second *aloo paratha*. My mother smiled.

'I'm glad you like it.'

'Yes, Mum, it's wonderful,' I added. 'Really tasty. I've missed your cooking!'

'Thank you Shalini,' my mother nodded politely.

'Aren't you going to eat with us, Sharmi?' said Jeremy. 'I feel guilty sitting here while you're standing over there, doing everything,'

'No, no,' my mother demurred. 'I'll eat later. But you go ahead, please!'

My father and Jeremy got on well from the start and I was pleased to find that Pop was keen to spend time with us both. There were so many places he wanted to show Jeremy, he said, and he would teach him how to make his famous *palak chicken*. As a child, I remember having friends round and my father would cook the chicken in the garden, on a typical African charcoal stove called a *jiko*. Gatherings like this are popularly known as *koroga* parties – *koroga* being the Swahili word for stir, because that was the secret of *palak chicken* – taking time to let the ingredients and spices blend into one as they were cooked slowly and stirred endlessly. This mouth-watering dish – always popular with me and my friends – was made with butter, finely chopped red onions, garlic and ginger, the freshest tomatoes, fragrant coriander, tender baby spinach leaves and a whole chicken cut into its various parts. My father never measured the ingredients, he just threw handfuls of herbs and spices into the pot with a confidence brought about by years of practice.

'Your father is lovely,' Jeremy said to me, as we climbed into our separate beds later that night. It was the first time we had slept apart in many years.

'Yes, he is,' I agreed. 'He really is.'

The rest of our time in Kenya passed in a blur of sightseeing and meeting relatives - including my father's eldest brother - and spending time with my Ushamasi and her family. My father was keen to drive Jeremy around Nairobi to show him the city I had grown up in. He took us to meet his friends one evening at their usual drinking hole – a lovely open-air bar with tables and chairs dotted on a grassy lawn with the warm, balmy air thick with the sound of cicadas. He took us to his favourite Indian restaurant, Ismailia, so that Jeremy could try all my childhood favourites - *falooda* (a bright pink Indian milkshake flavoured with rose water, basil seeds and vermicelli) *paan* (a sweet after dinner mouth-freshner consisting of a betel nut leaf filled with sweet syrup, desiccated coconut and fennel seeds) and *maru bhajia* (spiced potato fritters covered in gram flour batter and deep fried, crispy on the outside and hot and soft on the inside).

A couple of days later, we left for the long and notoriously dangerous drive down to Mombasa. At the end of the journey Jeremy shook my father's hand in appreciation of his superior road skills, which had been acquired through many years of navigating Kenya's treacherous roads as a navigator and organiser for national car rallies. The country has some of the most dangerous roads in Africa and you need all your wits about you when you attempt a drive of any distance. Hazards can rear up from any angle and with no warning and the roads are lined with upended vans and crumpled cars: gruesome evidence of accidents that may have only just taken place a few minutes ahead of you. To Jeremy, the boy from Surrey, it probably felt as though we had only just survived the trip by the skin of our teeth. To us, however, it was just a normal day on the road and, though surprised, my Dad was inwardly pleased by Jeremy's praise. I giggled at the serious, ceremonial handshaking between the two of them. *That's my Jeremy*, I thought, *a real English gentleman!*

My English gentleman was clearly captivated by Kenya. On the drive to the coast, he had taken dozens of photos and spent most of the journey with his face glued to the window.

'Are you okay?' I'd ask him during his quieter moments.

'I'm great, Shal,' he smiled. 'Just soaking it all in.'

Afterwards, when I saw the wonderful, evocative pictures he had taken during these journeys, I realised how different Kenya appeared to him. To my familiar eyes, the sight of women sitting by the side of the road selling giant mounds of tomatoes or red onions was as familiar as a black cab on the streets of London for Jeremy. Seeing a two-piece sofa tied to the back of a rickety old bicycle as the cyclist cycled precariously on a country road was a common sight to a Kenyan. To Jeremy, it was worlds away from anything he had seen before. The whole trip was a happy assault on his senses.

Metaphorically, there were a couple of little bumps on the road, but with Jeremy by my side, we sailed over those too. During check-in at the hotel in Mombasa that my father had booked through his contacts, there appeared to be a question over whether I would stay in Jeremy's room. But I wasn't going to take any of that nonsense. Similarly, when my parents came down in the early evening to find Jeremy and I enjoying a quiet beer together at the bar, they seemed somewhat taken aback. Indians, generally, do not smoke or drink in front of their parents. It is a sign of respect for one's elders. But I felt so distant from these rules and conventions. I only knew how to be myself, and over the course of the few days we spent together my parents seemed to accept that.

Other than a few uncomfortable moments, Jeremy and I enjoyed a wonderful holiday. My friend Cheeku, whom I'd known since Switzerland, was now living in Mombasa and she took us out several times to see the sights. I even ran a couple of Just Jhoom! classes at a fitness centre while I was there and my mother came along to watch. At first, she seemed a little reluctant, I think because she feared the class would be based on southern Indian classical dance and therefore full of Hindu references akin to the dances I did as a child. Bearing in mind that she was now a devout Christian I understood that she would be uncomfortable with this. But when she realised Just Jhoom! was based on Bollywood culture and music, and therefore completely secular, she was thrilled. After the class she came up to me and hugged me.

'This is brilliant,' she enthused. 'Very good, Shalini, I'm very proud of you.'

My mother's praise and acceptance made me realise how far we had come from the first time she had met Jeremy in my small kitchen in Guildford all those years ago. And, although I was conscious that my relationship with my mother would never be the same as it had been when I was a teenager, I was grateful that my parents were back in my life after such a long hiatus.

After Mombasa, we headed for Tsavo East National Park, only around an hour's drive from Mombasa. It was Jeremy's first safari and he got to see his first elephant in the wild, a pride of lions kill and feed on a buffalo and a couple of hippos amble across the savannah grasslands - all from the comfort of the viewing platform of the lodge in which we were staying. It was extraordinary. I recalled plenty of safaris from my childhood where we would pile into the car and drive through various parks and reserves only to see practically nothing the whole time we were there. Jeremy was like a wildlife magnet – wherever he pointed his camera, there was usually a wild animal.

'It's not always this good,' I warned him at the end of the first day.

'Yes Jeremy,' agreed Shivani. 'You are just so lucky!'

We then headed back to Nairobi and prepared for a long but scenic journey to Samburu, a remote game reserve in northern Kenya, and the place where Shivani was now based. Shivani drove us the full eight hours in her little white Maruti Gypsy. As we bumped through the changing landscape, Jeremy took hundreds of photos, capturing the people, the daily bustle of Kenyan life, the unique African light. We stopped briefly to have our photos taken on the Equator, just outside the market town of Nanyuki, which lay at the foot of Mount Kenya.

Samburu was as beautiful as it always had been, with the mighty Ewaso Nyiro River running through it, whole herds of elephants frolicking on its banks. We watched them, hearts in our mouths, from such close quarters that we could hear them breathing. That evening we arrived at what would be our home for the next three days: Sasaab, a luxury camp with airy, open-sided rooms perched on the hill-side that provided welcome relief from the relentless Samburu heat. Jeremy and I looked around in awe at the huge four-poster bed, enormous open-air bathroom and our very own private plunge pool. The managers, Tony and Ali, made us feel very welcome, plying us with ice cold beers and delicious chocolate brownies, as we sat admiring the view of the Laikipia Plateau that stretched towards Mount Kenya in the distance, the Ewaso Nyiro curling around the foot of the hill.

But we hadn't come here just to wallow in luxury. My sister ran a lion conservation project, Ewaso Lions, which she had set up in 2007 for the long-term conservation of lions by promoting the co-existence between the wildlife and the local communities that lived in the area. Over the next few days Shivani introduced us to the team that worked alongside her, gave us a tour of the campsite where she had been for a few years – a collection of motley, weather-beaten tents and structures made from wood and straw - and took us to meet the local Samburu community, who lived in the local Westgate village a few miles away from the campsite.

Many of the community were involved in Ewaso Lions through one of the many initiatives she had set-up over the years – targeting the different demographics including young men, women and children. Wherever we went, everyone knew Shivani. She was like a local celebrity. Even a three-year-old boy sweetly lisped 'Chivani' in response to our asking him who she was. It was hardly surprising, really, as Shiv had really integrated with the Samburu people, not just raising funds for the conservation of lions but also contributing to the local community by funding a library at a local school, providing employment for local people and starting a Warrior Watch programme which educated and trained the young Samburu warriors in lion conservation and instilling in them the notion that killing lions to protect their livestock was not a sustainable solution. It was truly impressive work. Through her dedication and determination, she had made a major difference to the lives of the lions as well as the Samburu people. Jeremy and I hugely admired her Ewaso Lions project, one which we could see contributed to the education, health and welfare of the whole community.

One of the highlights of our visit to Samburu came when we saw a pair of elephants mating. We were on a game drive early one morning when Shivani's assistant, a young Samburu called Jeneria, stopped the car to get a view of this rarely-seen occurrence.

'There!' He pointed excitedly to where a bull elephant in musth was mounting a female. 'This is the first time I have ever seen this. Jeremy, you are so lucky! I live in Samburu and have never seen such a sight and yet you on your first trip have seen this.'

And that became our motto of the visit - 'Jeremy, you are so lucky!' - because we really did get to see so many wonderful wildlife sightings, including the lions that were being protected by Ewaso Lions, the shy and elusive leopard and all of the 'Samburu Special Five' herbivores: the Beisa oryx, reticulated giraffe, Grevy's zebra, Gerenuk antelope and Somali ostrich. Jeremy was definitely our good luck charm.

'We must come back here,' Jeremy said on our last night in Kenya, as he did on the last night of every holiday abroad.

For once, I agreed whole-heartedly.

Chapter 11 – Thriving

"Shalini is incredibly competent at managing the artistic elements,
business elements and her own personal life.
Everything she does is with such enthusiasm and energy – that was
one of the main things that struck us about her.
She exuberates passion."
—Asian Women of Achievement Award Judges

*B*ack at home, the demand for Just Jhoom! kept growing. I had trained over 50 instructors and we began holding promotional events all over the country: a flash mob in Guildford, a silent disco at The Scoop, an outdoor amphitheatre located at the foot of City Hall in London, and a fitness convention in Blackpool, where I ran a class for over 100 people. In June 2012 we got a call inviting Just Jhoom! to appear on the ITV morning show, Daybreak. It was a golden opportunity.

On the morning of the shoot, Jeremy and I left home at 3am to make the three-hour drive to Newmarket in time for the show to start at 6am. Denise Van Outen interviewed me in front of Lanwades Hall, a beautiful historic Tudor-style manor house, as 50 of the local Just Jhoom! ladies danced on the lawn behind us. The live recording was then intercut with a video we had filmed earlier in the week. Despite the early hour, everyone was incredibly excited. I should have been nervous, I suppose, but I wasn't. Not at all. Just as I had been entirely focused for my *Arangetram*, as a young 16-year-old, so I directed my mind to focus on just one thought now: to make Just Jhoom! a success. I spoke with confidence and passion as I described why I started the business.

When the interview had finished Jeremy gave me a congratulatory hug. It had gone well. That day, the phones started ringing. And they did not stop! The Daybreak segment proved hugely effective in drumming up interest. We were even invited to appear on the Channel 4 show Sunday Brunch with Tim Lovejoy and Simon Rimmer in August. After that, things really took off. Along with my second trainer, Beccy, I travelled all over the country training up new Just Jhoom! instructors. We'd get up at the crack of dawn to drive the long distances to wherever we happened to be training that day – Wales, Nottingham, Manchester, Liverpool. And no matter how early it was, Jeremy would be up too, smiling and helping us load up the car.

I was working like mad to keep up with the demand. And, I suppose inevitably, it began to catch up with me again. Waking in the middle of the night, emotional over-eating, stress and tiredness. This time, however, thanks to the lessons I had learned at the Priory, I recognized the early symptoms of depression. But despite Jeremy's best efforts to make me relax at the weekends, I'd often find my way to the computer while he was out gardening… and I'd still be at my desk way after midnight. As anyone who has run their own business knows, being self-employed means that you never really switch off. But it was bad for my health and I knew that if I allowed this to go on, I would send myself spiraling back into a terrible depression.

Now that dance was my business, as opposed to a source of healing for me, I needed to find something else that allowed me to focus my mind and body and take away the stress of work. That's when I came across an online meditation course by Deepak Chopra. Meditation was always something that appealed to me, though I never believed I had the patience to sit and do it. But now I was determined to try. *Fifteen minutes*, I thought, *how hard can that be?*

Really hard, as it turns out! Sitting still for 15 minutes without letting my head fill up with hundreds of different thoughts was tough and I was convinced that I'd never be able to master the practice of 'stilling' my mind. But I pushed on, determined not to be defeated and, as the days passed, I realised that I could manage a little longer each time. Gradually, I got the hang of it and by the end of the course I was successfully meditating for up to an hour.

I decided to take it to the next level and began to practice mindfulness as well. To those who have never come across these terms, mindfulness and meditation are basically the same thing but where mindfulness is informal meditation, practiced as part of your daily routine, meditation is formal. You must take time out of your day to sit down and meditate. Mindfulness is about focusing your mind on the task you are doing in the moment, without letting your head get swamped by other thoughts.

For example, if I were washing up a plate I would focus my mind entirely on the task, taking time to notice my breathing, my hands and the way they moved in the soapy water and the bubbles as they slipped over the plate. You can eat mindfully, read mindfully, walk mindfully and take a bath mindfully. All it means is being in the moment and I loved it because it made me stop and slow down my brain. I remembered that when I'd been ill, I had actually (unintentionally) practiced mindfulness when I made *masala chai*. But I'd done that because it was all my befuddled brain could cope with at the time. In my 'well' state, I had to work hard to focus my attention on just one thing. To just be.

Incredibly, I discovered that mindfulness was something Jeremy had been practicing all his life, without realizing it. After returning from his fishing trips, for example, I'd ask him how it went and what he did.

His reply was always the same: 'I fished.'

There were many occasions when I'd find him sitting in the garden, staring at the pond or the trees and I'd ask him, 'What are you thinking?' only to be told, 'Nothing.'

I once began a conversation with the line, 'I was just thinking in the shower...' and Jeremy stopped me.

'You *think* in the shower?' he asked, nonplussed.

'Yes, it's the best time to think. There are no distractions. Why? What do you do in the shower?'

'I shower,' he grinned. 'I feel the water on me, I soap myself. I feel the day being washed away. I don't think anything in the shower.'

Jeremy practiced mindfulness naturally. I had to train myself. But with some effort, and a lot of practice, I was learning how to be more like Jeremy. I was learning how to simply be.

Then, in March 2013, I got some really good news that made the hard work all worthwhile.

'Oh, my goodness, I've been shortlisted!' I breathed in amazement when I read the email.

It was a Wednesday afternoon and I was having a meeting with one of my Just Jhoom! Instructors, when I decided to check my emails. And there it was:

I am delighted to inform you that you have been shortlisted for an Asian Woman of Achievement Award in the Arts & Culture category...

My eyes locked on those words: *... you have been shortlisted...* I had to keep reading that line, just to reassure myself it was true. Something inside me couldn't quite believe it. When Jeremy wandered in, I beckoned him over. He peered at the screen, reading the email over my shoulder. Then he started to laugh. It had been Jeremy's idea to enter me for the award.

'I knew it,' he smiled, squeezing my shoulders. 'I just knew you'd get through!'

The judging day was in mid-April and I was both excited and nervous when Jeremy dropped me off at the train station for my trip to London. I was usually very confident speaking in public, especially when it came to Just Jhoom! but the interview was unlike anything I had ever experienced before. It felt like a grilling in the Dragon's Den! I walked into the room to be faced with three judges - all with particular specialties in the arts and business - and they launched questions at me like well-aimed grenades.

'What's your five-year sales projection?'

'How did your personal history affect your decision to start this business?'

'What's your business plan for the next year?

'How many instructors do you aim to train in the next quarter?'

'What demographics are you catering for?'

By the time I came out of that room an hour later, my head was spinning.

'I don't think I did very well,' I told to Jeremy during a phone call on my way back home. 'I waffled a lot.'

I felt strangely flat for the next day, gutted that I'd blown the interview. But I didn't dwell on it too long and within a week I'd notched the whole thing up to experience, thinking that if I didn't win I could apply again the following year. In any case, Jeremy and I were excited about going to the awards gala, which was taking place in May at the London Hilton on Park Lane. Not only would it be a chance for us to have a glamorous evening out together, but a troupe of eight Just Jhoom! dancers were going to be performing in front of the 600 gala guests. Whatever happened with the awards, the gala would be a great chance to show Just Jhoom! off to a room full of influential movers and shakers.

On the day of the gala, I had my hair and nails done – a rare treat – and put on my favourite purple *churidaar*, a long tunic with slim-fitting trousers, and a scarf, while Jeremy donned his best black tie and we hopped on the fast train to London.

We had a quick aperitif at the wine bar in Waterloo Station, before catching a taxi to the gala. Jeremy squeezed my hand as we walked into the impressive Grand Ballroom, which was humming with excitement. There were plenty of famous faces milling around the tables, many dressed in beautiful saris, and I managed to spot Cherie Blair, Sarah, the Duchess of York, Nick Clegg's wife, Miriam Gonzalez Durantez and Maria Miller, who was the Conservative Culture Secretary at the time, among the throng before slipping upstairs to wish my dancers good luck. Then we took our seats for the start of the evening.

'Good luck!' Jeremy clinked his glass against mine and I raised one eyebrow meaningfully.

He knew I didn't have any illusions about my chances of winning. I was up against some very strong candidates, including the award-winning actor and playwright Lolita Chakrabarti, who was a regular on BBC TV and radio as well as having her on production company. She would almost certainly scoop the award; I was just happy to have been invited!

As the lights went down, the Bollywood music started up and my wonderful dancers opened the night with a spectacular show. They illuminated Just Jhoom! at its best and earned themselves an enormous roar of approval from the hundreds of seated diners. I quietly excused myself and raced upstairs to congratulate my dancers and thank them all for coming. They had come as a favour to me and I wanted them to know how much I appreciated their help.

Back at the table, I clapped and cheered my way through the long list of winners being announced by the gala hosts – an inspiring mixture of entrepreneurs, charity founders, media personalities and women in politics. Finally, at the very end of the evening, my category, Arts and Culture, was announced.

Sarah Ferguson was giving out the award and as she walked to the podium, Jeremy and I exchanged nervous grins.

'This has been a really strong category and we're pleased to announce there will be joint winners,' she said.

What? Joint?

'And the winners are...'

If there are two winners that means I'm still in with a...

'Lolita Chakrabarti and...'

chance.

'...Shalini Bhalla.'

Oh my!!

I leapt up from my seat in surprise and turned round to see that Jeremy had been filming me the whole time. His eyes were full of tears. For a brief moment, he put down the camera and we hugged each other.

'I'm so proud of you, Shal,' he whispered into my ear. 'So very proud. You deserve this.'

It was a genuine shock. I hadn't even considered the possibility that the judges might choose two winners in our category. My legs felt like jelly as I climbed the steps to the stage and shook hands with the Duchess of York and the other presenters, as well as with Lolita, my joint winner.

This meant so much to me, it was hard to even think straight as I stood on that stage, letting the applause and cheers wash over me. My heart swelled in my chest. It felt like everything in my life had been leading up to this moment. The award was a validation of my development - both personally and professionally. Despite losing everything in my early twenties, my family, my identity and even my mind, I had clawed my way back from the brink. With Jeremy's unwavering support, I had carved out my own path in life. And all the many hours I'd put into making Just Jhoom! a success were now being acknowledged. Those long, lonely hours working into the night on training manuals, or getting up in the pre-dawn darkness to travel the length and breadth of the country, not to mention the work planning, creating and marketing the programme itself. It had all been worth it! I'd never even taken a salary for myself, ploughing every penny I earned back into the business. And now, for the first time, all that effort was being recognized. In the eyes of my peers, Just Jhoom! was a serious venture and I, a serious businesswoman.

I thanked the Duchess of York for my award then stepped up to the podium to speak. Had Jeremy not been filming me at that moment, I would never have remembered what I said, so dreamlike was the whole experience. What came out of my mouth was entirely off the cuff and from the heart:

'Just Jhoom! which means Just Dance in Hindi, is all about changing people's lives. In today's society we have such problems with both mental and physical health. Dance and enjoyment - that's what Just Jhoom! is about; it is about changing lives. I definitely couldn't do that without my team - and you saw the Just Jhoom! dancers earlier on – they are a small part of the team. We have the MD and the office but the main people are the Just Jhoom! instructors. They go out there, day in, day out and run Just Jhoom! classes. Sometimes two people turn up, sometimes twenty – but they're there, running classes, inspiring people, making sure that we're changing lives. So, to them, the Just Jhoom! instructors, thank you so much, without you this would not have been possible. I'd like to dedicate this to my partner Jeremy because through all the ups and downs he's always been there. This one's for you. Thank you.'

It felt like something out of a film. I found myself being led to the side of the stage where Jeremy was waiting for me and we hugged each other in amazement. He was so proud, he couldn't stop telling me. Cameras flashed and the next thing I knew, I was being interviewed, trying to describe what it felt like to win the award. We were interrupted by a photo pinging onto my phone: it was a picture of all my dancers in the lift of the hotel with their thumbs up. The text read: *We saw the award while we were backstage and saw your name. Congratulations from your Jhoomers!*

I was so happy, I couldn't stop grinning. Jeremy and I returned to our table, plonked the award down between us and sat back as the waiter poured us each a large glass of champagne. The rest of the evening passed in a dazzling blur of lively chatter, congratulations and more champagne. At midnight, Jeremy finally poured me into a taxi to Waterloo. It was a memorable end to the evening. We sat happily at Waterloo, waiting for the last train back to Guildford, each clutching a bottle of beer, the award resting on my lap while the late-night cleaners worked around us.

'I can't believe it.' I sighed, staring in wonder at the heavy silver statue on my lap, the words 'AWA in Arts & Culture. Winner – Shalini Bhalla' engraved on the front.

'You're a winner,' Jeremy slurred in agreement.

'And you too – you're a winner!' I insisted. 'This award is yours too.'

'And I'm a winner,' he nodded, eyes closing. 'You're a winner and I'm a winner. We're both… *hic*… winners.'

We giggled all the way home.

It was true. My success was Jeremy's success. He had always been my biggest champion, but more than that, he had given me the confidence and the freedom to pursue my dreams, regardless of his own doubts that Just Jhoom! would ever prove a profitable business. He had backed me all the way. Not that I could ever truly rest on my laurels. I was always reaching for the next accomplishment. There were times when Jeremy couldn't understand this burning drive within me.

'Stop and look around, celebrate what you've achieved,' he'd urge. 'Why do you always want to do more?'

The truth was, it all went back to my childhood and the ambition that had been instilled in me as a young girl. It was never enough to be good at something, I always had to be the best. It wasn't enough to come second, I had to come first. I couldn't just have a good *Arangetram*, it had to be the most impressive one Nairobi had ever seen. It was deep within me, this burning desire to excel. It wasn't enough to win an AWA award, now I wanted to take the company global. I wanted to write a book, appear on TV.

What did Jeremy want for himself? Modest things, really. He wanted to retire at 60. He wanted to go fishing or golfing at the weekends and he wanted to tend to the garden and enjoy spending time looking after the pond. And then, in November 2013, he decided he wanted something else.

We returned to Kenya for our winter holiday that year. We often chose to go away in the winter because I suffered from Seasonal Affective Disorder which left me prone to low moods in the dark winter months. The excitement of a foreign holiday combined with some much-needed sunshine usually helped me over the hump of a cold, English winter. On this visit my parents were away - my mother in India and my father running the annual East African Safari Classic Rally, of which he was the general manager. Rallying was my father's great passion, something he had been involved with since he was a young man. He had a fantastic reputation in the rallying community, both in Kenya and abroad, a true icon of Kenyan motorsports.

After a short stay in Nairobi we travelled to Naivasha, a small market town northwest of Nairobi, to meet my father and watch the rally. Jeremy was fascinated with all the classic cars on display. After a couple of days, we left the rally and started an epic road trip from Naivasha to Samburu, stopping off at Nanyuki to stay one night with our friends, Ali and Tony, at their newly-built house on the outskirts of the town. With fantastic views of Mount Kenya and beautiful landscaped gardens which teemed with bird and insect life. It was quiet and peaceful – such a change from our lives back home. Truly idyllic.

As we left Nanyuki the next day, en-route to Samburu, Jeremy and I both had a strange sense that we were leaving home. Neither of us said anything at the time. We were both looking forward to once again visiting Samburu and staying at Sasaab. Just like last time we were warmly welcomed by Shiv's Samburu team and the local community.

Traditionally, the Samburu people were a pastoral, semi-nomadic tribe who herded sheep, goats and cattle. In the past they had come into conflict with lions that threatened their herds and over the years the lion population in the area had decreased dramatically. When my sister first set up her project, it was a few months before she actually saw any lions. This wasn't surprising as, at the time, there were only 11 wild lions left in Samburu National Park. Over the course of the first two years, my sister and her assistant, Jeneria, a young Samburu warrior, or *moran*, realised that the key to ensuring the long-term survival of this magnificent animal was to engage the local people. Their first step was to engage the warriors of the community – the young men who lived in the same areas as the animals and whose rite of passage on the path to manhood involved them killing a lion. Education and giving the local tribesmen a sense of ownership with respect to the wellbeing and protection of the wildlife was the first step in changing centuries-old practices.

Shivani also started working with local women, setting up a project called Mama Simba, which educated the women about conservation and the importance of preserving the wildlife. The Lion Kids Camp, for young Samburu herder children and local school children, soon followed. Now, instead of being in competition with the lions, the local Samburu communities were conservationists and it was up to them to ensure the survival of the lions. Watching my sister at work made me very proud. Jeremy, too, was hugely proud of her and in awe of all she had achieved in such a short time and at such a young age. From 11 lions Samburu now had 50 lions, testament to the hard work done by my sister through her project.

True to form, on our last night in Kenya, Jeremy announced: 'We must come back here.'

'Why don't we move here?' I suggested, gently.

'What do you mean? Now?'

'No. Why don't we live here when you retire? In Nanyuki. What's stopping us from buying some land here with a view to building our own home for the future? This is a life both of us would enjoy. Why don't we make it a reality?'

Now that really gave the boy from Surrey something to think about.

Chapter 12 – A Setback

"Life is thickly sown with thorns, and I know no other remedy than to pass quickly through them. The longer we dwell on our misfortunes, the greater their power to harm us."
—Voltaire[9]

'Right, I've had enough of this, I'm taking you to the doctor!' I couldn't watch Jeremy hobbling round the house, holding his sides, a moment longer. He had been his usual stoical self about a persistent pain on the right side of his back for a week, but it had gone on too long. For the last couple of days, he had been 'working from home', hoping the pain would disappear on its own with a little rest and some painkillers. This was clearly wishful thinking. It seemed to be getting worse and though he'd never admit it, I could see he was struggling.

I called the GP and made an appointment to bring him in that afternoon. If it had been me, I would probably have been there at the first sign of any pain. I was definitely the drama queen, ready with my cough drops and Vicks at the merest hint of a sniffle, ready to tell anyone who would listen that I had fallen ill. Jeremy thought this was always very amusing. He could have full-blown flu and still be trying to mow the lawn. On this occasion, however, he didn't object when I insisted he see the doctor.

'It's probably gallstones,' said the sympathetic GP after examining Jeremy. 'They can be very painful but I really can't do anything for you here. You'll have to go into A&E for further tests.'

Jeremy wasn't keen to go to hospital. It was July and the hottest day of the year so far - the last place he wanted to be was in A&E. But I insisted. So, we trundled down to the Royal Surrey County Hospital in Guildford, where Jeremy was given a battery of tests as well as some medication to help control the pain. After several hours we finally saw a doctor.

'We think it is gallstones,' he said. 'But you'll have to come back for an ultrasound in a couple of weeks just to confirm.'

We were both exhausted after so many hours spent in A&E, but relieved that the doctor seemed certain Jeremy was suffering from gallstones. By the time we got home it was nearly midnight but we switched on the computer as soon as we got in and looked up gallstones.

'Too much fatty food,' I murmured, reading the online NHS explanation of the causes of gallstones. 'No more cheese for you!'

Jeremy scowled. He loved cheese and would eat it with every meal if he could.

'Are you sure you don't want me to come with you?' I asked him two weeks later, on the morning of his ultrasound appointment.

'No, no,' he shook his head. 'You've got your work to do. No point us both missing work. I'll just get the ultrasound and then we'll figure it out once we know what it is.'

'Okay, I suppose you're right. Well, good luck. Hope it all goes well.'

We gave each other a quick kiss and then I was off out the door, my head already consumed with ideas for the series of meetings I had that day. It turned out to be a busy day and I didn't realise that my mobile was on silent. When I finally checked it at around 4pm I was surprised to see two voicemail messages and numerous texts from Jeremy, 'Call me!' 'Can you call me ASAP?' 'Please ring me!'

My heart started to race. Quickly, I dialed Jeremy's mobile.

'What is it?' I asked. 'Is everything okay?'

'It's fine. I've sorted it,' he said, his usual calm self. 'But I can't speak to you right now. I'll call you later.'

An hour later he called to say he was on his way home and by 6pm he was back in the kitchen with a cup of tea, explaining what had happened.

'I was lying down and the sonographer had the ultrasound probe on my belly; she was spending a long time looking at one place in particular on the screen, frowning. Then she said, "Hang on a minute, I just need to get the doctor in." She left and came back in with one of the doctors who took a very long hard look at the same place as the sonographer, before saying that there was something on my kidney but they couldn't tell what exactly. He said I needed to have a CT scan. I asked him how quickly they could do the scan under my private health insurance and he said immediately, which is when I started calling you – I was trying to get the details of my health insurance. By the time you called me back I was being wheeled in for the CT scan.'

I felt uneasy, but was pleased that Jeremy had managed to get the scan done.

'We have to go back in at 8pm tonight for the results,' he added.

'Eight o'clock this evening? Wow – that's late for an appointment.'

'Well, that's what you get with private medical cover – immediate tests, immediate answers. I'm not complaining.'

We grabbed a little light supper, fed Tabasco and then drove back to the hospital for our appointment. After a short wait, we were shown into the small office where the consultant was looking intensely at something on his computer screen. He got up, shook our hands briskly, invited us to take a seat then turned the screen round to face us.

'So, Mr. Lucas, you have a tumour on your kidney,' he said without any preamble.

'You can see here...' and he pointed at a grainy grey lump on the screen. '*That* is your kidney. And this,' he pointed at a lighter grey blob inside the kidney. '... *this* is a five-centimetre-long tumour.' I strained to see the blob he was pointing at. I wasn't totally aware of what was going on.

'Excuse me, but what do you mean a tumour?' I asked, confused. 'What type of tumour?'

'It's cancer.'

He said it so bluntly, like he was telling us that Jeremy had the flu. *Cancer? How can it be cancer?*

'But I thought it was gallstones...' I said in a small, shrill voice. I felt tears prickling behind my eyes but I forced them back.

'I'm sorry, Mrs Lucas, but this isn't gallstones. This is renal cancer and Jeremy will most likely need surgery to have the tumour removed. The good news is that it looks like we've caught it early. What we'll do now,' he said, turning back to Jeremy, 'is refer you to a renal oncologist and then...'

I couldn't hear him anymore. My head was full of that one word: cancer. Jeremy sat, as still as a statue, next to me. He remained fully composed and focused on the consultant's words. He spoke occasionally, to ask questions, but I couldn't take anything in. Tears streaked down my cheeks. A kindly assistant offered me a tissue and put a comforting arm around my shoulders as the consultant ushered us out of his office. It was all over in a flash and the next thing I knew we were getting back into the car. Jeremy took my hand and squeezed it tight.

All the way home, I sat in numb, disbelieving silence – neither of us speaking. It had never crossed my mind for a second that Jeremy's pain was anything serious. He seemed so healthy to me, so strong. When we walked back into the house that night it felt like I was walking into a different home. On the surface, everything seemed the same but something fundamental had changed. Tabasco came padding down the stairs and I scooped him up in my arms.

'Oh JumJums!' I held him close to my chest and gave him a big hug. Jeremy came in and took off his shoes. He seemed lost in another world.

'Are you okay?' I asked him, gently. 'You seem very calm.'

'I knew, Shal,' he admitted. 'I knew what he was going to tell us. I think… I think I knew when the doctor came in to look at the ultrasound. Listen, let's get some sleep and talk tomorrow. We're both very tired.'

Neither of us slept that night and since the following day was Friday we agreed to take the day off. We needed time to digest the news together and decide how to handle things. I knew nothing about renal cancer. I didn't even know that renal meant 'kidney'. The consultant had said he suspected there might be metastasis on Jeremy's lungs as he'd seen a spattering of tiny shadows that could be tumours, but he couldn't be sure at this stage. They couldn't be sure of anything until they carried out a biopsy. Jeremy decided to Google renal cancer, very much against the advice of the consultant. I didn't want to know. As far as I was concerned, if you Googled something that made it real and I didn't want this to be real.

'Whatever it is, we'll beat this thing,' I insisted. 'We're staying positive.'

'Of course,' Jeremy agreed, his brow furrowed as he looked at his laptop.

'You've got private health cover so they'll give you the best possible treatment as quickly as possible.' I went on.

'I know....'

'It's going to be fine.'

'It is.'

Jeremy looked up and patted the sofa. I went and sat down next to him and he took my hand in his and held it to his chest.

'You're scared, aren't you?' he whispered.

'Yes.'

'Don't be scared. I'm going to be fine. Really.'

On Saturday I had a class to teach in the morning. That afternoon I called Shivani and my parents to tell them and Jeremy's daughters came home so we could tell them too. It was very emotional, but we knew we had to tell those closest to us as soon as possible; we didn't want them finding out any other way. The rest of the day, we spent at home together, doing the things we loved the best. Jeremy pottered round the garden, while I sat in the conservatory reading and watching him work on the flowerbeds, which were blooming with colour in the July sunshine. It was another beautiful day that Sunday so we took ourselves down to the West Sussex coast for a long walk along Climping Beach. After the initial shock we both felt calmer. Whatever happened, I knew Jeremy would beat this disease. He was a strong, healthy man – he didn't smoke, he didn't drink much and we had a healthy diet. If anybody could beat it, it was him. Cancer had come into our lives unbidden but we wouldn't lie down and accept its presence. We would chase it away with everything in our power.

The longer we walked across the pebbled beach, hand-in-hand, feeling the warmth of the sun on our skin, watching the sunbathers and the excited children dipping in and out the sea, the more positive and optimistic I felt.

'We can overcome anything together,' I said, squeezing his hand.

We looked at one another and smiled. I was still shocked but I wasn't scared anymore. I knew that Jeremy would be okay.

The following day, Jeremy went in for the biopsy and I accompanied him for what was a relatively straightforward procedure. As I sat in his hospital room waiting for him, I worked on my laptop. I now had a million things on my plate. As well as the ongoing work for Just Jhoom!, I was launching a mindfulness and meditation course of my own.

Over the course of a year, I had delved deeper into the world of meditation and mindfulness and found they both helped hugely with regaining a sense of controlling my stress. I wanted to share this with others and I felt it would be a great addition to the Just Jhoom! brand. After training with London-based mindfulness expert, Shamash Alidina, I wrote my own course. I wanted to teach mindfulness myself but not in the way others were doing it. I found that most Western mindfulness courses were quite bland, but knowing that the teachings originated in ancient Buddhist texts, I was keen to share this knowledge with others. My course wasn't a religious one but I incorporated the Buddhist philosophies of awareness, non-attachment and acceptance into my courses. I felt that if people had a deeper, richer understanding of where these techniques came from and the ideas behind them, they'd have a better chance of mastering them successfully in practice.

I was due to trial my technique with a one-off workshop in August in a friend's barn, with a view to launching an eight-week course in September. But after Jeremy's diagnosis, I nearly ditched the whole idea.

'Do I need to do this now?' I wondered aloud, as I worked on a Facebook advert for the September course.

'Perhaps it's the wrong time,' I said, turning to Jeremy. 'I don't need to be adding to my workload while we're dealing with your health.'

Jeremy pondered this for a while - he never made decisions rashly.

'No. I think you should go ahead with it as planned,' he said evenly. 'Look, I think we need to keep our lives as normal as possible. We can't just stop everything.'

Two days after the biopsy we made our way back to Nuffield Hospital to meet Jeremy's renal oncologist to get the results. The oncologist confirmed that Jeremy did have cancer on his right kidney.

'The tumour is six centimetres in size and "clean", which means it has not spread to the surrounding organs, except the lungs,' he explained. 'Rather than attempt to treat the cancer, the best course of action is to remove the kidney. Functioning on one kidney should not be a problem.'

He went on to explain that what was of concern were the tumours in Jeremy's lung. He explained that these did not signify lung cancer but were, in fact, tumours from the kidney. But, because of the location of these tumours within the lung, it was going to be too dangerous to operate to remove them. The only way to treat them would be to use medication to shrink the tumours. Jeremy would then need to be scanned every three months for the rest of his life to monitor their growth.

We waited for a date for the surgery to have Jeremy's kidney removed. Perhaps idealistically, we hoped he could have it done over the summer so that we could both return to work in September without too much disruption to our lives. But, as it was the summer, all the surgeons were on holiday, so it was September before we could get an appointment. Our oncologist assured us that the tumour wouldn't grow bigger in a month. We just had to take his word for it, although by now I had decided that I wouldn't simply sit back and rely solely on the medical professionals to tackle Jeremy's illness.

If we were going to beat this disease together, we needed a whole arsenal of weapons.

Chapter 13 – Eastern Mysticism and Western Rationalism

"The real purpose of meditation isn't to tune out and get away from it all but to tune in and get in touch with your true self — that eternal aspect of yourself that goes beyond all the ever-changing, external circumstances of your life."

—Deepak Chopra[10]

'Now take the raisin and roll it between your thumb and forefinger,' I instructed gently. 'Look at the raisin, really give it your full attention. Imagine that you have never seen a raisin before – this is the very first raisin you have seen in your life. Really look at it, observe the deep black colour, the folds in the skin, the crumpled form, the grooves and hollows. Now *feel* the raisin and *think* about how it got here. How did this raisin start its life? As a grape growing on the vine, perhaps? Think about how it grew from a tiny seed, nourished by the earth, the rain and the sunshine. Feel it, squish it between your fingers, smell it. What does this raisin mean to you?'

It was the first day of my eight-week mindfulness course and I was leading a group of seven students in our first exercise: the Raisin Meditation exercise. It may have sounded a little nutty to anyone listening to us from outside the class, but I found that the Raisin Meditation, devised by mindfulness pioneer, Jon Kabat-Zinn, was an effective tool in training the mind to focus. The main reason many of us suffer from stress and anxiety in the modern world is that we are constantly juggling hundreds of competing thoughts in our heads. Our minds are constantly split between these thoughts and exhausted from the effort. Over time, we find it harder and harder to focus. But who can just empty their mind on command? Nobody, without practice. So, the first step was to learn how to focus on just one thing. The start of the course was all about clearing out the clutter, training the mind - and all the senses - to be present in the moment.

'Every time you get a different thought, tell yourself, "I'm not thinking, I'm just focused on this raisin,"' I directed.

For the next ten minutes, I instructed the class to feel, smell and then, finally, taste the raisin they each held. After a few moments I asked for feedback. The class exploded into life.

'Wow!'

'Oh my God!'

'That's amazing!'

There were laughs and smiles, as well as a couple of unhappy faces. Some people were astonished at the complex taste of the raisin, having thought about it so long and hard. To them, it offered an abundance of flavor. Other members of the group screwed up their faces in disgust, realising for the first time in their lives that they didn't actually like the dried fruit. Either way, as their first experience of mindful eating, the exercise was revelatory. By focusing 100 per cent on what they were doing, they were completely present in the moment and as a result, all their senses had been heightened.

'This is what we're going to train our minds to do,' I went on. 'We're going to become more mindful in all the activities we carry out in our daily lives. And by doing this – by staying in the moment, in the present, in a mindful way – we can find a way to inner peace and happiness. But we have to take it step by step. The brain is a powerful organ but you need to treat it like a muscle. You need to train it over time. It's like taking yourself to the gym – you don't start on the hardest equipment, you start easy and then work your way up to a certain fitness level.'

The mindfulness techniques I was learning had certainly helped me cope in the difficult early weeks of Jeremy's illness. On the day of my Raisin Meditation class, I had been at Frimley Park Hospital in Basingstoke, where Jeremy was recovering from the operation to have his kidney removed. Everything had gone pretty smoothly at first. I had driven him to hospital on the morning of 7 September and we had waited together while he had his vitals checked. We had a private room and all the nurses seemed very kind and compassionate. Certainly, compared to some of the NHS wards I had experienced, they weren't harried or stressed out. It was a peaceful environment and I think the calmness helped us both to feel more confident.

'See you on the other side,' he smiled cheerfully, just before they wheeled him down to theatre.

'What? You know what that means, don't you?' I replied.

'I mean, see you on the other side *of the operation*,' he corrected himself.

'Yeah, sure,' I laughed as I watched his bed disappear down the corridor.

While I waited, I felt relaxed and reassured. I knew he would be fine. We had met his two surgeons a few days earlier, during the pre-op consultation, and they were both brimming with the kind of professional confidence that comes from years of experience.

'This is a very routine operation,' they had assured us both. 'You have nothing to worry about.'

The nurses brought me tea and then lunch as the hours passed and finally, at 6pm, one of the nurses came to tell me he was out of theatre and in recovery.

'The operation has gone well,' she said. 'You can go and see him if you want.'

She took me down to the recovery room where Jeremy was lying, hooked up to various machines, a great big soppy grin on his face.

'Shal!' he exclaimed when he saw me. His face was puffy from the operation and his eyes were heavy and unfocussed. He was obviously completely off his head on morphine. 'There you are! I love you, Shal!'

'I love you too, Jem,' I said and took his hand.

He smiled weakly. It was a relief that he was awake and talking, though the nurse explained that his blood pressure hadn't yet stabilised and they couldn't bring him to the room until it had settled. I sat by his bed in the recovery room most of the night. His blood pressure just wouldn't stabilise and it was a worrying few hours. Finally, as dawn broke, he was stable enough to be transferred back to the room. I trudged alongside the bed as they wheeled him back, rubbing my eyes and yawning all the way.

'Why don't you go home and get some sleep?' one nurse suggested. 'He'll be fine. We'll call you if there are any problems.'

After driving home, feeding Tabasco and taking a quick shower, I fell straight into bed. As I pulled the duvet over my tired body, I felt myself sinking into the soft pillows, sleep dragging at the corners of my mind. *Just a few hours sleep, that's all I need and then I'll be okay. Just a few hours…*

I woke with a start. The phone by the bed trilled insistently as I groped towards consciousness, woozy and disorientated. I looked at the clock: 7.32. Urgh. I had been asleep for all of 15 minutes!

'Yes?' I answered, in a voice thick with sleep.

'Mrs Lucas?'

'Yes.'

'Just to let you know your husband is okay but he's had a bit of an incident. He's absolutely fine now but we just needed to let you know…'

'What do you mean an incident?' I asked, my heart thumping, fully awake now.

'His blood pressure crashed and we had to get the team in to recover him. He's fine, he's absolutely fine, but if you'd like to come in…'

I leapt out of bed and threw my clothes back on, before driving like a maniac all the way back to Basingstoke. The whole time I kept telling myself to stay calm but my heart and mind were racing. *What if he crashes again? What if I don't make it back in time?* I screeched to a standstill in the car park and ran all the way to his room. When I flung open the door I saw him sitting up in bed, smiling and sipping a cup of tea.

'Oh hello! he said, surprised by my sudden entrance.

Far from being at death's door, he looked very healthy indeed. His cheeks were pink and less swollen from earlier and he was wide-awake. *How can he just sit there, looking so damn healthy?*

I was furious.

'"Hello"? What do you mean "hello"?' I fumed. 'I've been so worried. They told me you crashed.'

'Mmm, I did,' he said, taking a sip of tea and stretching his arm out to me. 'I felt myself going so I pressed the button. And then... well, the truth is I don't know what happened. The next thing I woke up to 20 faces all around me and they said I'd crashed.'

I sat down next to him as he described his little 'episode'. It all sounded so benign but I knew it had been a close call. The nurse came in and explained how his blood pressure had dropped so low that he'd fallen unconscious and that's when the team stepped in. There had been a handful of them apparently, not 20! But Jeremy seemed perfectly fine. Later that morning, one of the surgeons came to see us. He said the operation had gone very well and they were sending the whole kidney with the tumour for further tests and a biopsy to confirm the exact type of renal cancer they were dealing with. That would take a little while. In the meantime, the important thing was Jeremy's recovery.

That evening Jeremy's daughters came to see him and I returned to Guildford to deliver my first mindfulness class of the eight-week course. It went well but I have no idea how I managed to get through the first class on only 15 minutes' sleep. After speaking to Jeremy on the phone later that night, I fell into bed and drifted into a long and heavy sleep. The next morning, recharged, I headed straight back to the hospital to check on Jeremy. He seemed comfortable there and not in too much pain. The nurses made a big fuss of him and he lapped up the attention.

'Don't get used to it,' I warned good-humoredly. 'I won't be as nice to you at home.'

'I know that!' he parried. 'Why do you think I'm making the most of it here?'

'He's one of our loveliest patients,' smiled a nurse taking notes at the end of the bed. 'Always very polite and appreciative. And he's doing so well!'

She was very encouraging but by that stage Jeremy couldn't even get out of bed. It took a few days before I could bring him home and even then he needed a lot of help just to get to the toilet and back. But his determination to get back on the road to recovery never waivered.

'The good news is that we've got it early,' said Jeremy's oncologist, when we went to see him two weeks later. 'Your wounds are healing well. You still need plenty of rest and definitely no strenuous exercise. The pathology results show that the cancer is not as bad as first thought, but we will take another CT scan in two weeks to see if there are any cancer cells left where the kidney was and also to keep an eye on the tumours in the lung.'

It was a long, slow process but gradually Jeremy regained his strength after the operation. At first, he had barely been able to walk from one side of the room to the other without getting out of breath, but with a lot of effort and perseverance, he recovered. The one thing the doctors were clear about was that he shouldn't physically exert himself or do any strenuous exercise. So, the day I came home from work to find he had mown the lawn, I saw red.

'They told you not to do any strenuous exercise!' I erupted. 'Do you want to send yourself back to hospital?'

'I feel fine,' he'd insisted. 'I don't see what the problem is.'

'You don't see the problem?' I was livid. 'You could reopen the scar, you fool!'

I couldn't bear it. I jumped in the car and drove to my friend Helen's house. She offered me a glass of wine and a few soothing words and eventually, I calmed down. It was one of the only times I had ever felt real anger towards Jeremy. Generally, he was considerate, easy-going and almost completely unflappable. If we got into a fight, he always chose to walk away or say something funny to make me laugh and defuse the argument. He did not like confrontation. Only once did I provoke him into fighting back.

'Don't walk away from me,' I had screamed after him. 'Stay and fight!'

So, he did. And boy, did I regret having said that. The shouting and swearing was so out-of-character and upsetting that I immediately crumpled into tears.

'Why are you shouting at me?' I bawled.

'You told me to!' he'd replied, completely justifiably.

It was a lesson learned. I never provoked him to 'fight with me' ever again. And, to be fair, he never gave me any real reason to be angry with him - until he decided to mow the lawn after a major operation. Later that evening, I returned home to a very unhappy and contrite Jeremy.

'I didn't want to upset you,' he said. 'I just couldn't stand looking at the overgrown lawn anymore...'

'Yes, I know your obsession with having a perfect stripy lawn, but I was worried. I thought you would hurt yourself and wind up back in hospital. Promise me you won't do anything so stupid again?'

'I promise.'

By early October Jeremy was recovering well and we went to see the oncologist. The biopsy on the full tumour had been conducted and the results confirmed that it was renal cell carcinoma. It wasn't one of the more common types of renal cancer and therefore wouldn't readily respond to conventional treatments, like chemotherapy or radiotherapy. So we would have to approach it with a targeted treatment, which would hopefully hold it at bay and stop it from spreading.

The good news was that, following the latest scan, there were no new tumours or cancerous growths around the area where the kidney had been removed. The tumours in the lung had not changed at all and Jeremy wouldn't need to start treatment unless and until the lung tumours exhibited any increase in size. We were asked to return in January for another scan and to ascertain if treatment was going to be needed. It all felt very positive and we were both buoyed by the oncologist's assurances. Back at home that night, Jeremy seemed immensely pleased.

'He's very good, isn't he?' he said to me.

'Mmm...' I murmured. 'But you know, your health isn't just about what the doctor prescribes for you. I've been reading these books and you can really help yourself by changing your diet, things like cutting out sugar, eating less meat. Taking a more holistic approach to your health. This isn't just about your cancer, it's about your whole body.'

'I'm not getting into any of that woo-woo stuff, Shal,' Jeremy waved at me dismissively. 'Woo-woo' was his word for anything vaguely alternative – from meditation to pranic healing, yoga, Reiki, massage, vegetarianism and anything else you couldn't get a prescription for; he lumped it all together.

'I have full faith in my doctor,' he went on. 'He's really very good.'

I sighed. I found Jeremy's approach to his health baffling. He believed that doctors were the only people who could help him and that he wasn't able to help himself. Not for the first time, I was annoyed at this blind faith in Western medicine. If this had been my cancer, I would have gone down a completely different route. In the weeks since his diagnosis, I had bought lots of books on a healthy lifestyle approach to cancer and one in particular had struck a chord. *Anti-Cancer: A New Way of Life* was written by Dr. David Servan-Shreiber who had been diagnosed with brain cancer. In his book he had explored how a Western diet of sugar and stress actually helped to create the conditions for the disease to thrive. He advocated traditional medicine combined with healthy eating, yoga and meditation.

To me, the Indian Ayurvedic approach made a lot of sense, whereby health and wellness is based on the balance between mind, body and spirit. Instead of looking at simply 'fighting cancer', I wanted to encourage Jeremy's general wellness. One of the first things I did was to cut down on the sugar we ate at home. I chucked away Jeremy's giant bars of chocolate - something he didn't appreciate. I was only trying to help, to give him the best chance possible of beating this disease, but he fought me at every turn. He wouldn't give up meat, he wouldn't cut down sugar and he point blank refused to meditate with me.

I needed more muscle in my corner, I concluded. It was no good me trying to go up against the entire medical establishment with just a few books in my arsenal. He would never take me seriously especially because many of the professionals we consulted seemed to be of the opinion that you could just eat and drink what you liked and it really didn't matter. Their attitude confounded me. I would rather they said, 'We don't know the answer, it's not our area of expertise,' instead of dismissing it out of hand. To my mind, this wasn't an either-or situation – Eastern Mysticism versus Western Rationalism. You could have both! All my life I'd fused the two approaches, why should health be any different?

On 10 October 2014, Jeremy's 58th birthday, I presented him with a card.

'It's a birthday present. Go on, open it!'

Inside the card was piece of paper confirming a reservation on a Living Well course at the Penny Brohn Centre in Bristol at the end of the month.

'What is it?' Jeremy looked confused.

'It's a centre where they help people with cancer, and their carers, take a holistic approach to the disease. There are talks about nutrition and meditation and you get to meet other cancer patients and...'

'I'm not doing it,' Jeremy scowled. 'Forget it. I'm not going.'

'Please Jeremy,' I urged. 'You don't even know what it is!'

He sighed and looked again paper in his hand.

'I really don't want to go,' he repeated. 'I just don't want to sit around talking about cancer. It's going to be depressing. I've had the operation, I feel fine, I'm not on any medication. Why do I need to go?'

'Think of it this way. This is a centre that helps not just patients but also their carers – and I'm your carer. So, I would like to learn more. I feel the need for some support. Do this for me, please.'

He shot me a doleful look. I knew I was winning him over.

'Look,' I softened my approach. 'We'll get a cat-sitter, go away for a few days, have a break. It's free and the place looks amazing! The food looks great, the grounds are beautiful. All the reviews are very positive. I think we'll enjoy it. It'll be good for us to get away.'

'Okay,' he relented. 'I'll do it for you. But just for you.'

It turned out to be one of the best things we ever did. I don't know why the Penny Brohn Centre is not recommended to every single person diagnosed with cancer, but it should be. A completely free centre, it explores all the different ways cancer can impact your life, giving you support and strategies to cope. The place is beautiful, too, in the middle of the pretty Somerset village of Pill, just outside Bristol.

When we checked in they gave us two rooms and I was surprised, saying that we would be sleeping in the same room.

'That's fine,' smiled the older lady on the front desk. 'We still give you two rooms and then you can decide on your sleeping arrangements. It's an option for you, in case one or both of you decide you need some space.'

We felt like naughty teenagers sneaking in and out of each other's rooms. They were basic, like a Travelodge, but functional and clean. In total there were 20 of us on what was a fully-catered residential course – ten cancer patients and their carers – and each day was filled with different workshops, on mindfulness, meditation, nutrition, the immune system as well as therapy sessions to explore how cancer had impacted our lives. It was the most wonderful environment and it opened our eyes to how we could build resilience into our lives and take control of our health.

Of all the cancer patients on our course, Jeremy appeared to be one of those not too badly affected. One young woman, Olivia, who had served as a nurse in Iraq, had a brain tumour. She described seeing people being blown up and stitching them back together. She had witnessed the horrors of that conflict and now she faced a huge battle of her own. It was heartbreaking because she was still so young, just in her twenties, but she was very upbeat and positive and wore colourful scarves around her head to hide the bulge from the tumour. She was a real inspiration to us both.

It is hard to overstate just how big an impact the Penny Brohn Centre had on us. Being among other cancer sufferers and their carers helped us both to feel less lonely in our respective struggles against the illness. During one very emotional therapy session, at which we were encouraged to open up to one another, I revealed to Jeremy just how helpless and scared I felt.

'I want to help...' I stuttered. 'All I'm doing is trying to help... all this stuff with diet and sugar... but you won't let me. I just don't know what I can do.'

I let the tears fall gently onto my lap. And then Jeremy started to cry too.

I had no idea how hard this has been on you,' he took my hands in his. 'You seemed to be coping so well. You seemed to be managing.'

It was the first time since the diagnosis that he had seen me in such a vulnerable state. Until then, I had been in project management mode, appearing very practical, very pragmatic.

He'd seen the manifestation of the worry, but not my actual feelings. In the safe environment of the Centre, I felt I could be honest with him, show him my weakness. And fear.

We cried, we laughed, we meditated, we walked in the gorgeous grounds and we ate the most amazing vegetarian, organic food. It was the best three days we'd had since the diagnosis and it completely changed Jeremy's attitude to his health. When we left he made a generous donation to the Centre – in fact, he became a lifelong supporter of the charity. He also bought a cookery book, which subsequently became his kitchen bible, as well as a visualization CD and a very expensive juicer.

'We must come back here,' he announced, as we took our leave.

Sadly, we never did.

Chapter 14 – A Secret Ceremony

*"What I know for sure is that speaking your truth
is the most powerful tool we all have."*
—Oprah Winfrey[11]

*A*s I gazed into Jeremy's eyes, everything around us seemed to melt away. We could have been alone or surrounded by a thousand people - I wouldn't have noticed. All I saw was him.

'I call upon these persons here present to witness that I, Jeremy Frederick Lucas, do take thee, Shalini Ashok Kumar Bhalla, to be my lawful wedded wife.'

In that moment, I felt closer to him than I had to anyone in my life. Our eyes were locked on one another, we were together in the moment. He looked so happy and proud and I felt exactly the same.

It was Tuesday 18 November 2014, just two months after Jeremy's operation and 17 and a half years since we first met. I hadn't expected to feel like this about marriage. I hadn't expected the moment to be so meaningful. The truth was that, after years of insisting I would never marry, I had now finally agreed to marry Jeremy for rather more prosaic reasons.

Shortly after his diagnosis, Jeremy had explained that I couldn't be considered his next of kin or be entitled to any support if anything happened to him. This had persuaded me. Although our relationship was a marriage in everything but name, I could see that it might be important at some point in the future to make it official. Jeremy had wanted to tie the knot before his operation but he couldn't locate his decree absolute, the legal proof that his first marriage was over. We had turned the house upside down looking for it but to no avail and so Jeremy had to apply for another, which certainly wouldn't reach us before the operation. So, we agreed a date of 18 November instead. Since the anniversary of our first date was 18 May, the two dates had a six-month symmetry in the calendar year, which pleased us. Since we had started going out together we had always wished each other 'Happy 18th' every single month. The date suited us perfectly.

The one thing I insisted on was that this wouldn't be a 'wedding' as such. No guests, no party. We were getting married for us and we didn't need to involve anyone else. So, we kept it a secret. I didn't even tell my sister. As far as I was concerned, it was simply a formality and a completely private decision made by Jeremy and me, together. For us, a marriage wasn't made in a church with the flowers and white dress, or a registry office with the celebrant and vows, or in a temple with the *havan* fire and seven *pheras* walking around the fire. We did not feel the need to have any religious or social ritual to tell us that we were married. For us, marriage was made in our hearts the day we decided to commit to each other for the rest of our lives. The love that we had for each other was far bigger than all the traditional rituals or practical necessities that society or the law imposed on us. But Jeremy was a realist and he knew that this meant nothing in the eyes of the law. It does not accept the concept of a common-law-wife. And so, to be practical, we felt it was important to take the legal step, though in our hearts and minds we had already been married for many years.

On the not-so-big day we had just two witnesses: Jeremy's golfing buddies, Terry and Peter and their wives, Sue and

Lizanne. I knew Terry and Sue but had never met Peter and Lizanne. Jeremy deliberately chose people he trusted, who wouldn't feel burdened by the secret of our marriage. If I told a close friend, or my sister, they might have felt laden with guilt at not being able to share the news with others. I didn't want anyone to have that on their shoulders.

Ours was a stripped-down, back-to-basics wedding, a ceremony at its most fundamental and about a million miles away from traditional Hindu marriages, where hundreds of guests attend elaborate parties for days on end. However, as someone who enjoys the customs and rituals that go along with ceremonies, there were certain aspects to our wedding day that fell into the traditional mould. For example, I arranged it so that I didn't stay with Jeremy the night before and didn't see him until just before the ceremony.

It just so happened I had to attend a MIND Media Awards ceremony the night before in London and so I decided to stay over at a hotel organized for by MIND. I had worked as a Voice of MIND, the mental health charity, for the past year as I was passionate about helping others to cope with many of the issues I had faced and overcome. I felt it was particularly important to talk to South Asian communities about mental health because, in my experience, it was a taboo subject in that world and rarely discussed. One of the reasons I had become so ill in my early years in Surrey was because I never had an awareness of depression before then. I simply didn't recognize it. In reaching out to others now, and showing them my route back to health, I felt I could help other South Asian families to open up and speak more honestly about these issues.

On the morning of our wedding I was met at Guildford train station by Terry, who took me to Peter's house, where I changed into a red *salwaar kameez* that I'd bought specially for the occasion. Red is the colour worn by Hindu brides and I wanted to honour this tradition from my heritage. I looked at myself in the mirror and was pleased with the outfit – a long red tunic over slim-fitting trousers and a green scarf thrown over my shoulder. I carefully applied my make-up and stuck a red *bindi* on my forehead and wore gold bangles on my wrists – all signs of a Hindu bride. I felt exhilarated and quite excited. I had spent my adult life adamant that I would never marry, but this was different. I was doing this for Jeremy – he had always wanted to marry me. I was also doing this for us. I wanted to spend the rest of our lives as husband and wife, together side-by-side, a strong message to Jeremy that I was his wife and we were a team who belonged together and would fight anything that was thrown our way – including cancer.

It was a bright day, sunny and cold. I walked with Peter, Sue, Terry and Lizanne the short distance from the house to the registry office and met Jeremy, who was waiting for us outside. He was wearing his best suit and a tie that I had bought him and he was beaming from ear to ear.

'You look lovely,' he smiled. 'I knew you would wear red!'

He gave his camera to Terry and we walked in, hand in hand. Just before we entered the room in which we would be married, Jeremy handed me a card.

'Go on, open it,' he whispered.

Inside, inscribed in his beautiful handwriting, I read:

My dearest Shal,

So here we are on our wedding day after 17½ years. How strange that it should come about after such a strange and difficult time this year. This is such a great way to turn all that unpleasant stuff into something wonderful.

I consider myself extremely fortunate to have you by my side, even more so this year, and especially today. They say you have to wait for the best things in life and I had to wait until I was 40. I'm so proud to be able to marry you today and whatever the future holds for us we can face it all together as husband and wife and enjoy life to the full.

I love you so very much,

Jeremy

Until this moment, I had just felt happy, but now something stirred deep within me. I understood the true significance of the occasion for Jeremy. After all, he had wanted to marry me just weeks after we first met, despite having gone through a painful divorce. This was something he had yearned for, for many years. But after we bought our house together, I always felt our commitment to each other was rock solid. I didn't need marriage and I told him I didn't want it. To his eternal credit, Jeremy accepted this and never once pestered me. In fact, throughout our years together, neither of us doubted the other's commitment. So strong was our faith in each other, we'd joke about looking for other partners.

'Wait a second...' Jeremy would say when he saw an advert for an online dating company on the TV. 'I need to register on this!'

'I'll get you the iPad so you can do it straightaway,' I'd reply, deadpan.

Or when I was watching my favourite Bollywood star, Aamir Khan, in a film, Jeremy would make a big show of backing out of the room.

'So sorry... I forgot it was your time with Aamir now...'

The truth was, neither of us even *looked* at another person. He thought I was beautiful, no matter what, and he didn't shy away from telling me so. Even when I was going through my depression, when I felt fat and unsexy, he was patient and loving. In fact, as a lover, he was generous to a fault. There wasn't a selfish bone in his body. He put me on a pedestal and I enjoyed being there. At parties we socialized with other people but we always ended up with each other, often with me talking and him listening. He never failed to help me to make sense of things when they were a mess in my mind. He calmed me, slowed me down, made me more patient and more compassionate – with myself as well as others. In all, he made me a better version of myself and I trusted him completely, more than I trusted myself. Now, after nearly 18 years together, I had finally agreed to be his wife, and I couldn't help but be swept up in how important this moment was – for both of us.

I spoke my vows slowly and deliberately, staring directly into Jeremy's eyes as tears welled up in my own. If I was to be married, this was the wedding I wanted. Not big and showy but quiet, intimate and meaningful. We exchanged rings and then kissed. It had only lasted about 15 minutes, but those brief minutes really were the most beautiful of my life.

Afterwards, we were invited back to Peter's house for what I thought was just going to be a bottle of bubbly. They had a lovely Victorian house with a great big lawn and Lizanne mentioned that we could sit outside and have a glass of fizz in the sunshine. But as I walked through the kitchen, I saw to my amazement that they had laid out a huge lunch, the centerpiece of which was a stunning homemade cake decorated with real peach-coloured roses. It was a complete surprise.

'Oh Lizanne!' I gasped. I was overwhelmed by her kindness and hospitality.

'Did you do all of this for us?'

'We did it together,' Lizanne gestured towards Sue. 'We couldn't celebrate your big day without a wedding breakfast.'

I was so touched. We sat outside in the winter sunshine and ate and drank together. The whole day felt very special. Even when Jeremy deliberately annoyed me by calling me 'wifey', I let it go. Did I feel any different? Not really. In my heart, we had been married almost from the moment we had met.

We kept the news to ourselves. We both didn't feel the need to tell our respective families or friends. For us, the occasion had been private and intimate and something that we had wanted to share just with each other. Nobody else had to know about our change in status – I didn't change my name or alter anything else. I wore my wedding band on my middle finger and on my ring finger I continued to wear the sapphire ring Jeremy had bought me in the early days of our courtship. I had also bought him a ring very early on in our relationship which he wore on his ring finger.

Now, he just replaced the old ring with his new wedding band. To the outside world, everything stayed the same. We didn't have a honeymoon, as such, though we returned to Kenya in December as part of our long-term plan for a change of lifestyle.

This time, when we landed in Nairobi, we flew directly to Nanyuki. My parents were not in Kenya as they had gone to India for a couple of weeks' holiday. I had spent days over the past year researching land in Kenya and, thanks to the help of some friends and family, I had found several land plots to look at while we stayed at a hotel in town. It wasn't something we were rushing into - as long as Gladys was alive, we couldn't leave Cranleigh – and I had to find a way to make Just Jhoom! work remotely, which would take a fair amount of time to achieve. But Jeremy's illness had made us both more determined to turn our dream into a reality. Life wasn't a dress rehearsal and I thought that if we found the right place in Nanyuki, we should just go for it.

We found that place on the fourth day of our trip.

'This is it,' I whispered under my breath, walking round the two-acre plot of land. It had uninterrupted views over the rolling, vast Lolldaiga Hills to the north and was overlooked by the mighty Mount Kenya from the east. Nearby, a herd of zebra grazed on the rough grassy terrain whilst acacia trees and luscious green shrubs dotted the landscape. All was still and quiet and peaceful. All we could hear was non-stop birdsong and the rustling of the trees as a gentle northerly wind blew off the Lolldaiga Hills. We couldn't see another house or hear another (human) soul.

'What do you think?' I asked Jeremy. He nodded silently as he surveyed the land.

'I like it but let me think about it,' he said.

That night, back at the hotel, we talked it over and agreed that it would be a wonderful spot on which to build our dream home. But, never one to rush into a decision, we agreed to sleep on it before making a firm commitment. After all, the £80,000 purchase price had to come from Jeremy's pension pot.

I woke up the next morning and turned to see Jeremy, lying on his back, staring up at the ceiling.

'I haven't slept all night,' he said quietly, without turning to look at me.

'Oh no. Why not?'

'I want to make sure this is the right thing to do. It's been going round and round in my head.'

Oh dear. It sounded like he was having second thoughts.

'Look, as I said last night, I think this is a good deal,' I sighed.

I had done my research and knew that this was a good area to buy in.

'Nanyuki is going to grow, prices are going up. If we don't want it in a few years, we can sell it and make a profit. This doesn't have to be our home it we decide against it. It can be an investment.'

'I agree,' he said, now turning on his side to face me. 'I trust you and I trust what you're saying about Nanyuki. I wasn't thinking about pulling out, I was thinking about buying *two* plots instead of one. Think about it – if we buy two now, we can wait a little while to get our plans finalised and then, when it comes to actually building the house, we can sell one plot to finance the building.'

'That's genius!' I exclaimed. 'But are you sure? I mean, it's a huge financial commitment.'

'Actually, in terms of parking my cash somewhere, I think it's a pretty sound investment,' he said. 'Let's talk to the seller, see if he can do something for us on the price of two plots.'

We arranged to meet the sellers, Rob and Wendy, a British couple who had settled in Kenya many years ago. They met us later that day on the plot. It was part of larger area that was being sold off in packages, with ten acres of clear land between each plot, giving each one plenty of privacy.

'Our friend here has agreed two plots for £140,000,' Jeremy smiled as he returned from his little walk-n-talk with Rob. 'It sounds good to me. Shal? What do you think?'

'You know my answer – I say yes!'

And that was that. We shook hands on the deal and Rob rushed back to his car to retrieve a bottle of wine he had fortuitously stashed there. I was simply thrilled! Jeremy, true to form, got his camera out and started filming me as I spun round, glass of wine in hand, getting more and more excited at the prospect of building our dream home in the country of my birth.

'This is a celebration!' I shouted delightedly at the camera. 'We've just agreed to buy this beautiful plot of land to build our new house on, for our new life in the sun. So over here...' I gestured for the camera to follow me. 'This is where our house will be. This will be our view...'

'And that's where the sun sets,' Jeremy pointed out, towards the horizon.

'Yes! And this is where we'll have our verandah,' I went on.

We were bubbling over with excitement, talking over each other, making plans for our future. It had been a difficult year but we had come through it stronger than ever - and married! Now, finally, things were looking up.

Chapter 15 – Ahimsa

"The simplest things have the knack sometimes of appearing to us the hardest. If our hearts were opened, we should have no difficulty. Non-violence is a matter of the heart. It does not come to us through any intellectual feat."
— **Mahatma Gandhi**[12]

*O*ur happiness was not to last. In January of 2015 we were told that Jeremy's cancer was active and beginning to spread. The tiny spots on his left lung, the size of small lentils, had grown slightly so his oncologist started him on a targeted treatment in capsule form. We had already made some serious adjustments to our lifestyle, thanks to lots of research and all the excellent advice from the Penny Brohn Centre. We had cut right down on sugar, were slowly cutting out meat and dairy and only bought organic food. We had also switched from chemical-laden cleaning products to more environmentally-friendly brands for our washing powder, soaps and shampoos. Jeremy had become a big fan of his juicer and every morning he could be found in the kitchen concocting different blends of fresh juices. We also introduced a variety of superfoods into our diet including kale, seaweed, chia seeds and berries. Jeremy had started taking Pome-T, a capsule containing extract of turmeric, broccoli, pomegranate and green tea, all thought to contain anti-cancer properties. We started attending tai chi and yoga classes together and I had even managed to entice him to come on one of my mindfulness courses. He loved it and started practicing meditation on his own.

Meanwhile, I needed a distraction so that I wouldn't be consumed by the worry of Jeremy's illness. So, I threw myself into designing our new house in Kenya as the sale of the land went through. I knew exactly what Jeremy liked and I channeled all my energy into building our dream home. The news that the cancer had returned made us even more determined to change our lives and move away from the noise, stress and pollution of the urban, fast-paced world we lived in. We calculated that we could afford to live quite comfortably in Kenya on Jeremy's Barclays Bank pension if we also rented out our house in Cranleigh.

As for my work, I had the idea of putting the entire instructor training course for Just Jhoom! online. This would enable me to run the business remotely. By now I had trained over 200 instructors in the UK, but I felt that, nationally, we would probably reach saturation point in the near future. If we wanted to roll this out internationally, it had to be an online course which could be accessed from anywhere in the world. In fact, the whole structure of the business had to change. I could see that it was no longer viable to ask instructors for an annual subscription fee. Many taught a variety of dance fitness programmes so they simply couldn't afford a fee for each one. If I sold Just Jhoom! as a one-off training package then this would reduce my overheads and allow for new instructors to sign up without committing themselves to any ongoing costs. So, while I maintained the Just Jhoom! business I also started to develop the online training course and explored the possibility of adding a mindfulness course too.

Even though Jeremy and I were dealing with a permanent sense of worry about his cancer and we were working hard in our respective work, we began to make a lot more time for each other. We found small, romantic ways of making each other feel special or surprising each other. One Saturday afternoon, I was expecting Jeremy home around 1pm after his usual game of golf with his buddies, but by 2pm he wasn't back. It wasn't like him to be late or not to call and I started to worry.

'Where are you?' I asked, when I called.

'I'm on my way back,' he reassured me. 'I just had to go to Guildford to pick something up. Don't worry. I won't be long.'

It sounded all very mysterious. When he arrived back, he handed me a pretty white bag.

'Surprise!' he announced, grinning.

'What's this?'

'Just open it,' he urged.

I took out a heavy object wrapped in white tissue paper and started to unwrap it carefully.

'Oh my gosh!' I exclaimed, when I saw the gift inside. 'The treasure chest! You bought me the treasure chest!'

It was a stunning wooden box inlaid with painted purple, white and blue wood, with a curved lid that was decorated with cream and gold floral designs. No bigger than a toaster, I knew it would look perfect on our sideboard in the lounge.

'Oh Jeremy, why did you buy this?'

'Because you like it and I want you to have it.'

I felt myself welling up with emotion. It was such a kind gesture. We had spotted the little box when we had popped into one of my favourite shops, which sold elegant wood furniture and pretty objects d'art from India. The treasure chest had caught my eye the moment we walked in.

'I love it!' I had enthused, lifting up the lid to look inside. It was so charming and colourful – but I had no idea what I would put in it and the £70 price tag felt like an unnecessary expense.

'Get it!' said Jeremy.

'What for?' I had laughed. 'I'll never use it.'

'Get it,' he had urged.

'No, no, no… It's an indulgence. I don't need it.'

Nothing could persuade me to change my mind – and Jeremy, knowing me as he did, didn't even try. Instead, he simply went back a few days later and bought it for me when I wasn't there. Now I gave him a big hug and whispered, 'Thank you, it's beautiful.'

'You are beautiful,' he said simply. 'You deserve beautiful things. I wanted to get it for you.'

By April, Jeremy's reactions to the drugs were painful and extreme. He developed something called hand-foot syndrome which at first was just sore hands and feet but, as the weeks passed, the skin on his palms and the bottom of his feet started to crack and peel. It was incredibly painful for him, to the point where he struggled to put his full weight on his feet. On top of that he suffered from acid indigestion, nausea, fatigue and an upset stomach. The oncologist was worried at the level of toxicity that the drug was having on Jeremy's body and so he switched his treatment to a drug called Votrient. This was an anti-angiogenic drug.

Angiogenesis is the process within your body where you create new blood vessels from existing ones and is essential for growth and healing. It becomes a problem, however, in relation to cancer and tumours because new blood vessels feed tumours with oxygen and nutrients. Anti-angiogenesis drugs work by preventing the tumour from growing its own blood vessels. If the drugs could do this successfully, they would slow the growth of the tumours and perhaps even shrink them. I had read up on anti-angiogenesis and found some interesting articles about how we could assist this process with Jeremy's diet. Some foods were naturally more likely to inhibit the growth of blood vessels. Green tea, for one, is anti-angiogenic, so we started drinking powdered matcha tea. Red berries like strawberries, blackberries, raspberries and blueberries are all naturally anti-angiogenic. Turmeric, garlic and parsley – these were some of the foods found to be naturally anti-angiogenic. We were taking a holistic approach, trying to support Jeremy's own immune system to help fight off the spread of the tumours. Votrient was less toxic than the previous drug, although it made his hair grow grey.

'At least I'm not losing my hair,' said Jeremy, in his usual positive way.

Unfortunately, it didn't stop the tumour growth and in June he was switched onto Afinitor, a targeted chemotherapy drug. This one gave him painful mouth ulcers, sleepless nights, as well as flashes and floaters in his vision. Not that he ever complained. Jeremy was as stoical as ever but there was certainly a greater toxicity in this drug than previous ones, to the point where they had to stop the treatment for a few days.

We had heard about a new form of treatment called immunotherapy. This worked by boosting the body's natural immune system to help fight the cancer cells. It made perfect sense to me and there had been almost miraculous results in various different cancer treatments. The only problem was that it wasn't yet approved in the UK for the treatment of renal cancer.

'Do you think it would help?' we asked the oncologist during one of Jeremy's consultations.

'If it was up to me, I'd put him on a course of immunotherapy tomorrow,' he confirmed. 'But we have to wait for regulatory approval. I don't think it will be long. In the meantime, we have options. Let's keep going with the Afinitor and see how you respond to that.'

In August, Jeremy and I signed the final papers for the land in Kenya and we completed the deal.

'This is for your future,' he said to me solemnly after our solicitor confirmed the land was now ours.

'You mean, for *our* future,' I corrected him.

'Yes, but if anything happens to me, it will make you secure,' he said.

'Don't be so silly,' I replied. 'Nothing's going to happen to you. We are going to build our dream home together.'

He's being over-cautious, I concluded. Jeremy was a prudent financial planner, of course but in this instance he was being a little dramatic. I didn't doubt for a moment that he would beat the cancer. Not for a moment. He was so strong and we had the very best care thanks to his private health insurance. We started to make plans to return to Kenya in December.

In September, I went on a silent retreat at a centre in Herefordshire for 10 days. It was a course in *Vipassana* meditation, an ancient Buddhist technique that had long appealed to me. The central idea of *Vipassana* is to see things as they really are: self-purification through self-observation. It takes time and discipline to master the technique so each course lasts ten days. Just before I left, I sent Jeremy an email to say that the Dalai Lama was in London later that month and wouldn't it be great if we could go and see him. Then, with the excitement of going on the retreat, I completely forgot about the email.

The retreat was a revelation for me. Each day began at 4am and we were in meditation until around 7pm with rest periods and regular breaks through the day. In all, we did around ten hours of meditation each day. In the evenings we would all watch a video-recorded lecture by S.N. Goenka, the teacher who had brought *Vipassana* to the West. I found these lectures interesting and inspiring and was moved by Goenka's message that one needed to develop 'equanimity' to allow for a truly balanced mind.

For the first three days we sat cross-legged on the floor in a large hall, men and women separated, and focused on our breath. Our full concentration was focused on the area below the nostrils and above the upper lip. The purpose of this method, known as *anapana*, is to sharpen the mind so that when you move onto *Vipassana*, your mind is able to feel the various sensations in your body - even the most subtle ones.

On day three we were introduced to the meditation technique of *Vipassana*. *Vipassana* literally means insight and is a body scan that observes the sensations of the body with equanimity – a mental calmness, composure and evenness of temper. The basis of this is a true understanding of impermanence, the awareness that everything is constantly changing. In other words, you let go of that which you can't control. You allow things to just be. This does not mean that you are passive or indifferent. Far from it. However, you find that when you have a balanced and calm mind, you are able to deal with life's challenges with the same calmness and balanced approach that you cultivate during your meditation practice. Equanimity allows you to be completely open to life as it presents itself. Equanimity also allows you to overcome the fears that arise from the ups and downs of life.

In *Vipassana* I was required to move my attention systematically from the top of my head to the tips of my toes and then back again. As I did this, I observed each and every part of the body, taking note of the sensations. I experienced a huge raft of sensations - pleasant, unpleasant, neutral; intense or subtle; small or large. And with each sensation I was required not to react to them, not to create any craving for or aversion to the sensations, but to stay objective and observe them with equanimity. In time, the mind begins to understand the impermanent nature of these sensations and allows them just to be as they are.

Some days were harder than others. I hit a wall on around day six. I was missing Jeremy terribly. As it was a silent retreat, I had locked my phone away. It was the longest time I had gone without hearing his voice. But I persevered. And on day seven I began to really understand the method to which I had been introduced. I began to experience subtle sensations throughout the body, a type of energy that swept my body in one go and enveloped me with a calmness and sense of acceptance that I had never had before. As the energy became more intense, one-hour sessions felt like they were only minutes long. It was a powerful, empowering and moving experience.

On the tenth and final day, having spent the entire time in complete silence, we were allowed to talk. The first thing I did was retrieve my mobile phone and call Jeremy. I didn't want to speak to anyone else. But I had forgotten that, it being a Saturday, he would be on the golf course so the call went straight to voicemail. After leaving a message I went back to the group to start sharing our experiences. But I couldn't wait to see Jeremy.

When his car drove up the following morning I was eagerly waiting and flung myself into his arms. I had missed him like crazy. I showed him around the venue, the large meditation hall, the simple dining facility where they had served organic, vegetarian breakfasts and lunches and the small dormitory I had shared with twelve other ladies. I spoke non-stop for six hours, all the way back home, while Jeremy listened patiently, asking all the right questions in the all right places. It was lovely to be back with him, where I felt I truly belonged.

The following day, 14 September, was my 40th birthday and he woke me up with a cup of tea and a lovely card.

'Life begins at 40!' it proclaimed on the cover and, inside, Jeremy had written:

I can confirm it is true! I met you when I was 40 and look what a brilliant 18 years it has been!

All my love, Jeremy xxx

As a birthday treat he had booked us a spa day at the hotel I had worked in as a manager and wedding coordinator very early on in our relationship. We spent the day enjoying massages, an indulgent lunch and a bottle of fizz. After lunch he presented me with my second birthday gift: two tickets to see the Dalai Lama speak on *Ahimsa - India's Contribution to the World* at the London Coliseum. I couldn't believe his generosity, his having remembered my comment from nearly two weeks before.

It was one of the best days ever. We took the train up to London and our first stop was lunch at the wonderful Dishoom restaurant, modeled on the old Irani cafés that were once part of the fabric of life in Bombay but have now all but disappeared. I introduced Jeremy to some of my favourite Indian street food including *pau bhaji* – a true Bombay staple of spiced mashed vegetables served on a hot, buttered bread bun; *bhel* – puffed rice and Bombay mix sprinkled with fresh pomegranate, tomato, onion, lime, tamarind and mint and *paneer tikka* – an Indian cheese marinated and then gently charred with red and green peppers.

Satiated and happy, we then made our way to the Coliseum to hear the Dalai Lama speak. The minute he walked onto the stage a hush descended on the auditorium, followed by spontaneous applause for a good two minutes. This diminutive 80-year-old man had the presence of a giant. He exuded goodness, kindness and compassion. He talked about compassion and how the central idea for this comes from an ancient Buddhist principle of *ahimsa* which is also a feature of Hinduism and Jainism. *Ahimsa* can be interpreted in many ways – some people define it as 'non-violence' - but the way Buddhists understand *ahimsa* is that everyone contains a spark of divine spiritual energy and therefore to hurt another person is to hurt oneself. And this doesn't simply relate to your actions, but also your words, deeds and thoughts. *Ahimsa* is a way of life.

I was listening hard to this, trying to follow the Dalai Lama's train of thought, but as I leaned in, I noticed something out of the corner of my eye. Jeremy was taking photos! The organisers had specifically instructed us not to take pictures and it made me very cross that Jeremy had ignored this instruction.

'What are you doing?' I hissed at him.

'Nothing,' he murmured under his breath.

'I can see what you're doing. You're taking pictures. Stop it!'

'Dalai Lama says *ahimsa*,' he intoned solemnly.

I couldn't help it, but I grinned.

On our return to Surrey, I felt so inspired by the Dalai Lama's message of compassion that I felt compelled to do something - to spread a little compassion myself - even if on a very small scale.

As he articulates so eloquently in his book, *How To Be Compassionate*:[13]

In order to achieve peace, tranquility, and real friendship, we must minimize anger and cultivate kindness and a warm heart. As we become nicer human beings, our neighbours, friends, parents, spouses, and children will experience less anger, prompting them to become more warm-hearted, compassionate, and harmonious. The very atmosphere becomes happier, which even promotes good health. This is the way to change the world.

So, together with some friends, I created a free online course called *Compassionate Me*. The idea was that by using a series of techniques including meditation, performing acts of kindness, writing a daily diary and a gratitude journal, people would spend four weeks practicing self-compassion, compassion for friends and family, compassion for strangers and in the final week compassion for nature. I poured my heart and soul into the course and was thrilled to find that when we launched it, 100 people signed up for it straight away.

But, in spite of all the personal growth and positive experiences, the dark cloud of Jeremy's illness still loomed. At the end of November, Jeremy's drugs were changed again. This time he was moved onto Axitinib, a cancer growth inhibitor, and we waited hopefully to get the all clear for our trip to Kenya. The new drugs made him a little wheezy and his legs were swollen with fluid but the doctor signed him off for travel. By now, we had agreed that it was probably best if Jeremy stepped down as General Manager of the Golf Club in the New Year.

He needed rest and relaxation to help him fight the disease and, though he loved his job, we both recognised that it was an extra, unnecessary, stress with everything he was going through. Now that my family was back in my life we decided to go back out to Kenya to spend some time with them. In early December we flew out and spent our first day in Nanyuki, doing surveys on our land. It was exciting to be there and really start planning our future in Kenya together. We both felt completely at home in Nanyuki and could easily picture ourselves living there.

After a few days there, we travelled to Samburu to spend some time with my sister who had recently moved with her team to a new, more permanent camp a few miles from the last site. We were there for four days before flying on to Mombasa, where we stayed in a beautiful Lamu-style villa on Kenya's south coast. A beautiful white-washed, thatched building, it had four spacious bedrooms which all faced a small forest of indigenous trees with the warm, blue waters of the Indian Ocean just beyond. It was the perfect place to unwind, swimming in the sea or pool, playing table tennis or walking on the unspoilt and secluded white-sand beach.

We didn't have to lift a finger, as Stephen the cook and Katana the house manager did everything for us. We enjoyed three blissful days on our own before my parents and sister joined us for the rest of the week. The holiday in the villa was a gift to my parents as it was my father's 67th birthday on 18 December. On the day itself Jeremy presented him with a smart cashmere sweater and Stephen made a wonderful seafood feast and baked a cake. We had a relaxed, fun week and everyone got on really well (or so I thought). After a couple of days back in Nairobi with my parents, we were to fly back to the UK.

Sadly, once we were back in Nairobi, many of the old issues with my parents raised their heads again, casting a dark shadow over all the happy memories we had shared in Mombasa. Once again, I found myself in my parents' home, desperate to leave. Even Jeremy, that paragon of patience and kindness, said to me that night, 'I'm sick of this single bed nonsense.'

I agreed. By now we were actually a married couple and not, according to my mother's beliefs, living in sin, although she didn't know this. We had decided not to tell them until we moved over to Kenya and then, we thought we would have a big celebratory party in the gardens of our new home in Nanyuki.

Still, after 18 years, it astonished me that she couldn't acknowledge our relationship or allow us even a degree of respect.

Chapter 16 – Many Ways Up the Mountain

"This is my simple religion. No need for temples. No need for complicated philosophy. Your own mind, your own heart is the temple; the philosophy is simple kindness."
—**Dalai Lama**[14]

I had lost my faith in organized religion many years earlier. I was brought up as a Hindu by my parents and, until my late twenties, I really believed. I even taught Hindu theology in schools to children from the ages of eleven to sixteen. Hinduism is a hugely complex and ancient religion and it is difficult to pinpoint when it actually started, as scholars can't seem to agree on any one date. It is a religion that was not founded by one person but instead evolved slowly over millennia. Hence, there is no single 'book' or prophet – and each Hindu community has its favourite deity and there are many sacred scriptures including the *Vedas, Upanishads* and the *Bhagavad Gita* (The Song of the Lord). But, even with all the different gods and rituals and beliefs, Hindus also believe that there is one universal being, the ultimate reality: Brahman.

When teaching Hinduism in schools I would do a short exercise where I would take a large bowl of water and ask a student to put a tablespoon of salt into the water. I would ask them to stir the salt until all of it was dissolved. I would then ask the student to take the salt back out using a tablespoon. Needless to say, there were always calls of, 'We can't do that!' and, 'That's not possible, Miss!' The analogy I would draw from the 'experiment' was that the presence of Brahman in the world is like the salt in the water – invisible but everywhere.

Hindus believe that Brahman has three functions and these are personified by three gods: Shiva, Brahma and Vishnu, known as the *Trimurti*. Brahma is the Creator and source of all creation; Vishnu is the Preserver, responsible for restoring balance and goodness to the world in times of evil; Shiva is the Destroyer and is needed because change is necessary for the creation of new things.

Then you have Ganesha, the son of Shiva; Krishna an avatar of Vishnu, and of course all the goddesses, many of them wives and consorts of the gods: Laxmi, the Goddess of Wealth; Saraswati, the Goddess of Knowledge; Parvati, the Goddess of Household and Motherhood; and Bhumi Mata or Mother Earth. Hindus have a god for everything!

My training in Indian classical dance when I was young helped to reinforce my Hindu faith. The dances I learned represented mythological tales about the various gods, often with a central moralizing theme. They were colourful, vibrant and evocative stories which resonated deeply with me as I danced my way through childhood and young adulthood. They informed my world in every sense - physically, spiritually and mentally.

My favourite dances were those that told the stories of Krishna, the mischievous, flirtatious, beautiful blue-complexioned god of compassion and love; the brave, righteous Lord Rama and the *ladoo*-eating, cheerful and chubby elephant-headed Ganesha.

Krishna, considered one of the most powerful incarnations of Vishnu, was often portrayed dancing with his love, Radha, flirting with the *gopis* or milkmaids, playing the flute whilst herding his cows or stealing butter and blaming the theft on his friends, much to his mother Yashoda's dismay. But he was also seen as courageous, kind, wise beyond his years and a true teacher of his time. The *Bhagavad Gita*, one of the most popular Hindu texts, describes a sermon that Krishna gave Arjuna, a Pandava Prince. It is a famous discourse on ethics and morality and contains the essence of Hindu philosophy.

In fact, the basis for much Hindu philosophy is to be found in stories like the *Bhagavad* Gita, stories that continue to be passed down through generations and re-enacted through dance, as I did. Another Hindu epic which I often re-created through my dance, was the *Ramayana*, which tells the story of Lord Rama, another incarnation of Vishnu. The story goes that Rama was exiled to the forest for fourteen years by his stepmother Queen Kaikeyi and father Dasharatha, the king of Ayodhya. He was accompanied by his wife, Sita, and brother, Laxmana. Whilst in the forest Sita was kidnapped by the ten-headed demon king, Ravana. With the help of the monkey God, Hanuman, Rama defeated Ravana and rescued Sita. Rama, Sita and Laxmana then returned back to their homeland of Ayodhya where they were welcomed by their people. This triumphant return is marked by Diwali, the Hindu 'Festival of Lights'.

Diwali is usually celebrated in October or November and is one of the most important in the Hindu calendar, signifying the victory of good over evil, light over darkness and knowledge over ignorance. As a child I remember in the days before Diwali my mum cleaning and decorating the house, as we spent ages lighting *diyas* (oil lamps) and creating beautiful *rangoli* (coloured sand floor patterns) outside our home. We wore new clothes, performed *puja* (prayers) to Lakshmi and then celebrated by giving each other gifts, feasting and letting off fireworks.

Every Diwali my Ushamasi would present a half hour celebratory programme on Kenyan television depicting the Ramayana and I would always have a starring role in the programme – sometimes as Rama himself or sometimes as a dancer telling the actual story through my dances. But perhaps my favourite story was how Ganesha got his elephant head. There are many versions to this legend – but this was the one I was told as a child and when I was older created many dances to.

Legend has it that the goddess Parvati, Shiva's wife, created the form by which we know Ganesha from a paste of dust, oil and sandalwood that she took from her body. One day, she asked Ganesha to stand guard at the door whilst she went to bathe. Meanwhile, Shiva who had been in the forest meditating, returned home. Upon finding Ganesha at the entrance to the house, he demanded to be let in but Ganesha, following his mother's orders, refused. Unaware that they were father and son, the two began to fight. Ganesha was no match for the mighty Shiva who, in his anger, cut Ganesha's head off and flung it away.

Hearing the commotion, Parvati ran out of the house to find her son lying, headless, at her feet. She was distraught – and furious with Shiva who, when he realized his tragic mistake, was filled with remorse. He sent his men into the forest and demanded they return with the head of the first creature they found who had its head pointing North. The first creature they found was a sleeping elephant. They brought the head back and Shiva attached it to Ganesha's body, breathing new life into his son. Parvati was still not happy, worrying that everyone would laugh at Ganesha with his big tummy and elephant head. But Shiva appeased her by saying that Ganesha would be so powerful that all the people would pray to him first before they prayed to other gods. And so it is that today Ganesha, the elephant-headed god, is considered the Remover of Obstacles – and prayed to before any other god in the Hindu pantheon.

The stories of the Hindu religion are beautiful and evocative, with moral undertones that are undoubtedly appealing. When I breathed life into these stories through my dance I felt a connection to each god, an understanding of the meaning behind the story. But somewhere along the way I started to question the beliefs behind the stories. I began to feel that Hinduism seemed full of contradictions and rules that went against the new life I had created in England. According to Hinduism, I wasn't meant to marry a man outside of my caste, let alone outside of the religion.

Also, living with a man outside of marriage was a complete no-no. In spite of this, Hindus worship Krishna, who is only ever spoken of with regard to his girlfriend, Radha, not his wife, Rukmini. In a society where it is a taboo for an unmarried couple to live together, they worship a god whose main consort was a woman he never married! The love between Krishna and Radha is held up as eternal and sublime, a symbol of divine union – but what about his wife?

Many aspects of Hinduism also challenged the feminist in me. *Raksha Bandhan* is an annual ceremony, usually held in August, where sisters tie a sacred thread, *rakhi,* on their brothers' wrists as protection. In return, the sisters receive a gift and have to ask their brothers for protection and to assume responsibility for them. As a child I never questioned this annual tradition, but as a strong and independent woman I found it difficult to stomach – I did not need anyone to protect me. Another annual rite was *Gauri Puja*, where Hindu girls fast for five days straight and send prayers to the goddess Parvati (also known as Gauri) beseeching her to send them good husbands. It was a part of my childhood and yet now I could hardly believe how backward it seemed. Boys never had to pray for good wives. Similarly, during *Karva Chauth*, a festival celebrated mostly in Northern India, a married woman will fast from dawn until she sees the moon rise, praying for the protection and longevity of her husband. Once she sees the moon, the wife will then turn to her husband to ensure that his face is the first she sees. The fast can only be broken when the husband gives his wife the first sip of water and morsel of food to break her fast. Where was the festival when husbands starved themselves for a whole day for the safety and longevity of their wives?

Perhaps the story that vexed me most was that of the *Agni Pariksha* or Trial by Fire of Sita by Rama. Although there are many variants to the story, the essence of it is that Rama, listening to the discontented murmurings of the people around him, begins to doubt Sita's chastity. He forces Sita to walk into a burning pyre stating that the fire would not harm her if she had been faithful. Sita walks through the fire unscathed, proving her chastity and purity, and Rama accepts her back. In India today you often hear of women, sometimes rape victims, having to prove their innocence or chastity by doing certain tasks, such as walking long distances carrying rocks on their heads, so that their husbands will take them back. In spite of the fact that these women have been abducted, abused or raped, it is they who have to prove their purity; they who have to undertake their own *Agni Pariksha*.

As a young woman, living in England I began to realise that the life of an Indian woman – regardless of class or caste - is often predetermined. We are expected to become good, chaste wives, whether we liked it or not. That we would get married and have children was never in doubt. But what if we didn't want these things? I began to question whether there was something wrong with Indian society's norms and religious diktats or something wrong with me.

But despite my growing disenchantment, I still considered myself a Hindu right up until the day in 2007 when I read Richard Dawkins' groundbreaking book *The God Delusion*. It was on the list for our monthly book club in Cranleigh and it blew my mind. For the first time in my life, I was intellectually challenged to justify my belief in God – and I found I couldn't do it. Dawkins outlined just how improbable the existence of God was, to the point where it was unthinkable to continue believing. He shone a light into the murky waters of religious dogma and pointed out the great harm it was doing around the world. He argued that this continued brain-washing of whole societies was holding back the teaching of science and that outdated religious practices around the world undermined basic human rights, especially women's rights. It chimed with so much of what I had struggled with for so long and I found I could no longer justify my own somewhat hazy system of belief. So, in a great shrugging-off of my past, I decided from that point onwards I would identify as an atheist.

It was, coincidentally, around the same time that my mother underwent her conversion from Hinduism to Christianity – her own Road to Damascus moment. It was both sudden and dramatic and she subsequently wrote about the moment which changed her life in her memoir *Soul on Fire*.[15] In it, my mother describes how she felt lost and angry until she let God into her heart, and then, for the first time, she had new faith, new purpose and the peace she had always sought. My mother, by her own admission in her book, became quite evangelical in her belief in Christianity and would often send me and Jeremy emails to tell us why our relationship was wrong in God's eyes. This put further strain on my relationship with my mother and contributed to my own disillusion with organized religion.

I found it to be too dogmatic, where people with rigid views ended up putting their principles above their humanity. When I looked at all the ancient teachings by enlightened spiritual teachers such as Jesus, Mohammed and Buddha, it was clear that they all had the same unifying message of tolerance, humanity and compassion. To show humility, Jesus washed the feet of his disciples. Love, unity, tolerance, respect, humility - these were Jesus' guiding principles and the foundations of Christianity. And yet, there are some fundamentalist Christians whose practices are anything but tolerant and compassionate. Buddhism shares fundamentally similar philosophies and yet the world has been appalled to watch the persecution of Rohingya Muslims by Buddhists in Myanmar. History is, of course, riddled with wars, genocides and persecutions that have been carried out in the name of religion.

An event in recent history that relates directly to my own family and ancestors is Partition. In 1947, after 200 years of British colonial rule, India was finally going to become an independent nation. But centuries of Hindu-Muslim strife had also culminated in the Muslim League, led by Muhammad Ali Jinnah, demanding a separate Muslim state: Pakistan. Over the course of just one month, the borders of East and West Pakistan and India were drawn up and, overnight, people found themselves on the wrong side of the border. Muslims were stranded in India and Hindus and Sikhs found themselves stuck in Pakistan. And so began one of the largest human migrations the world has ever seen. With it came savage, senseless violence. It is thought that over one million people died in what is seen to be ethnic cleansing on a huge scale and it is estimated that around 14 million people were displaced. Hindus and Sikhs killed Muslim men and raped and murdered Muslim women; Muslim men killed Hindus and Sikhs and raped their women. The violence was on both sides, the anger and the savagery indiscriminate. Trains full of butchered, bloody bodies would arrive at stations on either side of the border.

Interestingly, the main players on this stage were Lord Mountbatten, the last Viceroy of India (a Christian), Muhammad Ali Jinnah (a Muslim), Mahatma Gandhi (a Hindu and huge advocate of *Ahimsa*) and Jawaharlal Nehru (an atheist). The inability of these men to agree on how India would become independent and the subsequent method in which India was divided into two contributed to the horrors that followed Partition. People who had lived side-by-side for generations, speaking the same language, eating the same food and dressing in the same way now turned on each other because they worshiped different gods.

Perhaps blaming Partition on religion alone is simplistic - there is so much more that caused these horrific events. But so ingrained is the trauma of this shared history that even today, as India and Pakistan are locked in a kind of cold war, many Hindu parents will warn their children to never marry a Muslim - just as I had been told as a child. So, our Hindu religion, strong Indian cultural upbringing and shared history played such a big part in our psyche and perhaps was why my mother had reacted so badly to Jeremy the first time she heard about him.

Atheism, to me, was a way to wipe the slate clean and a way to move ahead with my relationship with Jeremy, unencumbered by the restrictions of my religion, the cultural norms and the baggage of history. I had to throw out everything so that I could start again. Like many people, I still wanted answers to some of life's deepest questions: *Why are we here? What is my purpose?* Over the years I read, thought and meditated a lot on these questions. I had a sense that there was a higher purpose to humanity than simply 'the survival of the fittest' and although I was an atheist, I still felt myself to be a spiritual entity.

Throughout all my questioning and exploring, Jeremy was never comfortable with my assertion that I was an atheist. He had always been quite certain of the existence of God and would describe himself as being brought up in the Christian faith, though he too was suspicious of any faith claiming to be the only true religion. But, as always he was supportive of my need to push the boundaries and explore what I felt was important to me at the time. However, over time, I began to feel uneasy with my atheist beliefs. It wasn't sitting comfortably with me anymore. I had been searching for a long time and, through my meditation, I began to feel an awakening of my spiritual self to an ancient knowledge. This wasn't an intellectual stance, it was a feeling of a deep connection to the spiritual world. I felt the power and presence of a Higher Being, a connection to a consciousness that formed the very essence of ourselves.

Now, though I reject organised religion, I believe in this Higher Being. I choose not to call this Higher Being 'god' because that word has so many connotations. Call him whatever you like - God, Allah, Bhagwan, Khudah – but I believe there is a unifying consciousness in the world, of which we are all a part. I also believe that there is a spiritual life that exists beyond our physical world - an afterlife, to give it a name. But this is just my belief. I have the humility to see that. And I don't condemn or judge those who ascribe to a different set of beliefs, because I understand that, for many people, religion isn't just what they believe or have been taught from childhood. It is far more significant than that. For many people religion is their way of making sense of the world, or it is their community, their family, their comfort and their sense of place in society.

Religion undoubtedly plays a vital part in millions of people's lives. But, to those who say Christianity is the only way, or those who say Hinduism is the one truth or those who assert that there is only one god and he is Allah, I say *No*. Each of these religions is not *the* way, it's *your* way. If god exists then it is not in a book or scripture or in a church, temple, synagogue or *gurudwara*, but rather in a mother's love for her child, in a lover's embrace, in the kind deed to a person in need, in the laughter of children playing, in the compassion that we have for other human beings.

My favourite Bollywood actor, Aamir Khan, made a movie called *PK*, in which he plays an alien who comes to earth from another planet. The alien is baffled by the different ways that the humans on earth follow rituals and dogma in the name of their specific religions. He wonders at the fear that belief in religion invokes, or more accurately the fear in not believing in religion invokes. He questions which god humans should believe in - the god that man has made, or the god who has made man. These are the questions that I often think of: who identifies us as being Muslim, or Hindu, Buddhist or Christian? Not god, but man. Who imposes these differences? Not god, but man. Who causes these divisions? Not god, but man. All in the name of religion.

I remember my Ushamasi giving me a lovely visualization when I was a young child.

There is a mountain and at the top is God. Muslims are going up one way, Christians another and Hindus another - all on their own path. We're all going to the same place. We're just taking different paths.

I would take it a step further and say that on this mountain there are also atheists and agnostics and spiritualists and all the other religions and beliefs of the world. We are all on our own paths going to the top in search of Truth, *our* personal Truth, whatever that means for each of us. I believe that tolerance and acceptance of each other's beliefs, the humility and compassion to accept that we are all different, yet bound by our humanity, is stronger than any message that organised religion can give.

Until we fell out, my mother had always been a major influence in my life. I admired her. She was my role model and I wanted to be just like her. She was independent, she earned her own money and in the conservative Indian community in Kenya we grew up in, she was one of the few career-women we knew. Mum was ambitious, intelligent and driven. Sometimes it meant that work came first – and there were fights with my father about this because he wanted his wife at home, looking after the family -

but over time he accepted that she was her own person. My mother was devoted and loyal to the family in other ways, providing for us and pushing us to achieve and excel. She gave me things for which I'll always be grateful: my education, resilience and independence.

I was proud of her. She was different to all the other mothers in our community and I liked the way she was always direct and frank with people. I tried to emulate her at first but over the years I realised that this approach could also be hurtful. I wanted to be frank like she was, but I didn't understand how it came across. It was Jeremy who showed me another, more compassionate way of asserting myself and being honest.

After our trip to Kenya, which had ended in another disagreement with my mother about my relationship with Jeremy, I went through a range of emotions. Until that point, I thought that my mother and I were on the road towards healing, that the estrangement would one day be behind us. After all, Jeremy and I would be moving to Kenya in the near future; we would get closer and the warmth and love between us would surely grow, making up for those lost years. Now I knew for certain that this was a fantasy. What hurt most was that it was religion that had caused the rift. Without the rigid conventions and restrictions of both the Hindu and Christian orthodoxies, we may never have clashed in this way. After we returned to England I felt no anger towards my mother, just sadness and a sense of relief that I had spent so many years living in a separate country, far from her influence. In the end, the estrangement had been liberating and perhaps even necessary for me. The space had given me the freedom to work out my own beliefs. In Jeremy, I had discovered an individual with true compassion. Someone who allowed me to work my way through all my questions and accepted me for who I was, no matter what I believed. He not only gave me the space to grow spiritually, but he also completed me, making me a better version of myself in every way.

Without Jeremy I would not be who I am today.

Chapter 17 – Letting Go

*"Ever has it been that love knows not its own depth until
the hour of separation."*
—Kahlil Gibran[16]

I was cross. We both were. What did the nurse mean when she said we had to *consider hospice care*? She was a mobility nurse who had come to the house to assess Jeremy's physical needs. I thought she was going to try and help us to make the house more comfortable for him. He had been struggling with the stairs recently and was finding it difficult to walk because of his swollen legs. I thought that she would advise us about the various equipment we could install – a few rails, perhaps, maybe a stair lift – but, instead, she had surprised us both by saying that we could no longer meet Jeremy's needs at home.

I was shocked. Hospice care was for people who were dying and Jeremy wasn't dying. We told her that this wasn't our preference and thanked her for her time.

'You're not giving into this, are you?' I asked Jeremy.

'No, of course not,' he said crossly.

'No, you're just going through a bad patch,' I huffed, as I sat down next to him. He was sitting upright on the sofa, trying to stay cool in the summer heat, his feet up on the coffee table.

'It's the disease in your body fighting the medication,' I went on. 'That's why you're so weak.'

It was nearly seven months after our return from Kenya and Jeremy seemed to have gone rapidly downhill. He had lost a lot of weight and was tired most of the time. He spent every afternoon dozing in his recliner in the conservatory, looking out onto the garden which now, in the height of summer, was bursting with colour and life. But we still felt hopeful.

In the spring he had finally been put on a course of immunotherapy – the wonder drug we hoped would beat the cancer. We'd heard amazing stories about immunotherapy, miracle stories about people whose lives had been transformed, even when they were in the very advanced stages of the illness. Those who had been informed their cancer was terminal had been restored to robust health after the treatment. The approach was revolutionary, harnessing the body's natural immune system to fight off the disease and keep it at bay. Our problem had been that immunotherapy was yet to be approved in the UK for use against renal cancer. In fact, it still wasn't. But Jeremy's health insurance company had approved payment for the drugs, understanding that the license was imminent and further delay would only be harmful to Jeremy's health.

Jeremy received his first treatment through an infusion drip in April and we were both excited and relieved. He even took a picture of the infusion being pumped into him and posted it on Facebook with the words, 'Feeling Hopeful,' next to a smiley face. Two more treatments followed in May and June. The immunotherapy came with its own range of side effects, including a lack of appetite, tiredness and, most uncomfortable of all, oedema (a build-up of fluid under the skin) in the legs and stomach. Once again, Jeremy bore it all stoically and with a renewed sense of positivity.

But in the last couple of weeks we had been told that the cancer had metastasized. The scans showed a tumour at the base of his oesophagus, which made it difficult for him to eat, and his left lung had virtually collapsed, so he had trouble breathing. He felt sick all the time and he couldn't swallow. The only solid food we could get down him was watermelon so he had lost a lot of weight. Though he never once complained, I could see that he was often in pain. He asked me to perform pranic healing on him.

Pranic healing is a form of energy-healing that removes bad energy from the body and replaces it with positive energy, therefore helping to heal the physical body. The principles are similar to the more widely known reiki. During pranic healing the practitioner doesn't actually touch the person but instead absorbs energy from the air, ground and sun and then transfers the energy, using their hands, to the person who is pain or suffering by manipulating their energy centres, or *chakras*. This recharges the energy in the body which, in turn, heals the physical body. It can be very effective and, as the pain worsened, Jeremy had started to ask me to do it for him. 'Do your thing on me,' he'd say, waving his hands in front of his face in an impression of my healing. Afterwards he always said that he felt better. It was comforting to know I could help to take the pain away, even if just temporarily.

The mobility nurse came on 22 July. That weekend, I was due to attend a life-coaching course near London but I wasn't happy about leaving Jeremy on his own. I decided to cancel, but he insisted I go, so we asked Jeremy's daughters to take turns spending time with him over the weekend. But over the next 24 hours he became weaker and weaker. Swallowing had become so painful for him that by Monday morning he was very dehydrated. We called his oncologist, who advised him to come into the hospital to be rehydrated. I drove him to the hospital, where he was shown to a private room and put on a drip, then rushed home for a couple of hours to finish some urgent work on the new online Just Jhoom! course.

At 7pm, the phone rang.

'You need to come in,' said Jeremy. 'The oncologist is coming to see us.'

It wasn't unusual for the oncologist to see us so late in the day – after all, he was a busy NHS consultant at the cancer centre in the County Hospital, a research professor and a private oncologist. I drove back to the hospital to find that Jeremy had been moved to a room by the nurses' station. It was a bigger room than the last and he seemed settled and comfortable. I wasn't there long before the oncologist arrived.

'Hello Jeremy. Hello Shalini,' he gave us each a fleeting smile, then looked down at his notes. He read silently for a couple of seconds then looked up at Jeremy.

'How are you feeling?' he asked and Jeremy returned a weak smile.

'Not bad, not good… I've been better.'

The doctor sat on the chair next to the bed and asked Jeremy a few more questions about his symptoms. Then he frowned a little and spoke quietly,

'Jeremy, I'm really sorry but there's nothing more we can do for you.'

What? The words didn't seem to fit into my head. They swirled around in my mind but I couldn't make sense of them.

'But he's on immunotherapy…' I stuttered. 'Are you saying it's not working?'

'That's right. The treatment's not working. The cancer has spread.'

It felt like I had been punched in the stomach. *Why? Why hadn't it worked for Jeremy?* Suddenly, a horrible thought crept into my mind.

'What are we talking here - days, weeks, months?'

'Days or weeks,' said the doctor.

No.

No, that can't be right.

Not days. Definitely not days.

Jeremy is so strong.

We'll have weeks, maybe even months… and then, somehow, we'll turn it around. We'll find another drug, another form of immunotherapy that works. We are not giving in. We are fighting this thing all the way.

I turned to look at Jeremy, sure that he would be having the same thoughts. But in that moment, something shifted. His whole face and body relaxed. The strain of all the past weeks and months disappeared and his face slipped into an expression of calm repose. It happened in seconds. In the same few seconds it took me to decide that the doctor was wrong, Jeremy had accepted his prognosis. He wasn't going to fight anymore. I could see that straight away. He had had enough; his body had had enough and his spirit was tired. His doctor had given him permission to let go and he had accepted it. Calmly, quietly and almost imperceptibly, he let death become his new reality.

In the silence that followed I knew it was over.

'You have borne everything we have thrown at you with such grace and positivity,' said the doctor. 'In terms of your treatment there is nothing we could have done differently, except perhaps to have started the immunotherapy earlier - if that had even been possible.'

'Thank you, doctor,' replied Jeremy and, courteous to the last, he held out his hand to shake. 'Thank you for all your care and professionalism. It has been greatly appreciated.'

Later that night, in his private room, I lay next to Jeremy and we held each other. I had no questions any more, no answers. I didn't know what to say or do. It didn't make sense that after everything we had done, after everything we had thrown at Jeremy's cancer, the disease had still won. It wasn't fair. It wasn't just. Inside me, a storm of emotions raged and yet, next to me, Jeremy was an oasis of peace and tranquility.

'I'm not scared of dying,' he whispered in the darkness. 'I'm actually quite excited about what's on the other side. My only regret is leaving you and the girls.'

'You're not going anywhere yet,' I said. 'We still have time.'

The next morning, I started to make arrangements to bring Jeremy home. We would need equipment and a hospital bed ready when he arrived in order to ensure a comfortable transition. There was no way Jeremy was going to leave this world in a hospital. If there was one last thing I could do for him now, it was to ensure that he spent his last few days in the quiet and peaceful surroundings of his own home, looking out onto the garden he loved and tended to by the people who loved him.

In the meantime, we had to let our families know. On Tuesday morning I called my sister, who told me that she would be on the next plane out of Nairobi. I didn't even have to ask her to come. I texted Tom, Katie's boyfriend, and asked him to make arrangements for all three daughters to come to the hospital together that afternoon. Jeremy broke the news to his daughters and they were, of course, inconsolable. Jeremy also called his brother, Nick, and step-sister, Susie, to tell them the news. While he was with his daughters, I returned home to take delivery of the bed and all the equipment we would need for his care. I wanted to make sure it was all set up and ready for him to come home the next day.

But when I returned to hospital very early the following morning, Jeremy had made a decision.

'I don't want to come home.' he told me solemnly.

'Why not? I'll look after you.'

'I don't want to tarnish our home.'

I was devastated. I wanted to make him comfortable, I wanted to look after him. He was the one who was dying but all he could think of was me. How was I going to live in our home with those memories of his last days once he was gone? My mind couldn't even comprehend it. I simply couldn't see a future without him. The present was all we had and I wanted to do everything in my power to ensure he was happy. I tried to persuade him. I wanted to take care of him, I told him, to give him love and tenderness in the comfortable surroundings of the home that was our shared sanctuary. I wanted him to see Tabasco, too, to enjoy his company and his affection. But Jeremy's mind was made up. He would not go home and nothing I said would change his mind. I simply had to accept his decision.

'Okay, I'll come and stay here,' I said, my mind whirring. 'I'll get everything sorted. I'll come and stay with you from tomorrow night.'

If my sister was here by Friday she could look after Tabasco for us, while I stayed with Jeremy. I decided to make the hospital room as homely as possible. I brought in some of the wildlife photos he had taken in Kenya, as well as a Samburu tartan throw and some family photos.

Now we had to tell Gladys the news. It was heartbreaking. She didn't even know that Jeremy was unwell – we had put it off and put it off, arguing to ourselves that he would get better and so there would be reason to worry her unduly. Every time he had gone into hospital we told her he was away for work. But we were running thin on lies and Gladys must have noticed that her son was no longer visiting her every week. Over the past couple of months Jeremy had barely left the house. He'd hardly seen a soul. Jeremy's daughters went to the care home to be with Gladys and I stayed with him. Then, over Facetime, Jeremy broke the news to his mother. At first, she seemed confused, she couldn't grasp what he was saying. It was just too overwhelming. Throughout the conversation Jeremy remained calm and strong, but I knew that inside he was breaking.

I finally left at around midnight to feed Tabasco and get some sleep, which never came. I was back at the hospital very early the next morning.

Though never particularly devotional, Jeremy had taken up going to church on a Sunday in the past year. I think it had brought him some comfort and he loved to sing hymns. Now, in full organisational mode, he insisted on seeing the vicar who would be conducting his funeral. He had already written me a list of the things I had to take care of, like the car and the insurance, and now he was making arrangements for his service. Having organised many funerals through the golf club, Jeremy knew exactly who to contact and he wrote down the details of the people I needed to speak to in order to make the arrangements. On the phone, the curate Reverend Ian Maslin from St Nicolas Church in Cranleigh said he could either come to see Jeremy today, or on Saturday. The vicar was away and would not be back for a few weeks.

'Which would you prefer?' I asked Jeremy.

'Tell him to come now,' he replied decisively.

When he arrived, I decided to give them some time alone and had a cup of tea in the waiting room. Around forty minutes later the Reverend emerged from Jeremy's room and told me, 'I'll come back on Saturday and bring a gin and tonic with me. Jeremy was keen to have one.' I smiled at him as he left, amazed at how Jeremy's humour remained undimmed.

I decided to go back home for a short time, pick up my things and feed Tabasco. Jeremy's friend, Terry, was due to visit so that Jeremy could ask him to do his eulogy, much of which he had recorded on my phone earlier that day. I felt comfortable that Jeremy wouldn't be alone for long and I would be back that evening to stay for the rest of the weekend.

I kissed him and gave him a hug.

Just before I left, I turned to look at him.

'Now you're not going to do anything silly, are you? I'll only be a couple of hours. You'll still be here when I get back?'

'Yes,' he smiled.

'Okay, I love you. I'll see you shortly!'

'*Theenk hain*, Shorty!' he quipped, using the Indian term for okay.

I smiled at him and left. Then I rushed home, finished up some work on the website, packed my weekend bag and gave Tabasco enough food to last him until the morning. At around 5pm I called Jeremy's mobile but he didn't pick up, so I called the hospital and spoke to his nurse.

'Is he okay?' I asked.

'Yes, he's fine. He's sleeping. One of his daughters has just arrived.'

'Fine, I'll be leaving soon.'

Ten minutes later, Jeremy's daughter, Katie, called. She sounded distraught.

'Katie, are you okay?'

'No, Shal, you need to come in, the nurses are saying that this is it.'

I jumped in the car and drove like a crazy person, trying to negotiate the heavy traffic in Guildford town centre. When I got to the hospital I abandoned my car in the car park and ran up to his room. But by the time I arrived Jeremy had lost consciousness. His breathing was laboured and I could hear the rattle in his chest. Jenny and Amanda were now also at the hospital, their partners all in the waiting room.

'Please don't cry,' I implored the three girls. 'If he's ready to go, we shouldn't try to hold onto him. Sadness will only make this more difficult for him.'

I knew that the atmosphere should be as peaceful as possible for Jeremy. I believe that showing grief as a person is dying hinders the release of their soul into the afterlife and so it was hugely important that we did not show our distress.

We turned the lights down low and held his hands. I stroked his arm and said to him, 'You can go now, you don't need this body any more. Your soul can go up. You can let go.'

The time between each breath got longer and longer. Twice, he sat up in bed as if reaching out for someone. I felt that perhaps he was seeing his father who had died over 30 years ago.

'We love you. I love you, Jem,' I said again. 'Please don't worry about us. You must do what you need to. You can let go now, Jeremy. Your soul does not need this body anymore. Let your soul go up now.'

Staying as strong and as calm as I could, I continued, 'You can let go, Jeremy. Let go, my sweetie. I love you.'

For three hours he stayed with us and for three hours I spoke to him, completely calm on the outside, my heart breaking on the inside. And then, finally, he exhaled his last breath and at 9.20pm, he let go.

Finally, the girls let themselves cry. Then, after the tears, I told them to go home with their partners. There was nothing more they could do. I stayed with his body for the rest of the night. I didn't cry, I didn't feel sad. I didn't feel anything at all, in fact. It had all been so quick, so horribly, horribly quick. It was just Monday evening when we had been told by the oncologist that there was nothing more they could do. Three days from prognosis to death. Just 72 hours. It had been just one week since the visit from the mobility nurse who had talked about hospice care. I counted back even further in my mind. Two years! It was exactly two years to the day since his original diagnosis. He had been diagnosed on the evening of the last Thursday of July in 2014 and he left us on the evening of the last Thursday of July in 2016. I almost smiled at that thought. Jeremy liked symmetry; he would sometimes lie in bed with me at home, looking out of the window and lining up the window frame with a tree trunk outside, using his hand and eye, as if conducting a little survey. He would have appreciated the symmetry of this timing.

I sat on the sofa most of the night, just looking at him, my mind completely blank. I didn't sleep at all. I couldn't. I was in shock. Nothing seemed real and yet I knew that he had gone. I had watched him die. Jeremy's soul had finally been released from his body, a body ravaged by disease, a body that could no longer sustain itself. He had gone peacefully, with the blessing of all who loved him and he had appeared ready to go after all the suffering he had endured. I knew that in my mind. But I couldn't feel it. I was suspended on a different plane of reality, locked outside of myself.

The early morning sunlight crept in through the blinds. *My first morning without Jem.* There was no grief at that stage, no anger, no sense at all of the tsunami of pain that would eventually engulf me. I was like a woman standing alone on an empty beach after the tide has fled, staring into the distance, unaware of the gigantic wave that is forming far out to sea.

At 6am, Shivani landed at Heathrow and came straight from the airport to the hospital. She threw her arms around me before saying her own goodbye to my husband. The funeral directors came to take Jeremy away. There was nothing left for me to do.

Before I left the hospital, I removed the wedding band from Jeremy's cold hand, kissed his forehead and walked out of the room.

Chapter 18 – Numb

"A death is not the extinguishing of a light,
but the putting out of the lamp because the dawn has come...
Let the dead have the immortality of fame,
but the living the immortality of love."
—Rabindranath Tagore[17]

When it came to the funeral, I was very organised and clear about what I wanted. Jenny and Amanda had decided to do a reading each, his friend Terry would be giving the eulogy and I had planned the order of all the hymns, just as Jeremy had instructed. Jeremy loved to sing hymns and when he sang in church, he assumed a look of complete seriousness, his forehead set in a crinkled pattern that I found quite funny. Fortunately for him, his talent matched his enthusiasm and he had a lovely, deep singing voice. On the day of his death, Jeremy had told me exactly what hymns he wanted sung at his funeral and I had written it all down faithfully, determined not to let him down.

There had been practically no let up since Jeremy had passed away. After telling all our friends and family of his passing, I had so much to do: registering his death, getting the certificate, contacting the funeral directors and arranging the service and the programme. Jeremy's daughters and Shivani were there to help, but I felt I needed to do as much as I could on my own. He was my husband and it was my responsibility to organise a funeral that would honour him. But these weren't only my plans. I was carrying out Jeremy's last wishes. In the final hours before his death, Jeremy had given me a list of all the things he wanted for his funeral – where it was to be held, who was to speak on his behalf and all the music for the church service as well as for the crematorium.

Typically for Jeremy, a man with an eye for detail, he left nothing to chance.

'Don't spend a fortune on the coffin,' he had instructed. 'Get something traditional but not pricey. You know what I like.'

How strange to think that I would know what kind of coffin he would like, but I did. I didn't spend hours agonizing over the small decisions because I knew his taste perfectly. He also told me about his wishes for the wake at the Bramley Golf Club.

'Speak to Michael the chef,' he'd said. 'He knows what to prepare for the buffet and get him to serve the wine I usually pick.'

When I emailed the golf club to see if we could have the wake there, Jack Bayliss, the golf club Committee Chairman, emailed back:

I write on behalf of the whole Club, and also as a friend of Jeremy's, to offer you our deepest condolences on his passing. He was a friend of everyone at the Club, as well as being a long-standing, loyal and very able general manager. We have missed his cheerful face in the office...Of course the wake will be at Bramley Golf Club as Jeremy wished. It will also be with the compliments of the Club. I am sure you would also like to know that Michael has offered to do the food at his expense.

I was touched by the thoughtfulness of the club where Jeremy had spent so many happy years of his life.

A few days later, Terry took me to the golf club to discuss the details of the wake.

'Jeremy gave the club so much and we owe him a great debt of gratitude,' his colleagues all reassured me. 'We've talked about this, Shalini, and the board have agreed that we will take care of all the expenses. Just leave it to us and we'll make sure Jeremy gets a really top-notch wake. Don't worry about a thing - we'll sort it all out.'

What a wonderful gesture. It was lovely of them to do this for Jeremy and reassuring to know I could leave it all in their hands.

As the day of the funeral neared, I made the final arrangements, sorted out the seating plan for the church and had the order of service printed. Then, on the morning of 11 August, I dressed calmly in my room with Tabasco watching. No more colourful clothes for me. Now I would wear only white, the traditional colour of mourning for Hindus. No more *bindis* on my forehead and no more bangles. It felt wrong to wear the bright, colourful adornments that traditionally signify a married Indian woman. The day before I had chopped all my hair off. No longer did I want the long, black locks that Jeremy had so loved. I looked at myself in the mirror. I felt peaceful, calm even. Until that morning, I had been so busy organising and getting prepared that I hadn't really considered the reality of the day ahead.

As I turned away from my gaunt reflection, the hearse pulled into the drive and it then hit me: we were saying goodbye to Jeremy. This was it – this was the end. Just seeing the black car there, with the solid oak coffin I had chosen in the back, knowing Jeremy was inside, was a terrible shock and the tears finally began to flow.

'*Didi?*'

My sister, who had been staying with me, called out. I grabbed a pair of Jeremy's sunglasses to hide behind and went to join her downstairs. Standing at the bottom of the stairs next to her her were Jenny, Katie and Amanda.

'Are you okay?' Shivani asked, concerned.

'Yes, I'm fine. It's going to be fine,' I said and took a deep breath as we all walked to the car.

I clenched my jaw and clasped my hands together in the back of the car as we slowly followed the hearse to St Nicolas Church in Cranleigh. In front of us were several other cars and the funeral director told us to wait in our vehicle until everyone else had gone into the church.

'I just want to warn you - the church is packed,' he said quietly, as he helped me out of the car.

I nodded, though I barely registered his words. As we entered the church - Jenny, Katie and Amanda following the coffin and Shivani and me just behind them - the uplifting chords of *Amazing Grace*, a song chosen by Jeremy, filled the space.

I took my place in the pew next to my sister and gazed across the aisle, to where my parents were sitting. They had flown in from Nairobi the day before. Both of them had been distraught at the news of Jeremy's passing – especially my father who had really become good friends with Jeremy and had accepted him as my partner. As I knew that Terry would be mentioning our marriage in the eulogy, I had sat my parents and Shivani down the day before and told them about the secret ceremony. No one questioned me, they just accepted the news silently.

As I stood facing the altar, I was thankful that everyone else was behind me. It meant nobody could see my face or the endless stream of tears that came unbidden throughout the service. I focused my attention solely on Jeremy. It was just him and me, like at our wedding just 21 months earlier. *Had it only been 21 months?* It didn't make sense. Nothing made sense. But here I stood now, not with Jeremy by my side but staring at a wooden box, his coffin. I experienced a strange kind of tunnel vision. The world slid away and it was just the two of us there. You could have told me there were a thousand people behind me or none at all and I would have believed you.

Once we were all seated, the Reverend Ian Maslin took his place at the front of the church.

'I had promised to take Jeremy a gin and tonic when I next visited him in the hospital, but it was not to be,' he said. 'So, I hope you will allow me a small indulgence.'

He placed a small can of tonic and a miniature bottle of gin on the coffin.

Everyone laughed and the almost unbearable tension in the church was broken. The first hymn was *All Things Bright and Beautiful*. It was just the kind of hymn that Jeremy loved to belt out – joyful, rousing and a tribute to the wonders of nature. Everyone around me sung their hearts out.

Each little flower that opens, each little bird that sings...

I couldn't sing a note. I just let the tears flow freely and occasionally, while the church swelled with noise, I allowed myself to take in large, shaky gulps of air. There were poems, speeches and more hymns. Terry had everyone laughing and crying as he delivered his eulogy, which seemed to capture the essence of Jeremy so well: his humour, kindness and zest for life. The service seemed to go by so quickly and it was exactly as I hoped it would be – tender, sweet and loving. A fitting tribute to a warm and gentle soul.

Between the speeches and the hymns, I looked down at the simple white order of service that I held in my hands. I had spent hours choosing the photos of Jeremy through the years and now they were arranged in collages across two pages. At the back we thanked everyone for coming and for their wonderful messages of love, support and sympathy. Everyone had been very kind and I had been touched by the flowers, letters, emails, texts and cards of condolence that arrived at the house daily. We asked that if people wanted to make a donation in Jeremy's name that they send it to the Penny Brohn Cancer Centre.

After the service we followed the hearse to Guildford crematorium. On the way, we did a slow drive past Bramley Golf Club, as a mark of respect. It was a small, intimate ceremony at the crematorium: just myself, Shivani, Jeremy's three daughters and their partners, Terry, Peter and Jeremy's brother, Nick. The nursing home had arranged for Jeremy's mother to be brought over with a carer. We walked in to the sounds of the Indian song *Jhoom* by Ali Zafer. It was Jeremy's choice and acknowledged everything we had worked for together in setting up my business.

Before I knew it, the service was over and the velvet curtains closed around the coffin with the song *Time of my Life* from 'our' film *Dirty Dancing*. Again, I smiled at Jeremy's sense of humour – in that choice he had not only acknowledged our film but had also given me a message that he was alright, wherever he was now. I felt my heart breaking. It was so brutally final. The tears wouldn't stop and I felt my sister next to me, her hand rubbing my back. I don't know how long we stood like that but after a while, I turned to her.

'I'm okay, you go. I want to be here on my own for a little while.'

Everyone left and for a few minutes I stood there in the crematorium alone, watching the space where the coffin had been moments earlier.

Jem! My heart ached. *Jem, where are you?*

Silence filled the room. A large, looming silence. I was alone.

I felt oddly detached as I walked out of the crematorium and more alone than I had ever been in my life. The Reverend and the funeral director were waiting for me in the warm summer sunshine. I shook their hands, just as Jeremy would have done.

'Thank you both for everything,' I said sincerely. 'Jeremy would have been happy.'

For a moment I was conscious of my actions – in the depths of my despair I was behaving strangely normally, thanking people, functioning. I was reminded of the moment Jeremy was told his cancer was terminal and he shook his oncologist's hand and thanked him for everything he had done. I suppose if I had learned anything from 19 years with Jeremy it was to make people feel appreciated.

What a different woman I was to the one Jeremy had met all those years before. The old me would never have behaved this way. It wasn't just me - in Indian society people don't stand on such formalities. There's an old Indian saying, made famous by a Bollywood film in the early Nineties, which goes: *'Dosti mein no sorry, no thank you'*. It means 'No sorry or thank you between friends'. I think the intention is to make everyone feel relaxed, telling them not to stand on ceremony but, personally, I like manners. I like it when people show their appreciation, especially to those closest to them. Jeremy was unfaltering in this respect. He was naturally polite to everyone, especially those he was closest to, and I liked that. Jeremy was observant of others' efforts and behaviour. He took pains to acknowledge their feelings, to show that he valued them. Good manners, to Jeremy, were a way of life. It meant he never took anyone for granted. He even taught my sister how to shake hands! Before she met him, her handshake was limp and unenthusiastic. He showed her how to shake hands firmly.

We drove to the golf club for the wake and I saw that Jeremy's precious white Peugeot RCZ, with the number plate X4 JFL, had been positioned prominently outside. The number plate stood for 'Kisses For Jeremy Frederick Lucas'. I smiled when I saw it. He loved his car, even though everyone called it a 'hairdresser's' car it was his pride and joy.

There must have been around 150 people milling around in the large, bright dining room overlooking the Surrey Hills. The room looked beautiful with tables dressed in white linen, each boasting a centerpiece of purple and cream flowers. On a table to one side were the condolence books where people could leave their messages, alongside a couple of photos of Jeremy in frames and a lit candle. I had also arranged to have two books of Jeremy's wildlife photographs on the tables. I wanted everyone to see how talented he was. There were even pictures of Jeremy projected onto a big screen on one wall. The staff and members of the club had done Jeremy proud and for the first time I understood his affection for the Bramley Golf Club and why for so many years he had thought of it as his second home.

Brian, a friend from the club, said a few words and then, although I hadn't meant to, I decided to speak too.

'This is the hardest speech I will ever make,' I said through my tears, 'But I want to thank you so much for coming to say goodbye to Jeremy. He would have been so touched to see so many people here. I want you to remember Jeremy for the wonderful man he was and help me keep his memory alive. Thank you.'

Taking a deep breath, I pushed my grief to one side and began to walk round the room to shake every person's hand and thank them for coming. There were so many people, so many friends of ours who had been shocked by Jeremy's death. I tried to speak to them all. And after about an hour, I managed to catch a quiet word with Mark, a friend who had lost his wife to cancer in early 2014. He stood before me, offering me the same condolences I had given him two years earlier. His eyes were full of a deep sadness. Out of everyone there, he knew better than anyone how I felt that day.

'How do you do it?' I asked, searching his eyes for an answer. 'How do you cope?'

He sighed and looked down.

'It's as if somebody has turned the lights out and it's gone dark.'

'Yes, that's how I feel. I can't see a way out.'

'Shalini, trust me. You will learn to walk again in the dark.'

I grasped at his words like a drowning woman grasps a lifebelt. I made myself promise never to forget what he said. It seemed impossible, then, that I could ever learn to walk in the dark but I had to cling to some small raft of hope, however unlikely, that one day I would be okay. Because at that moment, I had no idea what my future looked like.

The rest of the day went by in a blur of handshakes, sympathetic smiles and quiet murmuring. I don't remember anything else that anyone said to me after I spoke to Mark. It was like it all happened in a dream. A bad dream. I was there but I was numb. Somehow, I got home. Somehow, I crawled into bed. It was done.

The next day I went through the two condolence books to read what everyone had written. The extraordinary tributes to Jeremy brought me a lot of comfort and I noted that the same words kept cropping up again and again. Jeremy was *a kind man,* they wrote. He was a *gentleman.* I nodded as I thought about how kindness was such an underrated quality in this day and age.

Suddenly, something occurred to me. I hadn't left a condolence book at the church, only at the wake. And yet there were people who had attended the church service but not the wake. Why hadn't I thought to leave a book for them to write in? How could I be so stupid! I had let him down.

I'm sorry, I'm so sorry, Jem.

Suddenly my guts twisted and all the air left my lungs. I fell to the floor and gasped; gasped again. But nothing… there was only a silent screaming wail that flooded over me and made me heave over and over.

JEM!

JEREMY!

Where are you? Why did you leave me?

I did nothing else that day, just slept. It was all I could manage. The following day I said goodbye to my parents who were going to stay with family in London. I knew they were grieving too – my father and Jeremy had become good friends in the last few years and his death was deeply painful to him - but it was a strain to have them around. Shivani decided to stay with me to the end of the month. She knew I would need her, even if it just meant going down to the shops to fill the cupboards with food. I knew she was suffering too but she never let me see it. In Jeremy she had lost a brother – one who had loved her, cared for her and always supported her. She, too, was grieving.

All around me lay a heavy and depressing silence. How darkly ironic, I observed. I had worked hard in the last few months to put all the training for Just Jhoom! online so that I could spend time with Jeremy. And it had worked. The course went live on 29 July, the day after Jeremy died and then I had all the time in the world. Just no Jeremy.

I woke each morning with the day stretching out in front of me like a vast, featureless desert. There was nobody to talk to, nothing to do. My world was nothing. Empty. A blank page.

So, I did the only thing I thought made sense to me – I started to clear the house.

Chapter 19 – Broken

"If you live to be a hundred,
I want to live to be a hundred minus one day so
I never have to live without you."
—**Winnie The Pooh (Joan Powers)**[18]

A large part of me died the day Jeremy passed away and every day after, a small part of me faded away until I no longer wanted to carry on living. I was broken. I had lost someone who could never be replaced and I had also lost the most cherished relationship I had ever had. I always used to think that I was in complete control of my life. Losing Jeremy shattered that illusion. Now I had no control over anything. I had no control over these feelings of vulnerability, loneliness, fear, anger, guilt and sheer disbelief at what had happened.

Organising Jeremy's funeral kept me focused and gave me a sense of purpose and control. But in the days that followed, all I could see was emptiness. An abyss of nothing but the distress and pain of separation. I needed to do something, fill my days and get some control back. I tackled Jeremy's possessions first. I asked his daughters to come and choose what they wanted from his wardrobe: shirts, ties, jumpers that reminded them of him. I kept the things that I had always liked to see him wear. The rest of the clothes and shoes I sent to Kenya with Shivani so she could distribute them to her community there; anything left over could go to charity.

When that was done, I looked at the list that Jeremy had made for me so I knew what he wanted everyone to have. He had asked that Jenny's partner, Tim, have all the DIY tools, which he had spent years and a huge amount of money collecting. You'd think he was a builder considering the number of gadgets and gizmos he had! Then there was all Jeremy's golfing gear. He had five sets of clubs and half a dozen pairs of golfing shoes. Some of it was too old to give away, but the good pieces went to Katie's partner, Tom. His fishing gear went to Jeremy's youngest daughter, Amanda. They had spent many happy times fishing together, so it meant a great deal to her. I gave Shivani much of Jeremy's photographic equipment, but perhaps his most precious possession of all, his camera, I gave to Amanda. Jeremy had taken so many wonderful photographs with that camera and after discussing it with Shivani we agreed that Amanda should have it. She was talented and would make good use of it. I wanted Jeremy's daughters to have as much as possible to remind them of their Dad and so I gave them photographs, the marquetry pieces Jeremy had worked on, the family piano, Jeremy's rifle, wine decanters to use at their weddings, their grandfather's war medals, their grandparents wedding photos – it was their family history, after all. I even gave Jeremy's beloved tortoise, Tommy, to Katie.

With the help of Shivani and Jeremy's daughters and their partners I began to clear out the house, garage and loft. Jeremy had always been the kind of person who said 'out of sight, out of mind', which meant he was a bit of a hoarder. We spent two weekends taking things to the tip and local charity shops. I was determined to streamline and declutter. Going through this process of clearing things out and organising made me feel like I was in control again. I couldn't control Jeremy dying, but I could control what I wanted to keep in the house and what I wanted to get rid of.

By the end of August I was on my own again as Shivani had gone back to Kenya. I started sorting through piles of paperwork in the house, things I knew I really didn't need any more – manuals, old bills, bank statements. After several days I had managed to fill over a dozen black sacks with rubbish to be sent to Jeremy's friend at the golf club, who would burn it all. I went through Jeremy's computer too, clearing his old folders and emails and sorting through the thousands of photographs he had taken. Once the girls had taken all they wanted, I looked at some of Jeremy's other belongings. I wanted there to be some benefit and value to the things he had used and loved. A fountain pen I had given Jeremy for our six-month anniversary went to a dear friend of mine, the only person who I knew still wrote with fountain pens. Another friend had a daughter with ambitions to be a music teacher so I gave her Jeremy's old guitar. Jeremy had a drum from Gambia that was his pride and joy. That went to a little boy, the son of one of my dance students, who has since started taking drum lessons. I even gave our lawnmower to the boy next door, because he loved to cut grass!

It felt good to give things away, knowing the things Jeremy had cherished would be well-used - and everyone was so appreciative. Clearing the house made me think about how much work there was to be done after a death. Imagine if I died with Jeremy - it would have been up to his family and mine to sort out all our affairs. I knew what Jeremy wanted done with all his things, but no one else did. How would the families have managed? I decided that I would leave everything as organised as possible so that when it was my turn to leave, those left behind would know my wishes.

I had one goal in the weeks after Jeremy's death: to organise my affairs as quickly as possible, so that I could join Jeremy. I was broken. I simply couldn't imagine a future on my own, without him. The only thought that gave me comfort was the knowledge that we would be reunited soon. For two weeks I worked like a demon, clearing the house. But some things I just couldn't hurry along, like Jeremy's probate, which was the financial part of settling Jeremy's affairs. In his will he had left everything to me, but he had asked me to give a little something to his daughters. Once the probate was arranged and the funds available, I had it in my mind to give them each a sum of money. Only then could I die.

Once my tasks were completed, I stopped. There was nothing left to do - and it was then that the emptiness hit me. For the first time in my life, I had no appetite for work anymore. I didn't want to go out, I couldn't face talking to people and, alone in the house, time seemed to slow down to the point of standstill. Every hour stretched out longer and longer. Even when I had things to do, I had no energy. Slowly and gradually I seized up, paralyzed by my grief. Every morning I woke I dissolved into tears. I cried in my bed, I cried in the lounge, I cried in the kitchen, the conservatory and the garden. Everything and anything made me cry, even something as mundane as brushing my teeth. I'd look at the toothpaste tube and it would spark memories of a hundred different conversations with Jeremy.

'Squeeze the tube from the end,' he'd berate me. 'Why do you insist on squeezing it from the middle?'

'What different does it make?' I'd reply, breezily. 'It's all the same stuff. It comes from the same place.'

'It drives me crazy! You know it drives me crazy. It makes it easier to squeeze as it goes down if you always squeeze from the end...'

And so on.

In frustration one day he'd attached a Post-It note to the tube that read, *'Squeeze my arse, not my stomach.'*

It made me laugh so much that I had kept that note, along with hundreds of letters, cards and little messages he'd given me throughout our years together. So now, of course, every time I squeezed the toothpaste I thought of him. My days were made up of these tiny shards of loss that stabbed at my heart over and over again.

Everywhere I looked, I was faced with reminders of his absence. There was a bottle of Bio-oil in the bedroom the sight of which filled me with helpless rage. We had bought the oil for Jeremy's scars after the operation to remove his kidney and somewhere along the line I had started using it for my face.

'It's gone down a lot,' Jeremy complained one day.

'Don't worry - I'll buy you another bottle when it's gone,' I had assured him.

And yet here was that same bottle in our bathroom, all these months later. It was an insult - it seemed to go on forever. Why? Why did this bottle of oil last longer than my husband? It was impossible, incomprehensible! The world had ended. Couldn't anyone see that? And yet these mundane items from a past life seemed to still exist. There were things in this world that had survived longer than him. How could that be?

Without Jeremy, my life made no sense. Getting out of bed each day became harder and harder. What was the point? Some days I couldn't manage it at all. At some point late in the afternoon, bleary-eyed, I'd summon just enough energy to haul my heavy limbs out of the bedroom to feed Tabasco before stumbling back to bed again. All I wanted was to close my eyes and forget the world. I watched rubbish American TV, the kind Jeremy had hated and I snacked on junk food all day: crisps, chocolate, cake, Bombay mix. It was all I could do. The box sets allowed me to switch off my mind and the rubbish food filled the gaping hole that had opened up within me. I took painkillers every day to numb my grief and at night I drank whisky to help me sleep. I abandoned all care of myself – I didn't put on make-up anymore, sometimes I didn't even get dressed. Mentally, physically, I had hit a wall.

At the beginning of September, I went back to teaching my adult Just Jhoom! classes. As the first one came to an end and we were doing the cool-down, I had to quickly turn away from the class as tears streamed down my face. But, although it had been difficult to stand up in front of the class, put on my best face and teach, that one hour of teaching had also given me a tiny sliver of respite from my grief. For that brief period, I could forget, escape from the pain. Teaching demanded total concentration: I had to remember the choreography, teach it to my students and correct them when they went wrong. But the three adult classes a week was as much as I could manage and so I stopped all my other school teaching and mindfulness courses. I didn't speak to a single soul from one class to the next, unless it was to my assistant Peta, who had taken on all the admin for Just Jhoom! I often asked her to run errands for me, as I found I couldn't walk down Cranleigh High Street anymore. I had only ever been in the village with Jeremy – it was Shalini and Jeremy. I always hated shopping so generally I had left it to Jeremy. When we did go into town together, we would walk into the shops holding hands. I missed having a hand to hold. It felt like a part of my own body was missing. I felt exposed, half of a person. At home I could sense him there more. There was a presence. So, I stayed at home.

Then I began to hit the milestones. On September 14, I woke up to my 41st Birthday, my first birthday in 20 years without him. My friends, Louise and Sue, came to spend the afternoon with me but I was a mess. I had never cried so much in my life. Every occasion, every birthday and anniversary, had been marked by a thoughtful, meaningful gesture: the mug of tea by the bedside, the accompanying card placed next to it, the little whisper in my ear: 'Don't let the tea go cold.'

I never heard his voice now. I wanted to, but couldn't. Sometimes I thought I heard his key turn in the door and my heart would lift. Or I'd see a car's headlights shine through the windows into the lounge and I would imagine it was his car. No. There was no key in the door, no card by my bedside, no car in our drive. My days were marked by the absence of these things, by the knowledge - the certain, unbearable knowledge that every birthday would now be like this. A year of lonely milestones lay ahead: his 60th birthday, our wedding anniversary, the first Christmas alone in the house, New Year's Eve, Valentine's Day – all without him. The empty milestones stretched bleakly into the future. I would never again wake to the sound of him walking up the stairs with a mug of tea, or listen to the sweet conversations each morning between him and Tabasco. The silence was unbearable.

Death became an obsession. I woke up every morning wondering why I was still alive. In small, subtle ways I tried to sabotage my health – I ate badly, drank whisky every night and took too many painkillers every day. I even abandoned my blood pressure medication. Perhaps I could kill myself this way? I scanned the papers for news of any recent deaths and when I found them I pored over every detail, searching the faces of grieving widows, wondering what their expressions were masking. I analysed their words and delved into their stories. How were they coping? Had death hit them as hard as it had hit me? Did they also feel battered and defeated? I measured my grief against theirs. Better? Worse? I needed to find a connection. I needed to know if I was alone in this terrible new world or whether there were others here with me.

I bought books on suicide. Yes, there are such things. I worked out the best way to do it and where. I had it planned. Only the knowledge of how much this would hurt my sister and parents stopped me from making those thoughts a reality. Still, the urge to end it all was so strong that on some days it was all I could do to resist. One long, lonely night, I sat on my bed surrounded by Jeremy's photos and held a whisky bottle in one hand and a bunch of pills in the other. How many pills were there? I counted them out. *Were there enough to finish me off? Why not? Why shouldn't I go now? What have I got to live for? Why put myself through this anymore?* I saw myself as if in a dream, taking the pills and drinking the whisky. I knew how it would feel to lie down on the bed and gently slip away in the night, to just drift out of my body and back towards him... But then Tabasco padded into the bedroom, jumped onto the bed and sat himself right on my lap and the spell was broken. The daydream evaporated. *I can't do it. Not while Tabasco's alive.*

One day in September I received an unexpected call.

'I just wanted to see how you were doing,' said Jeremy's oncologist. 'See how you're coping.'

Coping? I wasn't coping. What could I tell him? That I thought of dying every day? That I had nearly swallowed a bottle of pills? That when I drove my car I was often grabbed by the urge to swerve into the nearest tree? I had in mind three trees between Cranleigh and Guildford that would do perfectly. No. I didn't tell him any of this. I had questions of my own.

'You never said,' I replied slowly. 'You never said that he didn't have much time left. Not until three days before he died. Why? Why didn't you give us a prognosis?'

There was a pause.

'You never asked,' he said simply.

It was true. I suppose I had been so determined that Jeremy would beat the disease it hadn't even occurred to me to ask whether it was actually likely.

'But I would have thought you would have given us a bit more warning,' I said, desperately. 'We didn't know. I didn't know.'

'It's not like in America where the oncologist sits you down and tells you everything. Here, we wait and sometimes, if you've not asked for the prognosis, we don't give it to you. Do you think it would have made a difference to know?'

'I, I don't know. Maybe. Maybe I would have done things differently.'

'Or maybe not knowing helped you both.'

That last week of Jeremy's life had been so strange, so sudden. I'd gone over and over it in my head. Did I do the right thing? If I had known he was dying before that week I could have put my work to one side and spent more time with him. I'd been so determined to hit the deadline for the website launch and had deprived myself of those last few days and weeks with him. But if the oncologist had told me Jeremy was dying sooner, would I have believed him? Would Jeremy have lasted as long as he did without our shared optimism? I had seen how quickly he had given up when he had been given the news. Would he have given up sooner if he knew? I had so many questions - and no answers. All I knew was that I felt cruelly robbed of our time together.

People reached out – my parents and Shivani called often and my friends, neighbours and some extended family texted or emailed. They wanted to talk to me, to ask me how I was doing, but I had nothing to say, so I hid. I couldn't have a normal conversation anymore. I had no interest in other people's lives – their birthdays, anniversaries or holidays. Everything they said seemed to hurt. The most casual discussions served only to remind me of the life I no longer had so, instead of asking people to censor themselves, I did the easier thing and avoided them. Only occasionally did I let myself go out for a coffee after my Saturday class with the ladies who managed to keep conversations focused on safe topics like the news or a TV show.

I always imagined Jeremy would go before me because he was that much older. But his father Fred had died in his late seventies and his mum was still going at 96, so I also assumed he had many more years left in him. Jeremy was only 59 when he died. In the past, we had talked about death and I'd told him I didn't want to live to be more than 60. I don't know why, it was just a number I had in my head.

'Ah, but I want to live to be 100,' he replied.

'Okay, well you live to 100 and just for you I'll live to 80 and then we can kick the bucket together.'

In his last days, I had reminded him of this conversation.

'You were supposed to live to 100, remember?'

He only smiled at me, sadly.

Now even living till 60 seemed like torture. Another 20 years without him? I didn't even want to do one year. The fear of death is a natural instinct, hardwired into our beings. That is how we have survived as a species. But when you lose someone who means more to you than your own life, death holds no fear. I longed for death now – I held out my arms and begged it to come for me.

'You need to start taking anti-depressants,' my doctor told me when I visited her in late September. She had been able to gauge from my words and demeanor that I was suicidal.

'No.' I was adamant. 'They make me shake. I can't teach dance if I shake.'

Teaching was the only thing that gave me some respite from the constant, clamoring pain. For that brief hour, three times a week, I was myself again. I was a woman dancing and not a woman locked in deep grief.

'Well, you have to do something,' she warned sternly. 'Have you thought about bereavement counselling?

'Yes, Phyllis Tuckwell have been in touch.'

Phyllis Tuckwell was a local hospice care charity that had helped Jeremy with pain management through their Fountain Centre in Guildford. They had offered me and Jeremy's daughters free counseling and I was due to start in October.

'I'm glad to hear that,' my doctor nodded. 'You need to do it. And you need to go back on your blood pressure tablets. Your BP is 200 over 100. If you're not careful you could have a stroke or a heart attack.'

I looked at her blankly. *Well, wouldn't that be a blessed relief!* But I didn't say a word. Instead, I just nodded and left the medical practice in a hurry, anxious to return to the safety of my home and the comfort of my bed.

I couldn't face Jeremy's 60ᵗʰ birthday alone, so I decided to go away to a place we had never been before, somewhere which held no memories: Grenada in the Caribbean. I don't know what I had been expecting but it certainly wasn't a holiday from my pain. From the moment I started to pack my luggage, a barrage of happy memories from past holidays taken together resurfaced.

'We're all going on a summer holiday!' I'd start singing the moment we closed the front door behind us on our way to the airport.

'Is there something wrong with you? Are you in pain?' Jeremy would say, covering his ears.

I have a terrible singing voice, it's true, but that never stopped me. I was always so excited to be going away with Jeremy, to be sharing the adventure. Now there was no singing, no talking, and no laughing. Just a lot of crying. It was always the same when I went away with Jeremy. He took care of all the little details – carrying the luggage, paying the taxi driver, holding the passports and tickets. He did all these small things for us both. He'd hold my hand in the taxi and in the airport too, where we usually ate a light lunch of sushi before the flight. I would have a glass of bubbly and he'd have a beer - unless it was very early in the morning in which case he'd have a bacon sandwich and a coffee and I'd have scrambled eggs on toast and tea. Now every element of my solo journey was punctuated with the same thought: *I'm alone and I'll always be alone.*

My week in Grenada was quiet. I didn't speak to anyone, except exchanging a few odd words here and there with the staff at my hotel by the sea. I actively avoided everyone else. I went for walks along the beach, read, had massages and ate most meals in my room. If I ate in the restaurant I always took a book to read and requested a quiet table. One day, towards the end of the holiday, I was having lunch at the beach bar when one of waitresses who had been serving me all week approached my table. She pointed at my necklace, on which I had hung Jeremy's wedding ring, then she showed me her own necklace. Dangling on the end was a man's ring.

'I have one too,' she said. Her husband had died just a few months before, from a brain aneurism; he was 40. I told her my story. It was the only time I opened up.

On 10 October, I sat on the balcony outside my room and wrote Jeremy a birthday card, which I propped up on the table. Then I had a drink, just as we would have done together if he were here. First, I drank a beer for him and then I had a glass of champagne for me. Then, slowly and deliberately, I opened a small present. Inside was a silver tribute ring with a small amount of Jeremy's ashes layered into coloured glass crystals to create a

purple stone. The inscription on the inside of the band read '*Jem –
My Soulmate*'. As I slipped it onto the ring finger on my right-hand
I felt a fleeting sense of peace in the knowledge that now I had a
small part of Jeremy physically with me at all times.

I talked to him, I told him how much I missed him and I told
him how much he would have enjoyed this holiday. The sea here
were splendid and he would have loved snorkeling in the clear,
shallow waters of the bay. Then I fell silent, waiting for a reply
that never came. I sighed and stared out at the still blue sea.

All I wanted was to walk into it and never come back.

Chapter 20 – Doves

"Grief is a wound that needs attention in order to heal.
To work through and complete grief means to face our feelings openly
and honestly, to express and release our feelings fully, and to tolerate
and accept our feelings for however long
it takes for the wound to heal."
—Judy Tatelbaum[19]

There are doves in our garden!

I was sitting in the conservatory, staring out at the delicate pinky-brown birds pecking at the feeder. *How strange!* In all the years we had lived here, I had never seen doves here before and yet now they were visiting almost daily. Were they a sign from Jeremy? I hoped so. I so wanted to see signs from him. I knew he wasn't gone, that he had merely passed over to the spirit world, but I wanted to have some evidence of it. I wanted to *feel* it. Here, at home, I felt his presence more than anywhere else. Some mornings I awoke to a sort of tingling sensation running down my body, as if he was there, holding me. I stared out at the birds and smiled. Even in the depths of winter, Jeremy's beautiful garden teemed with life. And it was *his* garden. I barely set foot in it these days, only to feed Jeremy's fish in the pond or fill the bird feeder. Every two months a man called Ross cleaned the pond. The week before, I had remarked how happy Jeremy would be, knowing his pond was being looked after.

'It's *your* pond now,' Ross had replied. I stayed silent. No, it wasn't my pond. It was Jeremy's garden, his pond and his fish.

Shortly after I got back from Grenada, I received a call from the Phyllis Tuckwell organization confirming my counselling sessions. At the same time, the nursing home looking after Gladys called to say that she was dying. I went to spend some time with her, as did Jeremy's daughters, who were very close to her. When it came to looking after their 'Nana', none wavered in their devotion. The last two years had been a struggle for Gladys, following a bad fall and her move into the nursing home. Physically she was weak but it was only after she learned of Jeremy's death that she started to go downhill mentally. I had visited her two days after his death and she was distraught.

'I can't believe it,' she said over and over again.

It had only been a matter of days since finding out he had cancer in the first place. Now he was gone and she was in shock. Quite quickly after that, her mind came away from its moorings and in the last three months she wasn't always lucid. Thankfully, Jeremy's daughters were there for Nana, visiting her regularly and showing her the care and love she deserved. I tried, but I was struggling with my own grief and found it hard to be a comfort to her.

On the last day of October I went to see her. By then she had stopped eating and was barely conscious, her breath just a faint rasp.

'It's okay, Gladys,' I whispered as I held her cold, thin hands. The skin on her fingers was paper-thin, almost translucent. 'You can go now. You have nothing to fear. Go and see Jeremy and Fred again.'

Two days later, Gladys died.

'It's okay, she wasn't alone,' the nurse reassured me when she called to tell me the news. 'There were two of us with her, holding her hands.'

I was relieved to learn that she had had some human contact in her final moments.

'But it wasn't us,' I said to the nurse. 'Why did she go when we her family weren't there?'

'It's very common,' said the nurse. 'It's harder to leave when your loved ones are present. I think she had said all her goodbyes and felt ready to go.'

As I put the phone down, I had a strong feeling that just as Jeremy had looked after Gladys when she was alive, it was he who would have come to take her soul to the spirit world. He was the dutiful son both in life and death.

The arrangements for Gladys' funeral fell to Jeremy's three daughters and me, though it was Katie who took on the bulk of the work. We used the same funeral directors as the ones who conducted Jeremy's funeral just three months earlier. The body was taken to the chapel of rest and there we visited her to say our final goodbyes. I noticed how small and emaciated she had become in her final months. In death I could see no resemblance to the woman she had once been. It was so clear that this was just a body, a vessel to carry the spirit, and that Gladys' soul had long since fled. I thought about the sweet release that had, at last, freed her from her physical being, a being that in the last few years had become fragile and unreliable. In that moment, I felt a stab of envy. *She's with Jeremy.*

We held an intimate service at the crematorium on 11 November. I had chosen the date because it was when Gladys' parents had married and I liked the association. I was the executor of Gladys' will so I shouldered most of the responsibility of making sure her wishes were carried out. It made me realise how upended the natural order of things had become. She wasn't *my* mother. It should have been Jeremy doing this for her, not me! His mother should have died before him. None of it felt right.

Christmas approached. I dreaded it. I had always loved spending Christmas with Jeremy because he made it special for everyone. He was like a big kid, buying all the presents, making the Christmas cake weeks in advance and putting up fairy lights and baubles around the house. We'd stopped having a tree some years before because Tabasco kept pulling it down but aside from that, we always did Christmas in style. Gladys would come to stay with us from Christmas Eve until Boxing Day. On Christmas morning Jeremy would wake me with a card and a stocking filled with small gifts. He was always up early to get the food started and light the open fire in the lounge.

The festivities would kick off with a glass of bubbly and some pigs-in-blankets at around 9am. Then we'd open presents and enjoy a glass of sherry while Tabasco lapped up a bowl of milk as a treat. Jeremy would spend most of the morning beavering away in the kitchen and by lunchtime, the smells wafting out were incredible. It was a traditional Christmas in every sense: turkey, roast potatoes, trimmings, Jeremy's favourite brussels sprouts and parsnips, carrots for me, crackers and pudding followed by the Queen's Speech. Jeremy was the royalist in the house and a big fan of Her Majesty. We'd all help to clear away and then finally we'd fall asleep in front of a film. Boxing Day was for Jeremy's daughters who would arrive, arms loaded with presents. We'd spend a happy day together, munching on cold meats and stilton and playing traditional games like Articulate as well as a couple of rounds of Just Dance on the Wii.

It had been this way almost every year since we had become a couple and I loved it. Before I met Jeremy, I had never celebrated Christmas. The year before Jeremy died was the only year we hadn't spent it at our own home. Instead we were with friends. We had a lovely lunch and were grateful to be among friends but when we left, Jeremy confessed that he preferred making his own Christmas at home.

'Well, let's go back to doing it at home next year,' I had replied. The poignancy of those words filled me with regret.

The year of Jeremy's death Jenny, Katie and Amanda and their partners asked if they could come over and spend a couple of hours with me on Christmas Eve. Although it was lovely of them to come around, I found no solace in company. Without Jeremy there I felt that we were just going through the motions. But I wanted to give the girls what I hoped would be a meaningful present. Both Jenny and Katie would be getting married in 2017 and both would miss their Dad terribly on their respective wedding days. So, for each of them, I commissioned a blue glass pendant inlayed with Jeremy's ashes, as I had done with my own ring. On the back were inscribed the words 'Love You Jenny – Dad' and the same for Katie and Amanda. At the same time, I got a small red glass memorial paperweight with the words 'Jeremy – Forever in Samburu' for my sister to keep at her camp in Kenya. It felt good to know that the girls would have a part of Jeremy walking down the aisle with them and that he would also always be in Samburu.

Christmas Day itself felt like any other day to me - cold, lonely and empty, though I had a strong sense that Jeremy was watching over me. The Guildford Odeon never usually shows Bollywood films and yet, on that day, not only were they showing a Bollywood film, but one starring my favourite actor, Aamir Khan. *Dangal*, a true story about India's first female wrestling champions, was to be my route to escapism for a few hours that afternoon.

It felt odd driving into Guildford on Christmas Day; it was eerily deserted, with empty streets and shuttered shops. There can't have been more than ten people in the auditorium but I felt a certain camaraderie with my fellow Christmas refugees, washed up, as we were, on the shores of Bollywood. Here we were, all looking to escape, and we weren't disappointed. For three hours solid, we sat entranced, caught up in another world. We laughed, we cheered and we hummed along with the catchy songs. Immersed in the drama, I was about as far as I could possibly be from the memories of Christmases past and I sent a message of thanks up to Jeremy for sending Aamir Khan to me for those few hours! That night, I fell into bed, thankful that I had managed to get through the day relatively unscathed.

The rest of the holiday season wore on slowly. I struggled through the end of December, speaking to my sister occasionally, sifting through Just Jhoom! paperwork, tidying up my email inbox and sorting through Jeremy's photos. The New Year beckoned and I anticipated some relief that at least 2016 would soon be behind me. It had been a rotten year, the worst of my life. Neither Jeremy nor I had ever been keen on New Year's Eve parties; I tried one once and hated it. The big build up to midnight, people drinking too much and then standing round, singing Auld Lang Syne, which nobody knows the words for anyway… It was all too much for me. Instead we usually kept things quiet, just the two of us enjoying dinner at home, followed by watching the fireworks on TV. That year I didn't even wait for the fireworks. I went to bed early, impatient to start the new year.

Nearly 12 hours later, I still in bed, pinned down by the weight of my inescapable grief. I had woken early on 1 January 2017 expecting to feel different somehow, expecting to feel…what? That I had turned a corner? That today would not be the same as yesterday? That I could get up and feel okay, maybe not good, but okay? Yes, that's what I had expected. But the horrible truth dawned with the new day - nothing had changed. Everything was just as terrible as the last day of 2016. *It's just a date, after all. He's still not here, I'm still breathing. It's dark and cold outside. Why get out of bed?* I cast my mind forward to the year ahead and realised that a year of 'firsts' was about to hit me. The first Valentine's Day without him, Tabasco's birthday, our 'first date' anniversary in May, Father's Day, the anniversary of his death… On and on it would go. I screwed my eyes shut tight. *Oh God. This isn't living. I'm just lurching from one painful milestone to the next.*

I hibernated, I cleared out a lot of paperwork, sorted out my computer files, cleared the garage, ate a lot and watched hours and hours of TV. I couldn't even read any more because my mind wouldn't focus long enough to finish a page. Instead I did Sudoku, crosswords and Codebreaker. I binge-watched Pakistani soaps. My sleep cycle was all over the place – I would stay awake most of the night, fall asleep in the early hours, be woken by Tabasco at first light. The loneliness was unbearable. One day became two and then three and before I knew it, I hadn't seen or spoken to anyone in ten days. In early February I received a text message from one of my aunts in London.

I haven't heard from you for a while. Come over some time.

I looked at it for a while, confused, unable to process the meaning behind the words. I read it again. She hadn't heard from me? Come over some time? I was stunned by the apparent casualness of those two small sentences. They seemed so light, so breezy and offhand. Did she even mean to send this message to me, I wondered, or was it meant for another niece? Maybe the intended recipient hadn't lost their husband six months earlier and found it pretty easy to get out of bed in the mornings. Who was this person, I wondered, who had so thoughtlessly forgotten to contact their aunt? Who was it that could just jump in the car and drive two hours to north London for a chitchat without a second thought? I wanted to know because it certainly wasn't me.

Was something wrong with me? Should I have healed by now? Why was I suffering so much? I wanted to do this better. I wanted to 'get over' losing my husband but I couldn't. Every hour was filled with pain, every normal chore seemed like a Herculean task. *What's wrong with me?*

I did what I could – I found strategies to help alleviate the constant sense of loss, like putting the wheelie bins out on a Sunday morning rather than in the evening. It sounds like a small thing but it helped. Putting the bins out on a Sunday evening had been Jeremy's job. For nearly 20 years I hadn't touched them, so taking them out every Sunday evening was just another wretched reminder of his absence. So, instead, I did the bins in the bright light of a Sunday morning. A small thing, and my neighbours probably thought I was mad, but it helped. And after I found a small white feather on top of the wheelie bin one Sunday morning, I took it as a sign that Jeremy was telling me that I was doing okay.

The winter seemed to drag on; the dark days and nights seemed endless. Each time I closed my eyes to sleep I would be taken back to the hospital bed, to the last breath Jeremy took, the moment that the life drained out of his body. I would avoid my bed until exhaustion finally took over and when it did my sleep would be punctuated by nightmares and night sweats. I would jolt awake, sweaty, mouth dry, angry that another day had dawned for me, where each waking moment would be filled with an unbearable loneliness and isolation. I was furious at being forced to live in the world without him.

The one thing that continued to sustain me, that was my lifeline, was my Just Jhoom! classes. Sometimes when I was teaching I would get a strange sense that I was being watched. That Jeremy was in the studio encouraging me to carry on doing what I loved most. So with each dance I did, I imagined that I was dancing for him.

I didn't teach mindfulness anymore. I couldn't. I couldn't even meditate on my own. I would try. Sitting in the conservatory I would focus on my breathing and try to do a body scan where you concentrate on one part of your body at a time, starting at the top with your head. But within a minute or so, I'd be lying on the floor, weeping. I had no calmness in my heart, no silence between my thoughts – all I had was this bottomless well of grief. So, instead of meditating I would sit on the conservatory sofa looking out at Jeremy's beloved garden and pond and the doves that visited the bird feeder. Over time, a strange peace began to descend on me as I began to feel Jeremy's spirit present around me. But these moments were fleeting and their impermanence distressing.

The doves in the garden were no longer enough. I longed to feel him near me all the time, I longed for a real connection.

Chapter 21 – The Afterlife

*"Just as a little bird cracks open the shell and flies out,
we fly out of this shell, the shell of the body. We call that death, but
strictly speaking, death is nothing but a change of form."*
—Swami Satchidananda[20]

*Y*ou're going through waves of grief. You're stricken. He's saying that he has never seen you...'

Jamie paused and closed her eyes, listening to a voice that only she could hear.

'...he's never seen you fall to the ground before. He says these waves of grief paralyse you. That you have always been such a strong woman, but that you've forgotten how to be strong now.

'He wants you to know that he feels what you feel and that when you think of him, he senses what you are thinking. He believes that you are connected. Intertwined. He's clamping his hands together now. He says you belong together.' Jamie opened her eyes.

'Why did he leave me then? Why did he leave so early?'

It was not the first time I had consulted a medium. In fact, it was my fourth reading after Jeremy's death. I had been to three others before I found Jamie Butler and I had consulted them all for the same reason: to feel a connection with the spirit world that I could not achieve on my own. I had contacted my first medium within a few weeks of Jeremy's death but I had been too numb to take in what she was saying. Now, months later, I was in a more receptive state of mind.

I hadn't gone about it in a haphazard way; I had spent some time researching the subject online and found that Jamie Butler was a highly recommended psychic. She had published a good body of work on the internet, including blogs, podcasts and videos and had even written a book about her life. Her work 'translating' for the spirit-world appeared well-established and I desperately hoped that she could help me. I had always believed in the afterlife but after Jeremy died I began looking more closely into what may lie beyond the realm of the physical world. I had so many questions: Where was he? Why did he have to leave when he did? When would we be reunited?

The questions burned holes inside me and I needed to find someone who could help me answer them. Strangely, I had taken a Theosophy course the year before Jeremy died and had read a great deal on the nature of the afterlife. Theosophy, derived from the two Greek words *theos* (god, deity) and *sophia* (wisdom) is the study or knowledge of ancient wisdom, looking at the nature of divinity and the meaning of the universe. It is not a religion or a dogma, more a set of philosophies which encompass ideas about the spiritual world, the afterlife and the nature of being. These concepts are not new – many derive from ancient texts – and a belief in the afterlife is one shared by Hindus, Buddhists, Muslims and Christians. In particular, Hindus and Buddhists believe in reincarnation, the idea that you don't just have one life but many lives before you are united with the Higher Being.

The time between these lives is known as the afterlife. Even though I don't ascribe to a particular religion, the concept of the afterlife resonates with my own beliefs. I feel that is why, when you meet someone for the first time and they seem familiar, it is because you have shared a past life experience with them. Similarly, when you visit a place you've never been and have a sense of déjà vu. I believe I have known Cheeku in a previous life, which is why, when we first met in Switzerland, we had an instant dislike for one another before becoming firm friends. We knew each other! Connections like this are known as *soul groups*. Every person has a soul group of their own, which overlaps with others' soul groups. My soul group includes Jeremy, Cheeku and my sister, Shivani. All of us met before this life and we are likely to share more lives to come. And, although I miss Jeremy's physical presence every single day, I know that he and I will see each other again when I die and I also know that we will have many more lives on this earth together.

Kyunki, hum phir zaroor milenge.

Because, we will definitely meet again.

The more I studied Theosophy, the more I sensed that I already knew this stuff – that the knowledge was innate. Through meditation, I was able to feel a real connection to my spiritual self, to my energy. I believe that the spiritual world exists alongside our physical world but most of us cannot access it. Meditation can help us to feel the vibrations of our spiritual being but there are a lucky few, like mediums, who can actually interact with that world. Only on rare occasions do the rest of us get a glimpse of it, a small lifting of the curtain.

After a period of time in the afterlife, you are reincarnated - a soul enters a physical body and comes *through the veil*, at which point all past lives are forgotten. Linked to reincarnation is the law of karma which effectively governs all creation. In this present life we sow the seeds of our next personality in incarnation. Through the actions of karma and reincarnation, your soul learns new lessons in order to reach a higher, more enlightened state and in order to be closer to the Higher Being until you are ready to become One. Very enlightened individuals like the Dalai Lama are closer to this state than ordinary beings like me.

I asked Jamie about my *exit points*. I had read about these in many books about the afterlife. They are opportunities to cross over to the spirit world, points at which you leave the physical world and enter the afterlife. Exit points, effectively, are moments of death - or at least a chance of death. As I understand it, everyone has several exit points in their life and I wanted to know when my next exit point would be presented to me. I wanted to know when I would die, when I could be reunited with Jeremy. Jamie said that Jeremy refused to tell me so I asked her to consult another spirit guide, who said my next exit point would come in around seven years' time. *Seven years?* It seemed like a lifetime.

'I don't see you taking it,' Jamie said. 'Something will completely change between now and then. What is it? What changes?' She paused. 'You're the type of person who laughs all the time, aren't you?'

'I used to,' I replied, sadly.

'I see you getting back to that. Because when I see you in eight, nine years' time, you're laughing, in every image I see. Everything has changed between here and there. I mean, everything: location, home, work, friends. You're giggling. And yet, this whole connection with your husband is absolutely still prominent.'

This wasn't what I wanted to hear – seven years was so very long - but at least I had an answer. I could never kill myself, I knew that now, but this was not the same as suicide. An exit point could be caused by an accident, ill health - any number of things outside one's control. It wasn't necessarily a conscious choice to take that exit, but a decision taken by your spiritual, or higher, self. I had been told by another medium that suicide could prove cumbersome for my spirit and that it was important for me to learn the lessons of grief and bereavement in this lifetime.

Although the idea of dying had been one of my greatest comforts in the last few months, I had come to realise that suicide was not the path I would take. But I also don't agree that suicide is wrong or selfish. People can be very harsh about those who commit suicide – perhaps because they can't see that it is the ultimate act of desperation. Imagine being in such pain that death, oblivion, is preferable to life. As a society, we could be more understanding of the fact that, while there is an intolerable level of pain and indignity that human beings can suffer physically, so there can also be intolerable levels of mental anguish.

It is said that you cannot die from a broken heart, but I refute this – there are many stories of people who have been physically afflicted after suffering a terrible loss. My own grief caused me plenty of physical pain: my finger-tips and my jaw ached, my teeth were sensitive, I had pains in my breast, back, legs and head. But in spite of this pain, in spite of my grief, I began to understand that I would not end my life. One of the reasons was almost too strange to grasp.

According to one medium, Jeremy and I are *twin flames*: two spirits occupying the same soul. Before we were reincarnated into this life, our higher selves entered into an agreement that would help our souls to grow through lessons learnt in this lifetime. Jeremy's soul had to go through the pain of divorce and ill-health, while I would experience family estrangement and bereavement. If I took my own life, I would be breaking with that agreement, the consequences of which would be rebirth and the necessity of learning the same lessons all over again.

The idea of twin flames resonated strongly with me. My unbearable sense of loss suddenly made more sense than ever before. If Jeremy and I were one soul, then losing him really did mean that half of me was missing: mentally, spiritually and emotionally. No wonder I felt broken, incomplete. The mediums I saw in the darkest days of my grief helped me to understand the nature of our connection to one another and it was a great comfort. They all gave me good advice on how to overcome the paralysing sense of loss which had laid me so low. They recommended I write down my feelings, that I try lucid dreaming to reconnect with Jeremy, that I stay connected to nature and also continue with my teaching. All of them encouraged me to reach out to the friends who were offering their support and love.

I realise that some people reading this book may be sceptical of mediums and I won't deny that there are plenty of charlatans out there. But I consulted very carefully and I found their insights helpful. I believe that I received as much help through these readings as I did through my bereavement counselling. The reason many choose the path of suicide is that they are unable to see into the future. More pain? Happiness? Having even the slightest sense of what one's future may hold can offer a great deal of much-needed hope. If I learned one thing from consulting mediums it was that there was more to my future than pain. Perhaps all this pain was leading me to a higher purpose in this lifetime. Who knows how much that tiny nugget of information changed my attitude about taking my own life? They gave me back the one thing I had lost along the way – hope. Hope of a future beyond suffering.

They also helped me to see, without doubt, that Jeremy was not gone. I no longer needed to grasp subtle signs, like the white feathers or the doves in the garden, I finally knew that he was simply on another plane and he would wait for me there until my time came to join him. I imagined how we would be reunited as spirits… I saw him coming to meet me, in the same way he would come to meet me after all those long train journeys I took up and down the country. He would be waiting, just beyond the barrier, with a smile and hug. Then he would take my hand to lead me into the afterlife, where I would be able to rest and replenish my soul in readiness for my next incarnation to continue with my soul's journey. I understood that this cycle of death and rebirth would continue, with Jeremy as my twin flame, until we reached an enlightened state together, enough to be at one with the Higher Being.

Today, I don't fear death because I believe death is not the end; it is merely part of my soul's journey. And so, like with everything I do in life, I make preparations for my journey. When my time comes, my assistant, Peta, knows exactly where to find all my instructions, as well the items I have chosen to be included in my coffin. It may seem odd, but I have written the order of service and specified all the details. I am to be cremated in my red wedding outfit. There is a framed photo that Jeremy took of me dancing, which I want placed on my coffin. I am to be buried with a collection of items that represent important parts of my journey in this life: my dancing foot bells, bangles I wore on our wedding day, a picture of Jeremy, a packet of *bindis*, my favourite book, *A Suitable Boy* by Vikram Seth, as well as representations of Ganesha, Krishna and the symbol, Om.

Included will also be an excerpt from an article by Douglas Preston, entitled *I Took The Dalai Lama To A Ski Resort And He Told Me The Meaning Of Life.*[21] When a young waitress asks the Dalai Lama what the meaning of life is, 'The Dalai Lama answered immediately. "The meaning of life is *happiness*." He raised his finger, leaning forward, focusing on her as if she were the only person in the world. "Hard question is not, 'What is meaning of life?' That is easy question to answer! No, hard question is what *make* happiness. Money? Big house? Accomplishment? Friends? Or..." He paused. "Compassion and good heart? This is question all human beings must try to answer: *What make true happiness*?" He gave this last question a peculiar emphasis and then fell silent, gazing at her with a smile.'

Before losing Jeremy, I thought I had found the answer to this question but now I was searching all over again. If my future contained happiness and laughter then it was no good just sitting around, waiting for death to claim me.

I had to go out and find happiness again in this lifetime.

Chapter 22 – Walking in the Dark

"Not good news I'm afraid. Been given only a short time to go –
days, maybe weeks at most. Thank you for your lovely friendship,
which I have really cherished and the fun and laughter it has brought.
Take care and keep on doing what you
do so well – which is everything.
Enjoy your life to the full – it is too short not to.
Best wishes, Jeremy."
—Jeremy's text messages to friends
and colleagues on the day he died

*I*t was an article in the Guardian that started me thinking about the idea of *legacy*. The article, 'Top Five Regrets of the Dying', was based on a book written by a palliative nurse, Bronnie Ware. She had spent years caring for people in their final hours and they had shared their thoughts with her as they realised the end was close. Many felt they had worked too hard, not spent enough time with their loved ones or hadn't lived a life true to themselves. I thought about the regrets I would have on my deathbed. And I thought about what I would leave behind in this world. Jeremy's legacy was his children and the memories he had created by touching so many people's lives. But, as we had never had children, I wondered what would represent the two of us. What will live on, after my death? We are on earth for such a short time and I believe that how we are remembered is so important. *Did we love well? Did we live well? Did we matter?*

It was then that I recalled a time Jeremy and I had visited a secondary school in Samburu with my sister. She had shown us the 'computer lab' - a tiny hut containing one huge, old-fashioned computer that looked like a relic from the 1980s. It seemed ancient to our eyes but, to the schoolchildren, it was a wonder of modernity.

'We must find a way to support this school,' Jeremy said to me at the time.

And yet neither of us had done anything about it. Until now.

'Shivani, I want to set up a charity in Jeremy's name, to send children to secondary school in Samburu,' I told my sister when we next spoke. 'I'd like to release some money from Jeremy's estate to start the fund and then I will raise money to keep it going.'

'Wow, *Didi*, that's amazing,' Shivani replied enthusiastically. 'You know, we already have a scholarship programme with the Ewaso Lions project. We are currently supporting eight children. Why don't we set up the fund under the Ewaso Lions umbrella and integrate the current scholarships students into it?'

It was a brilliant idea. I started to research the education system in Kenya to work out how we could put the money to the best use and I spoke to the team at Ewaso Lions, who ran the scholarship programme. Together we worked out the details and in January 2017, six months after his death, we launched the Jeremy Lucas Education Fund.

Planning and setting up the fund was one of the first turning points for me in my grief. I was trying to make sense of losing Jeremy and focusing on giving to others in a charitable and compassionate way was my first step on the road to healing. Jeremy had loved Kenya and he especially loved Samburu – the land, the people, the wildlife. Just as he had taken Samburu to his heart, the Samburu people had taken him to their hearts. I strongly believed that Jeremy would have approved of a fund set up in his name – giving the Samburu children a chance to grow, learn, achieve, succeed and be independent. It was a legacy that I know would have made him proud.

We decided our strapline for the Fund would be *'Educating youth. Empowering communities. Encouraging conservation'*, highlighting our three-tier approach to the fund. We wanted to give an education to children from the Samburu area who did not have the means to pay, primarily for secondary education, but also for tertiary education - and in exceptional circumstances for private primary education. We also wanted to offer the children career advice at the end of their education and to help create an understanding of how the opportunities of a good education could be combined with positive action to benefit their own communities.

We implemented a system whereby the children being sponsored by the Fund would also be required to contribute to the Ewaso Lions project and their own communities, through internships and, where possible, future employment in the area. Underpinning everything we did was the philosophy of encouraging conservation. We wanted to inspire the children educated with money from the Fund to become the future guardians of the wildlife in Samburu – whether that be actively working in conservation or raising awareness and funds for conservation by other means, through their working lives.

With Shivani's team on the ground, we chose the first three children to join the programme and start the new academic year that January. Their names were Angeline, Veronica and Nicholas and they were recommended to us by their respective schools. The headteachers at their schools said they were bright and hard-working but didn't have the funds to go to secondary school. Fourteen-year-old Angeline's father had passed away the week before she was due to take her end of year primary school exams. Despite this terrible trauma she had come second in her class but her mother, who sold vegetables on the street, was too poor to send her to secondary school. So, Angeline, who dreamed of one day becoming a doctor, had chosen to repeat her final year of primary school in the hope of coming first the following year, which would earn her a scholarship to the secondary school. Her dedication and commitment, in the face of extreme hardship, meant that she was the ideal candidate for the Fund. A week after her interview, we secured a place for her in secondary school.

Veronica, also 14, was an orphan with eight siblings. Her eldest sister Monica could not afford to send Veronica to secondary school and suggested that perhaps it was time she found a job and contributed to the household expenses. Having achieved very high marks in her final primary school exams, this was very difficult for Veronica to accept and she suffered from depression. Her dreams of becoming a doctor began to fade away. At her interview she came across as very bright and determined, but hugely humble. She wanted to go to secondary school more than anything and would work hard to achieve good grades. She was perfect to join the programme and went, with Angeline, to the same secondary school.

Our third choice was Nicholas. At first, I had wanted the fund to be primarily for girls, because I knew that Jeremy would want us to support girls. He had always been surrounded by strong women including me, my sister and his mother. But after doing some research, I found that many similar organizations in Kenya were dedicated to helping girls and, as a consequence, many boys were struggling. After meeting Nicholas, who was 14, the team conducting the interviews found him to be a happy, determined young man who given the chance would work hard to make something of his life. Nicholas' father had been killed in 2015 during tribal clashes between the Samburu and another tribe, the Turkana. He was being brought up by his mother who could barely make ends meet. His aspirations to be a tour guide and work in Samburu and eventually contribute to his family and the local community were admirable and we knew that he deserved to be given funding for secondary school.

It was an almost impossible decision to choose just three children out of the dozens of applications I had been sent by the team in Samburu and the hundreds of children across the region who would undoubtedly have benefited from our support. But in those early days it was all we could afford to fund these three new children and the eight children already under the Ewaso Lions Scholarship programme. It costs £4,000 to fund a child through secondary school for four years in Kenya. This includes food, transport, uniform, books and tuition, as a well as personal items like toiletries and a mattress to sleep on at their boarding schools. The new Jeremy Lucas Education Fund was still just a fledgling venture, but I was anxious to help as many children as I could, as quickly as I could. I began to feel, for the first time since Jeremy died, a sense of purpose again.

At the same time, we merged the JLEF and Shivani's Ewaso Lion scholarship scheme so that there were eight children, ranging from age 12 to 19, spread across four secondary year groups, as well as one boy in primary school, our first girl to go to college and first boy about to start university.

As well as launching the fund we hired a part-time mentor to oversee the programme and to stay in touch with the three new children, as well as those kids funded through the original scholarship programme. We worked out that we had enough funds to maintain the project through its second year, but in order to put more children through secondary education after that, I had to start fundraising. It was then that an opportunity presented itself.

My friend, Sian Tyrrell, a portrait photographer and one of my Jhoomers, was planning an exhibition on 'faces' at the Cranleigh Arts Centre. Several months before his death, she had approached Jeremy to see if he wanted to take part, but when he became too ill we put it off. Now Sian asked if I wanted to display some of the photographs of animal faces that Jeremy had taken on his various trips to Kenya. The exhibition would also include portraits of local people, as well as sculptural papier mâché heads on the theme of family history. I readily agreed to having Jeremy's work exhibited; it would be a fitting tribute to a man who had so loved wildlife photography and the idea that his work would be helping to support the fund I had established in his name made me feel like we were coming full circle.

I decided to order one huge canvas of a particularly powerful image Jeremy had taken of two lionesses as well as four smaller images: a shy leopard hiding in a patch of sunlit shrub, a close-up of an elephant with its expressively-creased face and long eyelashes, two lions with their heads poking out from behind a bush and, one of Jeremy's favourite photos, a couple of Grevy's zebra looking straight into the camera. The exhibition was a huge success and I received so many positive comments about the photographs. We also sold small greeting cards with Jeremy's photos on the front and they were so popular I had to reprint them so I had enough to last the duration of the exhibition.

Over the following weeks, I began blogging about Jeremy's Fund on my Just Jhoom! website, posting messages on Facebook and generally starting to raise awareness in the press. Together with Shivani and my Jhoomers we managed to spread the fundraising message far and wide. Gradually, donations started to trickle in – a few hundred pounds at first and then more. After just a few months, and with sales generated from the exhibition, we had raised enough to put another two children through secondary education.

When the first report cards came in March, at the end of the first term, for Angeline, Veronica and Nicholas, I felt something that I hadn't experienced in a very long time: happiness. It took me by surprise, but reading that Veronica was getting A grades in chemistry and biology, Nicholas had achieved a mean grade of B in all his subjects and Angeline was consistent in her academic achievements, getting all B and C grades, put a huge grin on my face. It wasn't that I sought top grades from these children, it was more that they were making the most of this opportunity to learn. Good grades were simply the icing on the cake and made me even more sure that the Fund was a good and worthwhile endeavour – something that would change these children's lives.

We also came up with an idea that, during the school holidays in April, we would offer the children courses in IT, health and hygiene, household finance, budgeting and family planning. Every student would also be required to take part in a Lion Kids Camps that Ewaso Lions ran to educate and inform children about conservation. And finally, in December we would hold an Awards Day to acknowledge the hard work done by children during the year and to thank the parents for their support.

An unexpected outcome of setting up JLEF was the fact that it began to give me some of my confidence back. I had always been a very confident person with a strong sense of self. Jeremy's death had stripped me of all of that. But, with the initial success and hope that JLEF embodied, I began to feel that not only was I creating a legacy that was both mine and Jeremy's, but I was also beginning to find some inner peace and my own self-worth back. It was the first time that I really felt that my healing was beginning in earnest.

On 18 May that year it would have been mine and Jeremy's 20th anniversary. In spite of how far I had come through working on JLEF, it was a milestone that I could not face alone, in our house. So, I took myself away to Morocco for a week. Once again, I chose to visit a place that we had never been to together. And once again, as I took down my case from the loft and packed alone, my mind was flooded with memories of past holidays together. But this time I didn't cry when I got in the taxi, or in the airport, or even on the plane. The shock of going away alone seemed to have disappeared; this time, I could just about tolerate the dull ache of loneliness without succumbing to tears. And when I arrived at my hotel in the foothills of the majestic Atlas Mountains, just outside Marrakech, I felt rejuvenated more than I felt Jeremy's absence.

I kept to myself, mostly - walking around the hotel gardens, reading in the shade of palm trees, swimming in the pool. I even braved a *hammam* treatment, then wished Jeremy had been there to tell about the experience. It was just the kind of story we would have laughed about.

On the day of our anniversary, I wrote him a card and then had dinner at a Moroccan restaurant to celebrate the occasion. It was an amazing place and the spices were out of this world, so reminiscent of Indian cooking, and the décor and vibrancy of the restaurant was irresistible. Two musicians played drums and sang traditional songs, as I tucked into my vegetable tagine. I thought how much Jeremy would have liked this place. It was all so bittersweet. We had always wanted to visit Morocco together and part of me was so sad that we couldn't share the experience. Amazingly, for such a talented photographer, Jeremy was semi-colour blind. He struggled to distinguish between red, brown and green and yet he was drawn to colourful places. Morocco was a riot of exotic colours, smells and tastes. He would have loved it.

I cried that night, of course, but less than I did on the night of his birthday. The next day I swam and walked again; I even managed to meditate for a few minutes and, by the end of the week, I felt a glimmer of hope about my future. Maybe I could get through this. Maybe I was strong enough.

I wasn't exactly walking in the dark, as I hoped I might be by now, but perhaps, I had learned to crawl.

Chapter 23 – Always With You

"If ever there's a tomorrow when we're not together…
there's something you must remember…
You are braver than you believe, and stronger than you seem,
and smarter than you think…
But the most important thing is, even if we're apart…
I'll always be with you."
— Christopher Robin
(in *Pooh's Grand Adventure* by Crocker Carter)[22]

The warm July wind swirled around me as I stood on the verdant land. Majestic Mount Kenya towered in the distance and all around me were the sounds of the birds singing in the acacia trees and the gentle breeze blowing through the bushes. It had been exactly a year since Jeremy's death and I had returned to our land in Nanyuki to scatter his ashes.

Beside me were my parents, Shivani, five Samburu warriors and Ali and Tony, whose house had first inspired us to buy the land. They had all come to pay their respects. My parents had insisted on making the long drive up from Nairobi as they wanted to be part of this important day. The years of estrangement that we had had were now well behind us, and although it had come late, they had fully accepted that Jeremy and I had indeed been meant for one another. This place had represented our future happiness, it had given us so much hope and optimism at a time when we both needed it and now I'd brought Jeremy back here to fulfil a promise I had made to him on his death bed – that I would bring some of his ashes back to the land he loved so much.

'Thank you all for coming to say goodbye to Jeremy,' I said, as I looked gratefully at the little group around me. 'He loved this place. He loved Nanyuki and we were so excited to come and live here. If each of you would like to say something then please do.'

And they did. Everyone had a kind word to say about Jeremy; everyone shared a precious memory they had of him and everyone wrote him a small note. I scattered some of Jeremy's ashes around the lush grassy plot and buried the rest in the ground with our notes. Then we planted a small acacia tree on the spot. As the roots of the tree took hold in the ground and the little tree grew, I knew that Jeremy would always be there, part of the land he so loved.

It was a small but symbolic gesture - a way to honour Jeremy and his last wishes. He had told me before he died that I was free to do what I wanted with his ashes as long as some were scattered on our land in Nanyuki and some in the Maldives. I hadn't got around to the Maldives yet, but at least I'd honoured his first wish. When I returned home I would also scatter some ashes on the anniversary of his funeral to mirror the final journey he took: a small cupful around the garden, then at the church where his service was, in the crematorium gardens where his mum and dad were, at the golf club near the small starter hut they had built in his memory and finally at his favourite fishing lake close to the house. But here in Kenya, in a strange way, I felt like I was bringing him home. This was, after all, the land he loved so much and one that I knew I would return to live on one day in the future.

After the ceremony on the land in Nanyuki and a quiet lunch held at Le Rustique, a small local family-run restaurant, I said goodbye to my parents, who had to return to Nairobi, while I set about meeting a local surveyor and a log-cabin builder. Shivani and I had been talking for a while about constructing a small house on one of the plots so that she could stay there on her many work-related visits to Nanyuki. But, more importantly, I wanted to honour another of Jeremy's wishes that he had asked of me on his deathbed.

'Go out to Nanyuki and build our dream home,' he had said to me in the final days before he died.

I couldn't even countenance it until now. The idea of trying to build a house on my own was too daunting and the thought of it only made me feel more alone. But the more involved I became in the Fund and the children's lives, the more I longed to be in Kenya. Jeremy's words kept going around and around in my head and I started to wonder what was actually keeping me in England. My connection to it had always been defined by what I called "the three 'J's": Jeremy, JumJums and Just Jhoom! Jeremy was gone, Just Jhoom! was now online and Tabasco - JumJums - had settled into old age. It wouldn't be long before he, too, left me and then what? Our land in Nanyuki was still there, waiting for me, as were the house plans that I had long since abandoned. *Was I mad to think it or could I really build our dream home on my own?*

I didn't know when I was going to move back to Kenya but I knew that it was going to happen at some point. Until I made the permanent move, I decided to erect a small prefabricated wooden cabin on the first parcel of land and when I eventually moved for good I would live there, while managing the construction of 'our' bungalow on the second. There was much preparation to be done to prepare the land, even for just the small wooden cabin, and after the memorial for Jeremy I set about organising things in earnest.

Part of my trip to Kenya in July also involved meeting Peter, the JLEF mentor and co-ordinator. We spent a whole day discussing the children and future plans for the fund. I knew that when I got back to the UK I would have a lot of work to do to put everything in place. Unfortunately, I didn't have time to go to Samburu to meet all the children, but I promised to return in December to meet them and celebrate our inaugural JLEF Awards Day. I was beginning to feel that JLEF was perhaps where my future lay– it was the only thing that made me happy and I knew I could also put my teaching skills to good use on the ground, running holiday workshops, as well as computer and financial management courses for the older children once they had graduated.

After my two-week trip to Kenya, I finally felt strong enough to look at the pictures I had taken of Jeremy in the weeks before he died. It struck me, now, how thin he looked, how strained his smile was - I could see that he was grimacing through the pain. *Why hadn't I noticed at the time?* I wondered. *How could I have been so blind?* I never saw Jeremy's illness, only those beautiful eyes that I had fallen in love with 19 years earlier. Even in the depths of his illness, when the steroids made his face swell or his hair turned white, he was just the same to me as he always had been – gorgeous. I shook my head in amazement and felt a flash of sadness that perhaps I hadn't been a supportive enough at the end because my own fear of losing him meant that I couldn't see he was dying. Cancer is such a cruel disease. In the end it takes everything from you until all you have left is hope. Blind, crazy hope. Then even that is taken from you.

Looking at the photographs made me aware, suddenly, of how far I had come. Six months ago, I would never have been able to look at his photographs, let alone imagine making plans for my future without him. Grief is a merciless master. It holds you in a vice like grip, causing unspeakable pain. In time, as the well-meaning but meaningless saying goes, the grip begins to loosen its hold and the pain gradually fades to a dull ache. But, that ache is persistent – it never truly goes away. You just learn to live with it or, as my friend said, you learn to walk in the dark.

'Has it really been a year already!' my friends exclaimed when I told them of the anniversary of Jeremy's death. 'It has gone so quickly!'

No, it hadn't. Not for me. The last year had stretched out like a lifetime. While everyone had been getting on with their lives, mine had stood still. People talk about a 'dark night of the soul' - that period of grief and misery when you wonder why you are living and whether death would be less painful. That 'night' could last for a few hours, a few days or a few months. My night lasted for a year.

But I had survived that year without Jeremy and I realised that perhaps I was stronger than I once thought. I wanted to build on this glimmer of hope and independence that I was beginning to feel. It was as if a light had suddenly been switched on or a veil lifted and one of the effects of this was that I started to notice little things that I could work on, fix, around the house: holes in the wall or pictures that needed mounting. These were the sorts of jobs Jeremy would do, but without him here, they simply didn't get done and I didn't want to ask friends to step in. The truth was, I found it difficult to ask for help. It was always Jeremy I turned to for support - physically, financially emotionally - in all ways, I leaned on him. But now I realised that I needed – and wanted – to re-discover my independence and, even though it was a tiny step, being able to fix things around the house held a strange significance for me. I also wanted to make Jeremy proud. I knew he was looking over me and I wanted to show him that I was coping and looking after the house and garden that we had both been so proud of.

That August I booked myself on a week-long DIY course to fill in some vital gaps in my knowledge and to fill in those damn holes in the wall! I learned how to use a hammer, something I had never done before, how to hang pictures, repair holes in walls and wire plugs. I learned how to use a drill and how to tile a bathroom. I was so excited when I found Jeremy's drill in the garage and practiced using it with all the different drill bits. Each day I became more confident in my abilities and, because I was the only person on the course, I was able to ask more detailed questions about house-building to prepare me for my future endeavours in Nanyuki. If Jeremy were alive it would be him checking on the surveys and foundations, while I would be picking out cushion covers and curtains, but now I revelled in the simple pleasure of doing these things myself. In addition to learning how to fill holes, I also grappled with the basics of laying house foundations, rainwater harvesting, plumbing, solar panels and septic tanks.

Spurred on by my newfound confidence I also enrolled on a gardening course, where I learned how to plant and store bulbs, about winter gardening and lawn maintenance. Gardening had always been Jeremy's passion and he had created the most beautiful garden at home, coloured with cosmos, marigolds, begonias, geraniums and dahlias, to name just a few. He had even single-handedly built the pond and stocked it with a dozen fish, which had reproduced and now numbered at least a hundred. The lawn was his great obsession! He wanted it to look like Wimbledon. I had often watched him in summers gone by clipping long stray grass strands with a pair of scissors. Discovering the joys of gardening made me feel closer to Jeremy.

I also attended a short Krav Maga self-defense course – an Israeli defense system that works on using natural and instinctive movements when one is faced with danger. If I was going to be on my own I needed to make sure I could look after myself. Some people come into your life for a reason. You may meet them only once and never see them again but the impact they have made remains with you. The Krav Maga course leaders were like that for me. They gave me my confidence back. I no longer felt helpless, but empowered, with an unquenchable appetite to learn new skills and try new experiences: car maintenance, off-road driving, scuba-diving and something I had wanted to do for as long as I could remember – learn to ride a motorcycle.

Around the same time I also lost touch with Jeremy's daughters. Without him we had lost our connection. I truly believe that relationships can be nurtured and can grow but they can also wither and die. Just because you know someone for a long time it does not mean they have to be a part of your life forever. If a relationship has run its course, then let it go gracefully. Do not fight to keep it going if neither party is going to get anything out of it. The relationships that are meant to be will be always with you – if not physically then definitely spiritually.

I started writing this book as I entered my second year of mourning. I wanted to pay tribute to Jeremy, to express what he meant to me and to show exactly what kind of a man he was. Though hard at times, it has been a deeply cathartic experience, allowing me both the pleasure of reliving the years we shared and the ability to come to terms with the changes in my life since he passed away. Slowly, as a result, something in me shifted. The haunting image of Jeremy on his deathbed faded, the shattering grief softened and at last I could feel his presence everywhere around me. But, perhaps more importantly I realised for the first time that I was no longer living in fear. The thing I had feared most in life – losing Jeremy – had happened. Nothing else could be as bad.

After many months in the dark, I can finally see a future for myself, a future filled with hope and optimism – one I never imagined would be possible. I want to live again. I want to laugh again. And yes, perhaps one day, I might even want to fall in love again.

As I sit here in the conservatory overlooking our garden, my garden, I can feel Jeremy is here with me. Our journey together is not over – it has barely begun. One day, when it is my time to join him, he will come to meet me. I can see him now walking towards me, arms out, a wide smile lighting up his face…

But not yet. Not just yet.

Right now, I have a life to live. I think about him watching me now - wielding his drill, putting up pictures and buying slug pellets for the garden.

Slug pellets?! I hear him saying. *Wonders will never cease.*

He is surprised, yes, but also proud.

And that makes me smile.

Epilogue

"Yeh toh zaroori nahin hai ke zindagi lambhi honi chaiye.
Yeh zaroori hai ke zindagi badi honi chaiye."

"It is not important that the life we live is long.
It is important that the life we live is big."
—Shalini Bhalla

The first of the families began arriving just after 8am. They had been collected by the Ewaso Lions bus from their homes up to two hours' drive away and brought to my sister's camp in Samburu. Seeing them all arrive, I felt excited and a little apprehensive too – today I would be meeting all the children who had been sponsored by the Jeremy Lucas Education Fund for the first time and I so wanted it to go well. The day before I had sat down with the mentor Peter Lenasalia to go through a list of all the children, eleven in total now, in order to write a little speech for each.

It was 16 December 2017, our inaugural Awards Day, and an amazing milestone for our fledgling programme. We had brought the children and their parents together to explain the ethos behind the fund, to talk a little about the man who had inspired it and to celebrate and reward the children for their hard work throughout the year. But it was also more than that – today, the families and our organization would be joining together to create a new community.

As I made my way across the camp to the mess tent where everyone was gathered, I felt a light fluttering in my heart – it was packed with people. I looked over at the children – yes, I recognized their faces from their pictures. There were Nicholas and Angeline and over there, Junior and Solomon. Sitting next to their families, they looked nervous and shy. At the front, seated as guests of honour, were my parents and Shivani. The sight of my family filled my heart with happiness, as I realised how far we had come from the heartbreaking years of estrangement. I took my seat next to Shivani and smiled at my parents.

I was pleased that Jeneria had agreed to make the initial presentation. It allowed me to collect my thoughts. He explained about the conservation work at Ewaso Lions before going on to describe Jeremy, with whom he had been good friends.

He was a good, kind man,' Jeneria said, his voice cracking a little. 'And he was my friend. I called him *Apaya* – as to me he was a respected elder and part of our Samburu family.'

Jeneria then showed the children and their parents some of Jeremy's wonderful photographs of Kenya, before holding up a picture of Jeremy himself. In the photograph, he was smiling with delight as he held his camera ready to take photos of the elephants in the background. My heart skipped a few beats. It was wonderful to hear Jeremy's name and to hear him being spoken about with such high regard and affection. After Peter had spoken about the Fund and how we planned to support the children, not just financially, but also by providing a structured way into a future career, it was my turn to say a few words, which Peter translated into Samburu.

'Thank you for coming here today,' I began, my voice quivering with emotion.

'The reason we're all here is very bittersweet for me because I've lost somebody I loved very much. But he has allowed us to do something very special. For me personally, I believe education is really important.'

I gestured towards my parents.

'My parents – who are with us today as guests of honour - gave my sister and me a very good education. We were lucky because we had the opportunity not just to learn at secondary level but also at university. And because of that education my sister – who is just one person - has made such a difference to the whole Samburu community here. Not just in protecting and growing the lion population, but also in the lives of the warriors and, the *Mama Simba* (Mother of Lions). I had an education which allowed me to set up a business which helps others. My education enabled me to set up this fund. So, you see, education isn't just about yourself and earning money for your family. It is also about improving your community; it's about doing good things for society as a whole.

'Children, you have a fantastic opportunity and I urge you to work hard and make the most of it. Once you get through secondary school we will help you in your chosen profession. Whatever your dreams, we will support you and find a way to help you achieve them.'

I encouraged the parents to support their children in their endeavours so that the whole community would work together to raise a new generation of future leaders. Finally, I thanked Jeremy, who had given all of us this new start.

I sat down, tears pricking my eyes, but almost immediately two Samburu mothers stood up to embrace me. It was a lovely moment and I accepted their hugs gratefully. They could see how emotional I had become, talking about Jeremy, and they offered me their love and support.

After the speeches, we decided to have some fun. I had brought with me several games which I knew the children had probably never seen before –Connect 4, Hungry Hippos and Buckaroo. We split the group into three stations and for the next hour the groups took turns on each game. I watched in delight as the families threw themselves headlong into the activities. It was wonderful to see them so animated and excited. The games, though common in the UK and aimed at younger children, had not yet reached Samburu and our students were thrilled with the novelty. Soon the noise in the tent reached cacophonous levels.

'I'm not used to this,' Shivani exclaimed as hippos clattered and families whooped with excitement. 'Our camp is usually such a quiet place!'

'It's only for a short time, Shiv,' I grinned indulgently, watching all the excited faces of the children. They had all seemed so shy and quiet on arrival, it was heartening to see them relax and enjoy themselves.

For lunch we treated the families to grilled goat and mounds of rice - a luxury many could not afford - and, as their culture dictated, the men and women ate separately. In the afternoon it was time for the awards ceremony itself. To begin, three of the children got up to speak. Angeline, the first child to be taken on by the fund, spoke first, followed by Painoti, our first student attending teacher's college, and then Solomon, our first university student. All three of them spoke of their appreciation and happiness. Then the parents were invited to speak. Angeline's mother stood up.

'When the fund came into Angeline's life, we were going through a really hard time,' she said. 'Angeline's father had died and his family had disowned us. We had nothing, no money, and Angeline was doing the last year of primary again because I couldn't afford to send her to secondary school. That's when you came into our lives and brought hope. I believe the fund came into our lives at that moment for a reason. At a bad time for us, it was a blessing.'

I was very touched by her words and of course my heart went out to her as a woman who had also lost her husband. When Nicholas' mother spoke, she said how happy she was that Nicholas had the fund to support his education and then started to sing, a song filled with sheer happiness. Everyone began to clap and before I knew it three more Samburu mothers had also come to the front to dance and sing with her. It was an extraordinary moment. The women, wrapped in their *shukas* (sarong-like coverings), heaved their chests back and forward in traditional Samburu style so that their many beaded necklaces shook and rattled. Then, even more surprisingly, my mother stood up and started to dance with them. It was the most wonderful, spontaneous expression of joy and I couldn't help laughing and clapping along.

Afterwards came the presentations themselves. For each child we projected their photo on the wall and highlighted their achievements. Each student got a certificate and a goody bag, containing pens, a water bottle and a notebook, as a reward for their hard work. The children appeared very proud of themselves and I really enjoyed celebrating them, rewarding all their hard work and instilling pride in their achievements.

Over the course of the day, many of the children came up to speak to me and it was wonderful to get to know them a little, to discover a little bit about their personalities. The brother of one student, France, told me very solemnly how emotional the day was for him. He assured me his brother would work really hard. The children themselves were so bright and lovely. It felt so right to have this opportunity to help them, to put something back into the community. Jeremy and I had always been made to feel welcome here – that is why we loved it so much – but now, with the JLEF, I felt I could be a real part of the community.

My sister was already firmly embedded in the locals' lives and I'd discovered that many Samburu mothers had named their daughters after her as a tribute to her work. But I was stunned when one of the women told us that she had a granddaughter called Shivani - and one called Shalini too. How remarkable that these children from traditional African tribes now carried our Hindu names! How humbling.

Finally, at 3pm, my sister thanked everyone for coming and reminded them of all the hard work we would do over the next year. Just before the families boarded the bus, one of the village elders asked to say a prayer for our new community. We all stood up while the village elder spoke in Samburu, his sentences punctuated by everyone intoning the word *ngai*, which means god. On and on it went in this way, with the word *ngai* swirling around us all, like a soft, low hum reverberating through us. It was incredible, like a meditation, very spiritual and peaceful. In that moment, I felt Jeremy's presence strongly in the room. We were one – as a group, we had come together and formed a new community - and he was there too. Deep in my bones, I knew that what we were doing was right. This was how it was meant to be.

A few days later, I travelled to Nanyuki to start the process of building the log-cabin as a tribute to Jeremy. 'Jezza's Cabin', as it has been christened, would be completed in the Spring of 2018. I had fulfilled my promise to Jeremy to build our dream home on the land we loved so much.

In early February 2018, my father lost his own battle to cancer. In the space of 18 months I lost Jeremy, Gladys and my Pop. But this time I did not fall apart. Instead, over time, I have become more pragmatic. I now understand that this is the cycle of life and death and we must all go through it. I know that I will see Jeremy, Gladys and Pop again when the time is right for me.

***

Following my father's passing, I made two monumental decisions that would help me move forward with my life.

On my return to the UK that March, and after a lot of soul-searching and deliberation, I decide to close Just Jhoom! I began the process of winding down the business in June 2018, although my dance classes, so very important to me, will be the last aspect to go. The news has been met with sadness but also some lovely messages of love and support. People seem to understand my need to move forward in life. Although Just Jhoom! sustained me in the immediate aftermath of Jeremy's death, I have decided that I cannot take it with me into my new life.

The irony is that, as we are preparing to shut it down, Just Jhoom! has truly now become a viable business, something Jeremy always doubted it would be. The courses are sold online and because all the material is already there, I don't have to do anything except provide the marketing and web hosting. But Jeremy was so integral to the business that I cannot move it forward without him. We started it together and he was there for every decision, every event and every occasion. Just Jhoom!'s success was part of what we achieved as a couple. It was our project and it used to bring me so much joy but now it is a reminder of my loss. Without him, I have no heart for it. Just Jhoom! will always hold a very special place in my life but now I need a fresh start.

I have also decided to train as an End of Life Doula - a person who helps the dying, as well as their families, by making them feel safe and supported as the dying person makes the transition from this life to whatever is next. I have always believed strongly in my instincts and I feel that there is a reason I have endured so much loss in my life. If I can sit at Jeremy's deathbed and encourage him to let go then I feel sure I can do this for anyone else. I now feel that this is my true calling and the first step to this is the formal training which I will begin in September 2018.

As for moving to Kenya, I leave that open for the moment. Whilst Tabasco is alive I will not be moving anywhere. He is still my constant, loving companion. And I am not yet ready to leave the house in Cranleigh that Jeremy and I shared for so many years. My mother, meanwhile, has decided to move to India, which means the closing of another chapter as the main family home in Nairobi, the home which I grew up in and have so many happy childhood memories, will be rented out.

I have learned so much in the past few months. Not just how to fix the hinge on a door, but also how to fix the things in my life that are broken. I have learned how to rely on myself and how to give myself the compassion and love I need to make my life better.

These things I know to be true: life is short and fragile. If a relationship is not nurturing you or it feels toxic, end it. If a job does not make you happy, look for something that does. If a situation is not right for you, change it. Don't wait for tomorrow because today is all we have. We have choices and we owe it to ourselves to choose things that make us happy. We owe it to all those who have gone before us to live life fully, compassionately and to make a difference – however small. Go within and listen to your inner voice. Trust yourself and trust your instincts.

Against all odds, against my own family's advice, I chose Jeremy all those years ago. I'm so glad I did, because if I didn't I would have missed out on the best thing to have happened to me. I would have missed out on the best and happiest two decades, with the most beautiful person I have ever known. Loving Jeremy was not just a decision, it was my good fortune, it was my destiny. For that, I will be forever grateful.

I have lit a candle in front of a photograph of a smiling, happy Jeremy every morning since the day he died. As I look into his beautiful eyes I speak to him.

I'm thinking of you today Jeremy. I'm remembering how often you came through for me when I needed you most – how you always gave so generously of your time and so freely of yourself.

I'm thinking about how easy it was to be with you, how funny things seemed even funnier and ordinary pleasures felt special because we shared them together.

I'm thinking of how your belief in me made the difference between me giving up on my dreams and trying even harder to reach them. I realise how so very special you are and how much richer my life has been because you were in it.

I'm thinking of you, of all the good things you did, all the kind things you said and all the beautiful ways in which you filled my life. I'm asking for your guidance, your love and help as I move forward.

I love you with all my heart... and more.

Each day, as my energy clears and the dark cloud of grief lifts, I begin to hear Jeremy more and more. I begin to feel the hand of his guidance on my head.

I hear him whisper *'I am here. Always with you.'*

And so, I know he will be with me for the next part of my journey, wherever it may take me – and that fills me with hope.

Hamari Adhoori Prem Kahani

Jab hum mile to zindagi mili
Do dil, do jaan ek hue
Jab hum mile to hamari jahan ek hogayi
Hamari prem kahani ko dhadkhan mili

Lekin takdeerne hamarisaat bewafi kee
Kuch pal ke liye humko judaa kargayi
Ehsaas huan ki hum ek doosre ke bina saas nahin lesakte
Aur hamari prem kahani adhoori regayi

Lekin sache pyar ki kahani ka kohi anth nahin hota
Puri kayanat humko judaa nahin karsakti
Hum phir zaroor milenge
Hum phir zaroor milenge

Kyonki yeh rishta roohani hain
Kyonki yeh rishta janum janum ka hai
Kyonki is rishte ko hum ayat mante hai
Kyonki is rishte ko hum ibadat mante hai

Yeh mohabat ki kahani janum se pehle shuru hui
Puri kayanat humko judaa nahin rakhsakti
Hum phir zaroor milenge
Hum phir zaroor milenge

Jab hum milenge yeh judai ka mausam pura hojayega
Yeh intezaar ki ghari thamjayegi
Jab hum milenge yeh dooriyan, yeh khamoshiyan, yeh tanhaiyan mitjayengi
Do jism ek jaan phirse hojayenge

Hamari ishq ki kahani ko phirse dhadkhan milegi
Puri kayanat humko judaa nahin karsakti
Hum phir zaroor milenge
Hum phir zaroor milenge

Translation: Our Incomplete Love Story

When we met, we got life
Two hearts became one, two souls became one
When we met our worlds became one
Our love story got a heartbeat

But destiny betrayed us
For a few moments we were separated
We realised that without each other we couldn't breathe
And our love story remained incomplete

But there is no end to a true love story
The whole universe cannot keep us apart
We will meet again...
We will meet again...

Because this relationship is a spiritual one
Because this relationship is for life after life
Because we believe this relationship is a prayer
Because we believe this relationship is worship

This love story began before birth
The whole universe cannot keep us apart
We will meet again...
We will meet again...

When we meet again this season of separation will be over
The time for waiting will finish
When we meet again the distances, the silences, the loneliness will melt
away
Two bodies will once again become one soul

Our love story will once again get its heartbeat
The whole universe cannot keep us apart
We will meet again...
We will meet again...

Help and Information

The charities and organizations I have listed below are those that have been recommended or that I have used personally. The books I have listed are all ones that I have read over the years and have helped me greatly. This information is for reference only – we are all different and what worked for me may not work for you.

Cancer Care

Penny Brohn UK – A charity that provides free integrative care to everyone affected by cancer. www.pennybrohn.org.uk, tel: 0303 3000 118.

Macmillan Cancer Care – A charity supporting people living with cancer. www.macmillan.org.uk, tel: 0808 808 0000

Phyllis Tuckwell – A hospice care service for adult patients and their families, covering the whole of West Surrey and part of North East Hampshire. www.pth.org.uk

Family Estrangement

Stand Alone – A charity supporting adults estranged from their families. www.standalone.org.uk

Mental Health

Mind – The mental health charity provides advice and support for anyone experiencing a mental health problem. www.mind.org.uk, tel: 0300 123 3393, text: 86463.

The Samaritans – A safe space to talk 24 hours a day, seven days a week. www.samaritans.org, tel: 116 123

Further Reading

Afterlife

Betty, Stafford. The Afterlife Unveiled: What The Dead Tell Us About Their World. UK: O-Books, 2011

Butler, Jamie. With Love & Light: A True Story About An Uncommon Gift. USA: Prime Concepts Group, 2009

Borgia, Anthony. The World Unseen. USA: Square Circles Publishing, 2013

Edward, John. After Life: Answers From The Other Side. New York: Sterling Publishing Co, 2010

Heath, Pamela Rae & Klimo, John. Handbook to the Afterlife. USA: North Atlantic Books, 2010

Martin, Joel & Patricia Romanowski. We Don't Die: George Anderson's Conversations With The Other Side. New York: Penguin Group, 1988

Schwartz, Robert. Your Soul's Plan: Dscovering The Real Meaning of the Life You Planned Before You Were Born. California: North Atlantic Books, 2007, 2009

Cancer

Bailey, Christine and Penny Brohn Cancer Care. Nourish: The Cancer Care Cookbook. London: Watkins Publishing Ltd, 2013

Moorjani, Anita. Dying To Be Me: My Journey from Cancer, to Near Death, to True Healing. London: Hay House UK Ltd, 2012

Servan-Shreiber, Dr. David. Anti-Cancer: A New Way of Life. USA: Viking Press, 2008

Turner, Kelly. Radical Remission: Surviving Cancer Against All Odds. New York: HarperCollins, 2014

Death and Bereavement

Bailey, Helen. When Bad Things Happen in Good Bikinis. London: Blink Publishing, 2015

Feinberg, Linda. I'm Grieving As Fast As I Can: How Young Widows and Widowers Can Cope and Heal. USA: New Horizon Press, 1994, 2004

Gawande, Atul. Being Mortal: Illness, Medicine and What Matters in the End. London: Profile Books Ltd, 2014, 2015

Ginsburg Davis, Genevieve. Widow to Widow: Thoughtful, Practical Ideas for Rebuilding Your Life. USA: Da Capo Press, 1995, 1997

Ironside, Virginia. You'll Get Over It – The Rage of Bereavement. London: Penguin Books, 1997

Kalanithi, Paul/ When Breath Becomes Air. London: Penguin Random House, 2016

Yalom, Irvin D. Staring at The Sun: Overcoming the Dread of Death. London: Piatkus, 2008

Depression

Brampton, Sally. Shoot The Damn Dog: A Memoir of Depression. London: Bloomsbury Publishing, 2008

Cantopher, Tim. Depressive Illness: The Curse of The Strong. London: Sheldon Press, 2003

Marshall, Fiona and Cheevers, Peter. Coping with SAD: Seasonal Affective Disorder. London: Sheldon Press, 2002

Williams, Mark; Teasdale, John; Segal, Zindal; Kabat-Zinn, Jon. The Mindful Way Through Depression. New York: The Guilford Press, 2007

Spiritual Awareness

His Holiness the Dalai Lama and Cutler, Howard C. The Art of Happiness: A Handbook for Living. London: Hodder and Stoughton, 1998

His Holiness the Dalai Lama. How To Be Compassionate: A Handbook For Creating Inner Peace and A Happier World. UK: Rider, 2011

Gilbert, Paul. The Compassionate Mind. London: Constable, 2009, 2010, 2013

Kornfield, Jack. Bringing Home the Dharma: Awakening Right Where You Are. Boston: Shambhala Publications Ltd, 2011

Morley, Charlie. Lucid Dreaming: A Beginner's Guide to Becoming Conscious in Your Dream. London, Hay House UK Ltd, 2015

Rinpoche, Sogyal. The Tibetan Book of Living & Dying. UK: Rider, 2008

Tolle, Eckhart. A New Earth: Create A Better Life. London: Penguin Books, 2005, 2006

Mindfulness and Meditation

Alidina, Shamash. Mindfulness for Dummies. West Sussex: John Wiley & Sons Ltd, 2010.

Hanh, Thich Nhat. Peace Is Every Step: The Path of Mindfulness in Everyday Life. London: Rider, 1991

Hart, William. The Art of Living: Vipassana Meditation. India: Embassy Book Distributors, 1987

Kabat-Zinn, Jon. Full Catastrophe Living: How to Cope With Stress, Pain and Illness Using Mindfulness Meditation. London: Piatkus, 1990, 2013

Williams, Mark and Penman, Danny. Mindfulness – A Practical Guide to Finding Peace in a Frantic World. London: Piatkus, 2011

Quote Credits

Every effort has been made to correctly credit the quote sources, but if any have been inadvertently overlooked or incorrectly referenced, please contact the publishers.

Chapter 1

[1]Weiss, Brian; Weiss, Amy. Miracles Happen: The Transformational Healing Power of Past Life Memories. London: Hay House Ltd, 2012 (Pg 238)

Chapter 2

[2]Gibran, Kahlil. The Collected Works of Kahlil Gibran. 21 Books in One Edition. Musaicum Books, 2017 (Kindle Edition)

Chapter 3

[3]Barren, Stan. Inspiring Legends: Real Life Inspirational Stories (Book 1). InspirationDB.com, 2015 (Kindle Edition - Pg 59)

Chapter 4

[4]Price, Steven D. The Most Inspiring Things Ever Said. USA: The Lyons Press, 2017 (Pg 154)

Chapter 5

[5]Rumi, Jalal ad-Din Muhammed. Rumi's Book of Poetry: 100 Inspirational Poems on Love, Life and Meditation. CreateSpace Independent Publishing Platform, 2016 (Verse 86)

Chapter 6

[6]Eliot, T.S. The Cocktail Party. 1935 (Playscript)

Chapter 7

[7]Haig, Matt. How Books Saved My Life. www.telegraph.co.uk/news/society/11918745/Matt-Haig-how-books-saved-my-life.html. The Telegraph, 2015 (Online - accessed 18 June 2018)

Chapter 8

[8]Exley, Helen. Dance Is The Air We Breathe: Dance Quotations – A Helen Exley Giftbook. UK: Exley Publications, 1993 (Pg 5)

Chapter 12

[9]Sreechinth, C. The Laughing Lion Quotes: Quotes of Voltaire. UB Tech, 2018 (Pg 7)

Chapter 13

[10]Chopra, Deepak. 7 Myths of Meditation. www.huffingtonpost.com/deepak-chopra/meditation-myths_b_2823629.html Huffpost, 2013 (Online - accessed 18 June 2018)

Chapter 14

[11]Russonello, Giovanni. Read Oprah Winfrey's Golden Globes Speech. www.nytimes.com/2018/01/07/movies/oprah-winfrey-golden-globes-speech-transcript.html The New York Times, 2018 (Online - accessed 18 June 2018)

Chapter 15

[12]Easwaran, Eknath. Gandhi The Man: How One Man Changed Himself To Change The World. Canada: Nilgiri Press, 1972, 1978, 1997, 2011 (Pg 138)

[13]His Holiness the Dalai Lama. How To Be Compassionate: A Handbook For Creating Inner Peace and A Happier World. UK: Rider, 2011 (Pg 5)

Chapter 16

[14]His Holiness the Dalai Lama. How To Be Compassionate: A Handbook For Creating Inner Peace and A Happier World. UK: Rider, 2011 (Pg 120)

[15]Bhalla, Sharmi. Soul on Fire: A Testimony of God's Love. Kenya: Flamekeepers Publishing, 2008

Chapter 17

[16]Gibran, Kahlil. The Forerunner: Ever Has It Been That Love Knows Not Its Own Depth Until The Hour Of Separation. A Word To The Wise, 2013 (Kindle Edition)

Chapter 18

[17]Price, Steven D. The Most Inspiring Things Ever Said. USA: The Lyons Press, 2017 (Pg 226)

Chapter 19

[18]Powers, Joan; Milne, A.A. (Inspiration). Pooh's Little Instruction Book (Winnie the Pooh). USA: Dulton Children's Books, 1995

Chapter 20

[19]Tatelbaum, Judy. The Courage To Grieve: Creative Living, Recovery and Growth Through Grief. UK: Vermilion – Random House, 1983, 1997 (Pg 9)

Chapter 21

[20]Price, Steven D. The Most Inspiring Things Ever Said. USA: The Lyons Press, 2017 (Pg 225)

[21]Preston, Douglas. I Took The Dalai Lama To A Ski Resort And He Told Me The Meaning Of Life. www.businessinsider.com/i-took-the-dalai-lama-to-a-ski-resort-and-he-told-me-the-meaning-of-life-2014-11?IR=T, 2014 (Online - accessed 18 June 2018)

Chapter 23

[22]Crocker, Carter. Pooh's Grand Adventure: The Search For Christopher Robin. https://youtu.be/9tRepZdoRmY Buena Vista Worldwide Home Entertainment, 1997 (Online – accessed 18 June 2018)

Photo and Design Credits

Cover Design by Angela Basker

<u>Front Cover:</u>
Top Image (Shalini the Dancer) © 2012, Jeremy Lucas
Bottom Image (Jeremy and Shalini) © 2014, Malcolm Roberts
<u>www.castlestudios.co.uk</u>

<u>Back Cover:</u>
Author Photograph © 2018, Sian Tyrrell <u>www.siantphoto.com</u>
Top Image (Shalini and Jeremy - Wedding Rings) © 2014, Terry Newman
Bottom Image (Moon) © 2016, Jeremy Lucas (This was the last
photograph that Jeremy took with his beloved Nikon camera)

A Word of Thanks...

Shivani, for being the best sister a girl could ever have. You inspire me every day with your passion, dedication and hard work. You make me so very proud of all you have achieved and continue to achieve. I love you.

Mum and Pop, who gave me the best start in life, with a wonderful education, fantastic opportunities and experiences and inspiring in me the courage to be independent, fearless and strong, so that I could make my own way in this world.

Ushamasi–Mom, for believing in me and Jeremy when no one else would.

Cheeku B, for being the best friend a girl could ever need.

Katy W, without whom there would be no beginning, middle or end. You asked all the right questions, listened and really understood.

Tatiana W, for being an amazing copy-editor and proof-reader. I couldn't have done it without your support, advice and encouragement.

Alex W of Reviewed and Cleared, for his excellent, clear advice on all things legal and his wonderful encouragement.

Sian T, for her photography skills, all publicity photos and her friendship.

Angela B, for her design skills and designing the book cover and her friendship.

Louise G, for endless cups of coffee and much-needed walks.

My Jhoomers, for their constant support and encouragement and for turning up to Just Jhoom! classes when I needed you most.

Peta P and Clare D, who were my business support and my buffer from the world when I couldn't face anyone.

My neighbours, Rosemary, David H and Paula H, who knocked on my door to check I was still alive and fed me when they saw I needed it.

Viv P, for listening to me in my darkest days, when I was at my most desperate.

Terry N, for being a true friend to Jeremy and for the wonderful tribute starter hut at the Bramley Golf Club.

Peter G, for being such a support to Jeremy and being there for me when the legalities seemed all too much.

You have all been there to celebrate the highs in my life and you have seen me in my darkest days. Through it all you have stayed by my side. I will be forever grateful.

In My Thoughts...

Cancer is a cruel disease. It has no barriers and does not choose based on age, colour, race or gender – it just invades one's body, life and mind.

I have known many strong women who have lost their fight to cancer and I pay tribute to them here: Joan N, Gill P, Chrissy M, Val H, Rashmi B.

To Paula H and Louise H – keep fighting the good fight.

To my father, Pop: you too were taken from us far too early by cancer but you put up a bloody good fight. I know that you and Jeremy are up there looking down on us and wondering what all the fuss and tears are about. You are both free from pain and peaceful, now. More importantly, you each have a cold Tusker beer in your hands and you are making your famous *koroga palak* chicken, as Jeremy waits in anticipation for what promises to be a very tasty meal. You both loved food – and beer – and now you can enjoy both with no nagging wives or health problems to worry about.

Miss you. Love you.

Jeremy Lucas Education Fund

Educating youth, empowering communities, encouraging conservation.

More information about the fund can be found at www.ewasolions.org or by emailing education@ewasolions.org

About The Author

Shalini Bhalla-Lucas is an award-winning entrepreneur, trainer and the founder of Just Jhoom! – a Bollywood-inspired dance-fitness programme, with classes available nationwide. She is also an accredited Mindfulness and Meditation teacher – teaching people highly-effective, proven techniques to help combat stress, anxiety and depression.

Shalini has performed all over the world and has had TV appearances on ITV's Daybreak, Channel 4s Sunday Brunch and the BBC, as well as on numerous radio stations. She has been featured in publications such as RED magazine, Top Sante and Dance Today, discussing dance and Just Jhoom! but has also been called upon to discuss how she beat depression with dance, meditation and mindfulness.

As a result, of being so open about her depression, Shalini was chosen to be one of ten people in the country to be a "Voice of

MIND" – campaigning for better mental health provision in the UK, and has spoken in the Houses of Parliament to MPs about wellbeing and resilience to Mental Health problems as well as on a roundtable discussion for the Huffington Post and at the IAPT Therapist Convention 2015.

In 2013 Shalini won the Asian Women of Achievement Awards in Arts and Culture (in association with RBS) and was recently named as "One of 20 Female Entrepreneurs Energising Britain" by Real Business. In January 2012 she won the local Business Accelerator Award through the Surrey Advertiser, and was also included in the 2009 Young Business Leaders edition of Who's Who of Britain's Business Elite and the Who's Who of Britain's Business Leaders 2010 and 2011. In January of 2016 Just Jhoom! was shortlisted as one of six finalists at the inaugural Cranleigh & District Business, Innovation & Growth (BIG) Awards.

Always With You is Shalini's first book.

99011068R00176

Made in the USA
Columbia, SC
08 July 2018